Acclaim for
Malcolm X: In Our Own Image

"Engaging, entertaining, and thought provoking . . . Even the most impressionistic chapters should encourage researchers to go beyond the *Autobiography* and the film to reconceptualize and ask new questions about Malcolm X."

—*San Francisco Chronicle*

"This book is a struggle to take Malcolm with us on the long road to assessing who, why, and where we are."

—*Essence*

"Some of the essays are beautifully composed and soothing, while others are angry; all are thoughtful and lend valuable depth and solidity to the contemporary debate on the revered, manipulated, monumentalized, and commodified leader."

—*Booklist*

"An anthology important not just for its topicality but for its look at ferment among late-20th-century black intellectuals."

—*Entertainment Weekly*

"An excellent new collection of essays by prominent African-Americans. Wood is ideally suited to help shed a penetrating light on the mystique surrounding this controversial figure."

—*Elle*

"Reading [these essays] is like looking at Malcolm X through a kaleidoscope; one is left marveling at his complexity and constant willingness to re-invent himself . . . *Malcolm X: In Our Own Image* conveys the astonishing capacity for growth and change that is one of the most enduring lessons of Malcolm's life."

—*Phoenix Literary Supplement*

MALCOLM X

IN OUR OWN IMAGE

JOE WOOD, EDITOR

ANCHOR BOOKS
DOUBLEDAY
New York   London   Toronto   Sydney   Auckland

Dedicated to:

Pamela
Elizabeth
Joseph Sr.

An ANCHOR BOOK
PUBLISHED BY DOUBLEDAY
a division of Bantam Doubleday Dell Publishing Group, Inc.
1540 Broadway, New York, New York 10036

ANCHOR BOOKS, DOUBLEDAY, and the portrayal of an anchor
are trademarks of Doubleday,
a division of Bantam Doubleday Dell
Publishing Group, Inc.

Malcolm X: In Our Own Image was originally published in hardcover
by St. Martin's Press, Inc. in 1992.
The Anchor Books edition is published
by arrangement with St. Martin's Press, Inc.

Book design by Jaye Zimet

Library of Congress Cataloging-in-Publication Data

Malcolm X: in our own image/Joe Wood, editor.—1st Anchor Books ed.
p.   cm.
Includes bibliographical references and index.
1. X, Malcolm, 1925–1965—Influence.   I. Wood, Joe.
BP223.Z8L5763   1994
320.5′4′092—dc20   93-26310
CIP

ISBN 0-385-47141-6
Copyright © 1992 by Joe Wood
All Rights Reserved
Printed in the United States of America
First Anchor Books Edition: January 1994

1   3   5   7   9   10   8   6   4   2

Contents

Acknowledgments

Shouts of praise and thanks to the people who made this book possible: Faith Childs, Alan Bradshaw, Scott Malcomson, Adolph Reed, Matthew Countryman, Mike Hanson, Andy Hsiao, Lee Smith, Lynne Tillman, Darius James, Joy Glidden, Muna El-Fituri, Amelie Littell, Charles Mahorney, Lisa Kennedy, Esther Kaplan, Tanya Coke, Ed Morales, Ben Mapp, Micaela di Leonardo, Greg Thomson, Kellie Jones, Lisa Jones, Lisa Sullivan, Renee Green, Gary Dauphin, Desirae Foston, John Coltrane, Stanley Crouch, Pat Cochran, Sandhya Shukla, Jim Hoberman, Martha Southgate, Jeff Phillips, Jennifer Steinhauer, bell hooks, Michael Eric Dyson, Marcia Dyson, Jerry Watts, James Cone, Harold Cruse, Sabine Guez, David Bradley, Sam Anderson, Lawrence Wells, Elizabeth Moore, Barbara Christian, Connie Aitcheson, Joan Morgan, Veronica Chambers, Jon Larsen, Joe Delaney, Hattie Lee Davidson, Matt Diehl, Carol Diehl, Blackside, Inc., Film and Television Productions, Caroline Kerrigan, Playthell Benjamin, Elizabeth Higgenbottham, Deborah Yates, Michelle Wallace, Philomena Mariani, David Leeming, Eric Yadven, Evette Porter, Paul Gilroy, Garrett Kiely, Laura Heymann, Mustafa Jackson, Donelle Gladwin, Roberta Goodman, Michael Kelly Williams, Shirley Abrahamson, Philip Nobile, California Newsreel, and Drew Dunphy.

Excerpt from Larry Neal poem, "Malcolm X—An Autobiography," on page 155, originally appeared in the book *For Malcolm: Poems on the Life and Death of Malcolm X* (Detroit: Broadside Press, 1969), and is reprinted by permission of Broadside Press.

Lyrics from the W.C. and the Maad Circle song, "If You Don't

Work, You Don't Eat," on page 174, are reprinted by permission of Priority Records.

Lyrics from Tiny Grimes song, "Romance Without Finance," appearing on pages 169–170, are reprinted by permission of EMI/Mills Music.

Editor's Note

It's about letting these writers speak, and not shellacking them, but letting them speak. Understanding: people's voices, like people's bodies, are not meant to be perfect. In form: mine, a line, my artifice, to discard if you want. Take these voices in the order you want, structure and restructure them as you please. Only converse with them—be talkative and Black.

Read.

Malcolm X and The
New Blackness

=

JOE WOOD

When I was a child I wasn't Black enough, but Malcolm X helped me turn things around. My first Malcolm speech was in a tattered book on a shelf in my parents' bedroom. I read it when I was twelve, in 1976, the year of the Bicentennial. Malcolm was making blackness Black: *The masses of Black people today think in terms of Black. And this Black thinking enables them to see beyond the confines of America.*[1] Quietly, without fully realizing how much, I began to embrace this thinking, despite its strange incongruity—no one in my black, working-class neighborhood seemed to be spending much time thinking about America *or* Blackness. Or Malcolm. Still, I quietly embraced him, at home, far away from the classroom. Riverdale, my school, was white and located in an affluent neighborhood just inside the Bronx county line; its pantheon was populated by JFK and similar figures. Rumor even had it that Kennedy was once a student there, which contributed to the feeling that we were better than students at other schools, especially those poor, black kids I watched from the window on the bus going home.

I remember not wanting friends from school to visit my side of the Bronx. My family and neighbors were not Kennedys—we worked and we were too black. Our skin color and what we ate and how my parents talked and what we talked about and didn't talk about and the magazines—*Ebony, Jet, Essence*—we kept on our table made my home black. In school, I had white friends and I learned to like their music and talk like them. Back at home my friends accused me of slowly turning white, and then we had a big fight, and then we lost our friendship.

One summer my parents took my sister and me to Washington to visit the monuments. My father was born in Birmingham, Alabama, in 1934, which was a different time. I remember: We were at the base of George Washington's obelisk and I was thinking about Liberty and Justice and so on, when my pops looked at me and shook his head and said: "And he owned slaves." I already knew this; and Riverdale had taught me not to dwell on it. I guess I put this lesson on my face, because it stopped my father's shaking head. He said, "He still did some good things." My young black face: my father had put that Malcolm X book on the shelf, and he had raised me Black, and now, to his horror, he saw that Riverdale had taught me something else.

Just before I entered college I was stopped on Madison Avenue and 52nd Street by a White cop who told me I should get out of the area because "This is White man's land." Malcolm was making more and more sense to me; by senior year I had read *The Autobiography of Malcolm X* three times, reading and rereading its most angry passages. I'd found out that JFK had been soft on civil rights, Abraham Lincoln had said that he never meant Negroes weren't inferior, George Washington wasn't even a very *bright* slaveowner. I no longer wanted to hide my home, my blackness, our Black culture: yams, Zora Neale, Al Green—I got downright romantic about it.

I took one of the college's few classes on Black literature. The teacher taught the class as if she was leading a family gathering, and I liked the class and did not like it, accordingly. I liked feeling as if I had found a Black sanctuary. But I also worried about whether I belonged in it. My dirty past, my latent whiteness—I tried to put a cap on them, and the conflict made me question the use of these terms, of "race" talk generally. I asked myself: Do Black and White adequately describe my life?

Inside and outside of class we danced with the question, using Black literature and music as spiritual waystations. I kept my focus on Malcolm, conducting research at the college's enormous library. It was there I found out that the best books on him were written by White people: Goldman, Breitman, Wolfenstein. I wanted to know what

Black thinkers were thinking, but they were being quiet—they were keeping quiet.

Today in my old neighborhood you can see Malcolm X on people's chests and heads, on their TV screens and on their CD boxes—Malcolm X sells out. Around the city I see White children wearing his image and his X, the Nation of Islam's marker for our stolen names. I wonder what the commodified Malcolm is saying to our people, and I wonder how he speaks to Whites. I've looked to the *Autobiography* for answers, but an autobiography can't respond to everything. I listen for the voices of our fractious Black family.

This book is Black thinking on the subject of Malcolm X; it is brothers and sisters talking. I've invited some of our thinkers to critique Malcolm X and to make sense of Malcolm X's currency among us, and to make sense of *Blackness* itself—its meaning today and its usefulness as a concept to African America. We speak because we dare to look in the mirror and see our heroes and ourselves; we speak because Blackness has come to mean so many things, and nothing; we speak because we seek to name ourselves, and our lives.

When the phone rang, the sky was as gray as a dying White man. A friend was on the line with an invitation to "Objects of Myth and Memory: American Indian Art" at the Brooklyn Museum. An hour later we were at the museum. The show's featured objects had been collected by a curator named Culin; he had received (bought, traded, stolen) the art in 1903 from members of the Navajo, Zuni, Pomo, Maidu, and Osage groups in western America. My friend and I knew little about these people, and the exhibition didn't do much to help—the explanatory descriptions told more about how the art had been acquired than about what it meant.

I couldn't help thinking about the extent to which Malcolm X is being bought and sold, and about how he has become iconicized in the shuffle. Malcolm was back on the brain: *How does Malcolm's icon work? And what does it say?* I told my friend I needed a sip of water and went alone upstairs to the American Art room to compare thoughts about the "American" art there, the "native" art downstairs, and Malcolm. Upstairs, there was a bench, a guard, and walls of paintings, including a Gilbert Stuart portrait of George Washington.

The portrait brought the dollar bill to mind, so I pulled one out to see which George I preferred. I liked the dollar's George more. Why?

Neither image was exactly moving—I chose the dollar because of its more pronounced plainness, which contrasted with Stuart's officiousness: he had painted a George who would be king. But there was also more to my choice—why did the bill's *plainness* make it more attractive to me?

Because that plainness helps along the process by which an official, shared thing becomes *my* thing. While Gilbert Stuart wanted viewers to know the painting in front of me was his, down to the last garish stroke, the dollar *had* to be plain—it was supposed to help me feel as if I had "authored" a share of American wealth and power.[2] Governments worldwide use the same strategy, giving similarly significant people similarly plain portraits on currency. When I see those blank faces, however, they usually mean little to me, except to signal another community's authority and my momentary "capture" of it. In the case of the dollar, I think I know the story, and I insert "my" George behind George's face, and consequently, I am more encouraged in the belief that the icon serves me.

I sat down and recalled my introduction to iconology: Helen Gardner's *Art Through the Ages*, her chapters on Early Christian and Byzantine art. *To advertise the new faith in all its diverse aspects—its dogma, scriptural narrative, and symbolism—and to instruct and edify the believer*, she says, *acres of wall in dozens of new churches had to be filled in a style and medium that would most effectively carry the message*.[3] Constantine and the churchmen looked to the mosaic as the medium, and the message mosaics conveyed was the meaning of the evolving and still fresh religion. *The content of Christian doctrine took centuries to fashion, and for a long time even the proper manner of representing the founder of Christianity was in question. . . . After some crucial theological questions on Jesus' nature were resolved, a more or less standard formula for his depiction emerged*.[4] By the sixth century this evolving discourse was being depicted by means of standardized images of saints and Biblical characters: the icons. Easily reproduced, icons made Christianity portable—when worshippers looked at the latest icon, they were viewing the present state of Christian discourse.

They were also being indoctrinated. "Christian discourse" names two grand rivers of conversations, one cultural and existential, the other political and organizational. "Believers" were swimmers in both streams; a shared ethos or "spirit," in the form of belief in the powers of God and the saints, made the swimming easier. The spirit had many faces—icons, it was said, contained the faces, these spirits. Viewing the icons gave worshippers a sense of communion, and simultaneously, a sense of "authorship"—spirits, after all, converse with the individual, with you.

It's easy to forget that one's authorship of an icon courts an illusion—my version of George is so dependent on dominant myths about George and Our Nation that I can't possibly separate "him" from the saint I'd admired in Washington. Young Americans learn the myths in school, and, through the dollar, buy them again and again. We become participants in American culture and political discourses, and are made believers in American spirit: *E Pluribus Unum* and *In God We Trust* make sense to us.

I pocketed the bill and left the room; admitting complicity is always taxing. Downstairs, my friend was still making his way through the "native" masks, which, like foreign currency, were icons of communities unfamiliar to both of us, and in this case, conquered nations: the beaten Navajo, the disempowered Pomo. The masks had been separated from their people and were displayed like stolen corpses, no longer living materials of a culture but captured symbols of communities the museum considered dying or dead. *The icon can no longer be the same meaning, goal and means that it was formerly: it has already passed on into the museum where it can be preserved under the new meaning, not of a religious conception, but of art. But as we go deeper into new creative meaning it loses even that significance and nothing can be invested in it, for it will be the soulless mannequin of a past spiritual and utilitarian life,*[5] writes Russian painter Kazimir Malevich. He could have been talking about the masks in these glass cases, and he would have been right, in a way. These pieces were unexplained: they were ciphers ripped from their original cultures: they were silenced, buried, dead. Art. Evidence of a murder.

Evidence: I looked at my friend's face—what was I looking to see? There was a certain naive fascination: He and I were trying, unconsciously, to decipher the muted messages of the masks—and we did hear something, the silenced cultures spoke. To us, these masks were more than "soulless mannequins"; they were still *materials of a culture.*" No matter how captured and misnamed, they spoke "native" humanity, spoke Navajo and Pomo, spoke tongues that the curator couldn't even name. They also spoke American—the curatorial descriptions ensured these masks a role in American cultural discourse, showed us, for instance, how *E Pluribus Unum* we are. The spirits and the cultures—they had blended, were mixing, no matter the politics, the domination, the oppression. Our attempts had failed, these human spirits were talking.

The day had cleared a little by the time we left the museum. I retreated home, thinking about Malevich the whole way. Although he'd said the icons didn't speak to him, Malevich's art betrays him; the icons *were* speaking to him, even if their principal discourse had switched from the Christian to the Russo-Christian to the Russian. *The icon as symbolic bearer of the message of Christianity, in every Russian Orthodox household,* writes art historian Margaret Betz, *gave a sense of ultimate purpose not only to the life of the individual believer, but to his nation as well. The concept of Moscow as the Third Rome crystallized this sense of national destiny and centered it in the very heart of modern Russia in the beginning of the sixteenth century.*[6] By the time Malevich and his twentieth-century contemporaries turned their attention to the icons, the icons' significance as national symbols had solidified. In making his own *anti*-iconic art, Malevich was engaging in the discourse of Russianness—he was advancing his ideological stance using its parameters, and despite his declarations to the contrary, was promoting the spiritual power of icons, as well. *Even today, pictures of Russia's political leaders serve a function similar to that of an icon.*[7] Even after the October revolution, after the official ideology changed, the discourse, its icons—their Russianness—remained.

But what is Russianness? Or Navajoness, or Pomoness? What is Blackness? In figuring the Malcolm icon, we can suppose a Black People. We can also suppose the discourse of Blackness flows in two streams, one cultural and existential, the other political. These streams, sharing ethos, spirits, diverge from, run into, shadow each other. Yet they remain distinct: African American culture and Black politics are not one, but two.

To understand the reemergence of Malcolm we begin by considering his iconic power. In these hostile times, many African Americans are hungry for an honorable sanctuary, and Black spirit fits the bill. When used as a shelter—as a tool for emotional alliance—spirit, despite being fragile as a ghost, helps people weather alienation, despair, and weariness. We drink from the ethos in our politics, and bathe in the spirits of our culture: these shared beliefs, they bind us together. But we also seek a map to a better society. Ideology does that. In the absence of a viable ideology, we settle with spirit;

with spirit at our sides, we seek its signs: Malcolm, once dead, returns.

When he was alive, Malcolm argued vigorously for one particular notion of Black spirit—a "true" Black spirit, meaning "militant," "proud," "angry." Malcolm's icon has consequently come to signify the "truest" distillation of this Black spirit, and therefore the best product to validate and express "real" Black anger: anger about the way Black People have been treated everywhere we are Black, anger about the way we are now treated in America. These are angry times for everyone—Malcolm's icon proclaims anger so forcefully it even attracts angry non–African Americans; fellow travelers, hangers-on, and other assorted buyers purchase Malcolm, too.

But are the buyers, African American or not, angry or not, Black believers? Not necessarily, because Black spirit has never meant one thing, or anything concrete, which is its great power *and* failure. Spirit has no spine; it bends easily to the will of its buyer. Black spirit has many faces—it can mean anything from "angry" to "kindhearted" to "cool." Even for those who purchase Malcolm with the spirit's current militance in mind, the meaning of the possession is very uncertain. When Public Enemy, in their "Shut 'Em Down" video, says *Screw George Washington!* and knocks him from the dollar bill, substituting Malcolm X (and Angela Davis)—this may be an act of defiance, but what's doing the defying and what's being defied are not certain. Some things are certain: Public Enemy's substitution is supposed to confirm the group's opposition to White racism, and, more broadly, to the way things are. To normalcy. But the reinscribed dollar also asks viewers to bow to its various other agenda. The other agenda—most noticeably, American nationalism—compete for dominance, make the icon's meaning unstable. Even as the Malcolm dollar promotes PE's notions of a resistant, "true" Black spirit, it promotes the worth of American economic institutions. And American spirits. PE's version of Black spirit, already vague, gets more mixed up in the mix: begins to mean what American spirit means. Are these meanings at war? Which meaning is most subverted? Doesn't American spirit, backed by ideologies such as consumerism, have the upper hand? So whom does the icon serve most?

As used today, Malcolm the icon is principally a form of Black mask. Like dreadlocks and kente cloth, Malcolm X worn on a T-shirt is an

African American cultural form; as such, it "speaks" African American culture. But it is also a political signifier—it is also an icon of Blackness, and, consequently, a Black mask. No matter how much disagreement there is among African Americans about Malcolm X, or about dreads, the wearing of either signals engagement in Black discourse, making both Malcolm and dreadlocks, in this sense, a Black thing—you're talking Black when you wear these things. When, for instance, New York's Mayor David Dinkins went to Crown Heights to calm rioting young Blackfolk, he wore a Malcolm X cap. When Clarence Thomas wants to tell Blackfolk he really is Black, he bears Malcolm.

Last year at a music festival in Jackson, Mississippi, I wore my Malcolm X AK-47 T-shirt around those southern Black people and their Whites, and I felt proud: I was telling everyone what seemed obvious—I am Black. I was also announcing that I—and not anyone else—was the particular bearer of this "true" Black spirit. Wearing that T-shirt made me feel "real" Black, lean and competitive with the rest (as if my Blackness could compete with anybody's, especially anybody who resided in Mississippi). This competition even extended to members of non–African American communities, to sympathetic members of those groups. Malcolm was making me Blacker than all, with little but the aid of his face, vested with the spirit of *my* people.

My people: On that day I wanted my people to be Black people; we definitely did not include Whites. On that day I woke up and for a thousand reasons wanted the Whites around me to feel me excluding them. And this was felt despite a set of apparently contradictory facts: I knew I would go to the concert with a group of White friends. I would spend much of my time there dancing affectionately with a White woman friend. We would all dance to Al Green, Tito Puente, Thomas Mapfumo: African culture. For a few songs, we would dance in a circle. I felt somewhat insecure about the grayness of these circumstances—the T-shirt was certainly an anticipation of this. But only in part. Putting on the T-shirt that morning, I was also feeling the kind of anger you need to stay sane: periodic anger; cleansing, defining rage. Sometimes one needs this—these Black acts. There were words on the back of the shirt: "It's a Black Thing. You Wouldn't Understand." But what other messages was I sending out—with which other communities was I identifying—voluntarily or involuntarily? The community with which I *intended* to identify was "angry pro-Black

African Americans"; but this intended community and the other communities with which I was identifying are not the only communities that use Malcolm as a totem: His icon is transferable, the spirit blends with other spirits: enraged people who are not pro-Black, for example, can wear the Malcolm mask and feel identified with *their* enraged communities. (A German friend tells me he's seen neo-Nazis jamming to "anti-White" rap music because they like its anger.) The image on my shirt could even serve other *non-angry* communities—young African American posers, liberal Asians, fashionable Whites—almost as effectively, and just as disposably, as it served my Black self.

Other people's choosing community this way, by wearing Malcolm, does not mean that the icon is without African American value. Its roots are in African American cultural discourse, its African American origins help keep it useful to us. One communal profit comes from the way the image, even the X's on hats, suggests Malcolm's humanity. As with the memory of the Native American cultures preserved in the masks under glass, an echo of the originating humanity is preserved; Malcolm's mask thereby brings African American humanity to strange quarters.

There is a second profit, to African Americans and to Blacks generally. Though Malcolm's angry image gets overused by its communities—gets made more and more a thin and meaningless sellout each day—its proliferation also transmits some notions of Black political opposition. Whether or not the wearer brings her "authored" Malcolm to the wearing, she advertises Malcolm's antiracism stances, including both the nationalist ideology he eventually abandoned and his notion of militant Black spirit, with its current reconstructions. Malcolm's wearers become temporary participants in the struggle for Black realization, because their Black complicity is bought with their T-shirts. Still, this complicity is a shifty thing. For starters, the shirts perpetuate consumerism and the discourse of "race"—a big problem. Second, the shirts' oppositional meaning dissipates at the precise rate at which the shirts proliferate. If everybody's got 'em, nobody's being opposed—especially if the "oppositional" meaning is vague and spiritual in the first place. Third, T-shirts and hats are only T-shirts and hats; they get taken off whenever the wearer chooses, and they always get replaced, no matter how clear the ideology. All of which reminds us: "Culture as politics," in subtle and important ways, can contribute to a political opposition, but it is not enough.

* * *

We, the writers of this book, are trying to move the opposition forward
by considering more closely one site of our talk, Malcolm. We talk
about how Malcolm was the first author of his mask, how he intended
to make a "new" Black Man with "true" Black spirit, and he decided
to use his autobiography to tell this New Black Man's life story. Written
with the help of Alex Haley, Malcolm sensibly gave his life the familiar
shape of the Biblical Saul-to-Paul story—Malcolm as a lost man who
finds the truth through revelation. Unlike Paul, however, Malcolm
experienced two: first, the embrace of his Black Muslim identity;
second, the embrace of human commonality.

The autobiography tells a simple tale. Malcolm was born in Omaha,
Nebraska, on May 19, 1925. He was his father's seventh child, his
mother's fourth. His mother, Louise, was born in Grenada, the child
of a Black mother and a White father. Malcolm's father, Earl, was an
itinerant Baptist preacher, born in Georgia. Both mother and father
were followers of Marcus Garvey. Earl moved the family quite a bit;
they ended up in Lansing, Michigan, where Earl died in strange
circumstances—Malcolm said he was murdered. It was a different
time, the 1930s—the Depression raged, and Malcolm's family, already poor, suffered even more. Within a few years, Louise lost her
children and was put in a mental hospital in Kalamazoo. Malcolm and
his siblings were shuttled between several foster homes; he eventually
found his way to Boston and New York. There Malcolm Little became
Detroit Red, a small-time hustler. He took drugs, he turned tricks, he
danced with White women. In February of 1946 Detroit Red began
serving an eight-year prison sentence for petty thievery. He was twenty
years old. Malcolm spent the next six and one-half years in prison,
during which time he read voluminously and became a convert to
Elijah Muhammad's Nation of Islam.

After 1952, the Nation of Islam grew considerably, due in large
measure to Malcolm's recruiting efforts. Dropping his "slave" name
in accordance with Nation philosophy, Malcolm Little became Malcolm X. He married Betty Shabazz on January 14, 1958; they would
have six female children. In 1959 the Nation was catapulted to the
American stage by the CBS television documentary *The Hate That
Hate Produced*. By 1963, Malcolm was the second most requested
speaker on the college circuit, after Barry Goldwater. Later that year,
Elijah named Malcolm National Minister of the faith, but he silenced

him soon after for saying that John F. Kennedy's assassination was "a case of 'the chickens coming home to roost.' " (*Autobiography*, 301.) During his Nation of Islam period, Malcolm had been saying such things as: *To those of us whose philosophy is black nationalism, the only way you can get involved in the civil-rights struggle is to give it a new interpretation. That old interpretation excluded us . . . now you're facing a situation where the young Negro's coming up. They don't want to hear that "turn-the-other-cheek" stuff, no. In Jacksonville, those were teenagers, they were throwing Molotov cocktails. Negroes have never done that before. But it shows you there's a new deal coming in. There's new thinking coming in. There's new strategy coming in. It'll be Molotov cocktails this month, hand grenades next month, and something else next month. It'll be ballots, or it'll be bullets. It'll be liberty, or it will be death. The only difference about this kind of death—it'll be reciprocal.*[8]

By the middle of the following year, Malcolm had separated from the Nation altogether and made a religious pilgrimage, a *hajj*, to Mecca. In Mecca Malcolm encountered "white" Muslims. He later said the *hajj* prompted his life's second religious revelation: Islam, and the rest of humanity, might include some Whites. Now he took a new name: El-Hajj Malik El-Shabazz. During this period, Malcolm broadcast a new message: *I [have] had to do a lot of thinking and reappraising of my definition of black nationalism. Can we sum up the solution to the problems confronting our people as black nationalism? . . . I still would be hard pressed to give a specific definition of the overall philosophy which I think is necessary for the liberation of the black people in this country.*[9] Malcolm traveled to Nigeria, Ghana, Liberia, Senegal, and Morocco. In 1965, he attempted to organize an ecumenical political organization of Black people, and he called it the Organization of Afro-American Unity: *And I dedicate myself to the organizing of Black people into a group that are interested in doing things constructive, not for just one religious segment of the community, but for the entire Black community. This is what the purpose of the Organization of Afro-American Unity is. To have an action program that's for the good of the entire Black community, and we are for the betterment of the community by any means necessary.*[10] Malcolm was addressing a small gathering of the O.A.A.U. when he was shot and killed on Sunday, February 21, 1965. He was thirty-nine years old.

A simple tale, this story, as Malcolm and Haley told it, but it also hides a lot of information Malcolm wanted hidden. An obvious example is Malcolm's trip to Africa in 1959, when he visited Egypt, Saudi Arabia, the Sudan, Nigeria, and Ghana. Because Malcolm almost certainly encountered "white Muslims" on this trip, and because the trip occurred almost four years before his voyage to Mecca, his later revelation seems more than a little suspect. Malcolm's autobiography, moreover, merely glances over this first trip, quietly suggesting that Malcolm's failure to notice the "whiteness" of many of the Muslims he saw was the result of an infirm mind. *I was a zombie then—like all Muslims—I was hypnotized, pointed in a certain direction and told to march* (*Autobiography*, 429), he would later say about those years. A more satisfactory explanation would allow for Malcolm's doubts, although such doubting would have injured his smooth narrative of his early life as a firm convert to the Nation's narrow thinking.

There were other doubts, too. Just a few days before his assassination, Malcolm told a Harlem audience about a secret contact he had made with the Ku Klux Klan on the Nation's behalf. *I'm ashamed to say it, but I'm going to tell you the truth. I sat at the table myself with the heads of the Ku Klux Klan . . . who at that time were trying to negotiate with Elijah Muhammad so that they could make available to him a large area of land in Georgia or I think it was South Carolina. They had some very responsible persons in the government who were involved in it and who were willing to go along with it. They wanted to make this land available to him so that his program of separation would sound more feasible to Negroes and therefore lessen the pressure that the integrationists were putting upon the white man. I sat there. I negotiated it. I listened to their offer. And I was the one who went back to Chicago and told Elijah Muhammad what they had offered.*[11] In confessing this, Malcolm was implying that he had had doubts about Elijah's strategy; he later said that Elijah's concerns about Malcolm's belief in direct action—and Malcolm's doubts about the Klan deal—were strong enough to keep Elijah from letting him return South. Yet none of this conflict, which puts the Nation's ideological confusion into high relief, can be found in the autobiography, the official text of Malcolm's life.

This is partly the result of the autobiography's fractured construction. Malcolm changed direction during the autobiography's writing, but the book doesn't keep up. Instead, its primary narrative, its Saul-to-Paul Black conversion story, ends abruptly with Malcolm's departure from the Nation and his Mecca revelation. At Haley's insistence, Malcolm agreed not to revise the pre-Mecca sections of his autobiography. Rather than retelling the myth as he later saw it—as the tale of his struggle toward a coherent Black ideology—Malcolm allowed the book's earlier chapters to remain a face for the Nation's "true" Black spirit and nationalist ideology. As a result, the autobiography iconizes Malcolm twice, not once. Its second Malcolm—the El-Hajj Malik El-Shabazz finale—is a mask with no distinct ideology: It is not particularly Islamic, not particularly nationalist, not particularly humanist. Like any well-crafted icon, or story, the mask is evidence of its subject's humanity, of Malcolm's strong human spirit. But both masks hide as much character as they show. The first mask served a nationalism Malcolm had rejected before the book was finished; the second is mostly empty, and available.

Readers are left with two choices: Raise up the ideologically dead icon, or make of the second Malcolm what you will. The best writers on Malcolm, from the Trotskyites to the liberals, have done the latter. For most African Americans, however, the first icon seems more true: Malcolm, a strong Black face to counter the Whites. Unfortunately, his Black mask's ideological failings—its sexism, for example—remain as well; giving the appearance that Malcolm held these ideas until the day he died. *Domineering, complaining, demanding wives who had just about psychologically castrated their husbands were responsible for the early rush. These wives were so disagreeable and had made their men so tense that they were robbed of the satisfaction of being men* (*Autobiography*, 92), he had written. But is this a fair representation of Malcolm's incremental growth or of his concerns about nationalism in general? It *is* this: a cinematic projection, a hyperbolic mask undappled by doubts or questions, and it persists.

Which may, in a way, be as it should be. Malcolm, after all, put a great deal of effort into projecting his first mask. His work paid off—Malcolm's autobiography does remind African Americans that Black was a mask conceived by Europe as a designation for what Europe is not; it also promotes Malcolm's attempts to reverse this given order, to remake Black into a "good" mask. Malcolm asked African Americans to see this good, and Whites to see and pay for the Black mask they had made. Like a slave narrator, he would often direct his words to European Americans, much in the way nineteenth-century narrators attempted to awaken Whites to the immorality of slavery. *It was right there in prison that I made up my mind to devote the rest of my life to telling the white man about himself* (*Autobiography*, 185), he said. Malcolm fashioned his mask and autobiography, then, with European

Americans in mind. Given the way Malcolm is usually understood, as quintessentially Black and anti-American, this other audience makes for a contradiction. And the contradiction raises the very question Public Enemy raised by placing Malcolm on the dollar bill: Which spirit does the icon serve most?

This contradiction, this question: They are the reason Malcolm abandoned his nationalist ideology, and they point to a new way of thinking about race and America. Both Public Enemy and Malcolm X may be oppositional icons in American cultural discourse, and signifiers for sundry spirits, but they are largely irrelevant to the politics of our communities, Black or American. Malcolm ended up saying that he wanted to organize Black people, but he never found an organizing philosophy to make it happen. This is still true of Black political discourse. We do have signs, but so many of them fail as reliable evidence of a politics opposed to the oppression of Black people. Our "biology" and culture—they move so quickly, infect so many; they are shared characteristics of communities often different from our Black political community. Since *color*, James Baldwin says, *is not a human or a personal reality; it is a political reality*, we might call our cultural communities African American, and the political community Black. (Racial "biology" is simply too illusory for community formation.) Even if these labels are arbitrary, and even if most members of both groups are often one and the same, the distinction is important.

The problem with "culture as politics" is that it isn't (and almost never produces) the sort of action that not only challenges, but *changes* political structures. It *can* change minds and it *can* remind people of the fact of human commonality—this is no small achievement. But culture shifts very swiftly. It promotes, confuses, destroys ideological arguments; but its materials are too easily transported, bought, and sold. It can help us name ourselves, it can remind us how to grow; but it is slippery, it is hard to pin down. It is an honorable shelter for the weary, but it is also a hiding place for the weak of heart, and the posers. Culture is our lives, culture is the way we are—but our cultural stream is more inconstant and directionless than its political counterpart.

We've buried Malcolm in our culture. Malcolm X figures in novels such as *The Man Who Cried I Am*; he stars in operas and films about his refusal to "sell out"; he is the subject of lengthy poetic tracts about Ideology. But he also sells T-shirts, hats, potato chips, brings in dollars for people who couldn't care less about African America.

Malcolm's spirit blends—it is a vague notion, an idea that can resonate everywhere, toothlessly. Malcolm's spirit has been and will be used and misused for as many purposes as there are people; his spirit will mix with many a community's ethos, good and bad. We can consequently expect many cultural battles over Malcolm's "real" spirit, and many resurrections, too.

We need to put Malcolm to better use. Malcolm, in the end, gave us no coherent ideology, but he did leave us a site for Black political discourse. Recently I asked Justice Thurgood Marshall what he thought of Malcolm, and he said, "All he did was talk." The Justice meant this observation as a complaint, but I see it as Malcolm's most appealing characteristic. He stands for Black talk about Black thinking; we use him as a starting point. We seek, as Malcolm did, to name ourselves, and we begin, as Malcolm did, with the Black mask given us. We take the baton from Malcolm: we take our humanity for granted, and we realize that our community is made up of people of all sorts of colors, genders, classes, ethnicities, sexualities, etc. We have always known that African Americans weren't the only niggers on this earth, and now we invite all other people who are oppressed to join us. We know there is a way in which choice has nothing to do with this. When I, for example, was stopped on Madison Avenue by that White cop with nigger on the tongue, I became Black. But I have also chosen to be Black, and determined to make my own name. "Race" is a dying category; Whiteness, and the Blackness it makes for itself, is dying too. We will seize the day and make a new Blackness.

Our new Blackness acknowledges the way each of us lives beyond the Black community. I am a multitude of names, masks, community memberships. Denying this is tyranny—"race" is not my only state. I am a Black and I can be a member of a circle made up of Mississippi Whitefolk: I make new communities all the time. Which does not make me a "multiculturalist" or a "cultural mulatto"—it makes me a human being in the world. Our lives—they are about choosing our communities, and making new ones. Growth. Our lives are about naming ourselves—we are electricians, poor people, Ellingtonians, entymologists, spelunkers, candy-store owners, Woods. We learn our communities' discourses and we speak, we act, we build the group and our selves. We Blacks will make our mask mean what we want it to mean, realizing how swiftly Blackness and Whiteness mutate, how the faces of oppression change, how we sometimes oppress others. How we are White, in instances—our new definition is expansive, our Black spirit has blended with others, with the spirits of other disenfranchised people: Latinos, gays, working-class Europeans. Whiteness is still the enemy, but look: There goes Clarence Thomas, eating pigfeet and collard greens, digging Miles, looking like an Asante elder—and so what? Clarence's preferred community, most of the time? *Eenie meenie miney mo*. One can be a woman and not a Feminist, an African American and not Black. *And if she hollers let her go*. Conversants who want to help Black discourse flow—this Black People is becoming real. Believers in speech and deed are believers, no matter the other signs. *But can they feel the spirit?* Black is about talking to other Blacks; Black is about being conscious of a certain political We, about wearing the mask with pride. Black consciousness is what Black is. Becoming. Black. Is about making Blackness— the next step is to create a new and compelling politics to push the discourse forward. We talk.

Today we need, even more than we did in Malcolm's day, to talk to ourselves, and to see ourselves—to tolerate our complex selves. People interested in a more tolerant society have little use for Malcolm's narrow (and tattered) nationalism, his lack of political program, his sexism. His fixation on "race." The first mask simply needs to be changed. The second Malcolm, Malik, will speak for our new community. We will give him ideology, something to say. The old mask—its moment has passed. It flakes from our faces like dead skin.

We are in transition, always. *Black People* still makes sense today, if only because so many of us still die younger than we should, and live lives far more difficult than we should, just because of who we are. To help stop our blood from spilling, we still need Black People, the idea. And a people needs to feel a spirit and to possess its own icons: African America and all Black people need Malcolm. But Black spirit and icons (and culture) aren't enough to fix things. Our talk will lead us to a clear politics that takes into account our changing character, and directly addresses our problems. And beware: This new political thinking might—will—result in a complete reworking of the very idea of Black People, and will put it to rest, such that we might, like any People, evolve and die and evolve and die and evolve and die and evolve and die.

"Race" is turning gray. Our book suggests this. All the people I've invited to write are Black, but this book shows us that this identity is not exclusive, or fixed, or even clear. *Malcolm X: In Our Own Image* reminds us that our ideas and our interests (instead of our "biologies" or our shared cultural practices) already make for bonds outside our acknowledged communities, and that we can move to acknowledge our ties and create new and better communities. We are talking and making a new Blackness.

NOTES

1. Bruce Perry, ed., *Malcolm X: The Last Speeches* (New York: Pathfinder Press, 1989), 45.

2. There is an irony here—the dollar portrait is actually a flattened version of a Gilbert Stuart original. All but the slightest traces of Stuart have been erased.

3. Helen Gardner, *Art Through the Ages*, 7th ed. (New York: Harcourt Brace Jovanovich, Inc., 1980), 218.

4. Ibid., 219.

5. Kazimir Severinovich Malevich, *Essays on Art 1915–1933*, vol. 1 (London: Rapp & Whiting, 1968), 170.

6. Margaret Betz, "The Icon and Russian Modernism," *Artforum* (Summer 1977): 139.

7. Ibid.

8. George Breitman, ed., *Malcolm X Speaks* (New York: Grove Press, 1965), 31–32.

9. Ibid., 212–13.

10. Perry, *Malcolm X: The Last Speeches*, 133.

11. Ibid., 123.

Malcolm as Ideology

≡

AMIRI BARAKA

Malcolm X continues today, twenty-seven years after his murder, to be at the center of ideological development and discussion in the Black Liberation Movement, the Black national community—and to some still broadening extent, America, the general.

There is, of course, the syndrome that Lenin spoke about when he said that once opponents of the bourgeoisie are dead, the rulers transform these class enemies into ciphers or agreeable sycophants of Imperialism (however "askew" they might have "seemed" in life) who are now "rehabilitated" all the way into being represented as the very opposite ideologically of what they actually were in life.

But Malcolm is also, himself, a figure of ideological development and change. So that it is easier to focus on some particular period or aspect of his life and make that the entire substance of who he was.

Because Malcolm's life was shaped by such continuous ideological development, if we take the whole of that development into consideration, analyze and explicate each period—what it was, why that was, given time, place, and condition, and why it changed, and what it changed to—then we will get a deeper biographical portrait of Malcolm, one that is not static and "ideal" but in motion.

The portrait Spike Lee had drawn, in his "fourth-draft script," is an instance of absolutizing the middle portion of Malcolm's life and trying to use that as a defining spine of the entire life.

Spike begins his proposed film of Malcolm with himself, apparently, as "Shorty" (a sidekick of Detroit Red's) running up the street, arms full of "Congolene" supplies. Shorty is about to "Konk" a big country boy's head, Malcolm Little, so that he can become "Detroit Red."

This is Spike's point of departure, as well as the perspective through which he shreds piecemeal the earlier aspects of Malcolm's life. In other words, Malcolm's young life is seen mainly as a memory in Detroit Red's mind.

In fact, Detroit Red holds center stage in Spike's screenplay. Even the character Shorty appears more than Malcolm's father or mother. So Spike sees the Detroit Red years as "real time" while the early years are just disparate flashes of memory.

This is because, to Spike, Detroit Red is the *real* Malcolm, and flashbacks are all that is required of the formative years.

This perception is further elaborated upon by Spike's treatment of the later "political" years. They are shuffled toward us, almost like cards, coming at us face down, so superficial is their use to us as drama or politics, which at their most powerful would be a single composite!

Each of us sees a thing or event according to our own experiences and interests and ideological stance. Malcolm's life itself was also an ideological statement, one that is ironically consolidated, made more explicit, by its specific changes.

But to understand the *overall statement* Malcolm's life makes, one must make a *material* analysis, an evaluation of concrete conditions, but one that is also dialectical, i.e., sensitive to the point and cause and dimension of change.

The Bruce Perry calumny (*Malcolm: The Life of a Man Who Changed Black America*,[1]) seems to me the action of one of George Bush's CIA "proprietaries" (subcontractors contracted to do a specific job) whose mission is to cover Malcolm's real life with a barrage of psychopathic untruths. So that Malcolm's life becomes simply the disoriented thrashings of schizophrenia.

Perry's "research," which consists of disconnected "interviews," half by telephone, dredges up irrelevant and fragmented "events" and strings them together as the proof of his "theory"—that Malcolm was "white" and that his "problem," the real cause of his "militancy," was his dissatisfaction with his false "Blackness" and the hatred of his mother and father. That, plus his continuing "cowardice" and pathological "criminality."

Malcolm's father, mother, Aunt Ella, etc., were likewise pathologi-

cal criminals. Indeed, the whole of the Black Liberation Movement
was (is) pathological.

It is significant that Pathfinder Press, the cat's paw of the Socialist
Workers Party (Trot), had Perry edit and write the introduction to its
edition of Malcolm's *Last Speeches!*

Why not? The Trots have never supported Afro-American self-
determination. Their suit against Abdul Al Kalimat and the Black-
owned Readers and Writers Press for publishing a Malcolm Reader
for Beginners is simply base capitalist business practice.

The irony is that here another white corporation is fighting Black
people for control of their lives. The SWP is historically and actively
opposed to Malcolm as ideology, yet it would go into the bourgeois
court to sue Black people to franchise Malcolm as property!

I was recently summoned to a Malcolm celebration in D.C. at
Howard University by Betty Shabazz. The gathering featured middle-
class Negroes of mostly backward persuasions. What was stunning is
how this assembly of Negro bureaucrats, academics, middle-class
"conscientious objectors" to Black struggle were furiously, if stiffly,
rubbing up against Malcolm like self-manipulated "firesticks" trying
to make at least a little smoke.

Sharon Pratt Dixon, D.C.'s outspokenly pro-capitalist mayor, led
a motley crew of small businessmen and half-hip promoters of "Black,"
the product, using Malcolm as if to sanctify and legitimatize their own
lives, and paths, as somehow, any way, connected to Malcolm.

It is like the paradox of "Blackness" as an ideology, in that it is
the most superficial i.d. of the nation, classless and ultimately deceptive. Both Buthelezi and Mandela are "Black." Like Roy Innis and
Malcolm X.

It is the ideology, the class stance, their acts, that define persons,
exclusive of nationality. So, now, to confirm Lenin's teaching, these
Negroes were serving the big bourgeoisie and themselves as apprentice
torturers, by distorting and hiding Malcolm's life to enhance their own
and U.S. imperialisms.

It made me remember 1965 when I returned to Newark and went
with Ben Caldwell and another brother up to Montclair to a gathering
of the Howard U. alumni where I had been asked to speak. When I
mentioned Malcolm X the Negroes actually booed! They even wanted
to throw Ben out because he had no tie. I gave him mine and talked
bad to these Negroes for thirty minutes.

These are the same kinds of Negroes who sat in the Howard student center rubbing up against Malcolm X because he had become not safe but clearly usable.

That is why Spike's "use" is so obvious and painful, since it is in neon. Spike's films reveal him as the apologist for this same sector of the Black petty bourgeoisie that holds Black life a caricature, Black struggle a ridiculous hypocrisy, whose incomes "prove" this, whose "Blackness" is only a job description.

Since this is a period of reaction, like the bottom of the downward stroke of the Sisyphus Syndrome of Black life in America, there is a retrograde trend, a specific sociopolitical tendency in U.S. society, expressed in all aspects of the society, with part of its social base a reactionary sector of the Black petty bourgeoisie, comprising a comprador class (that part of the Black bourgeoisie and petty bourgeoisie whose *market* is imperialism, not other Black people). Negroes serving imperialism and white supremacy as a sector of "black opinion."

For these, Black struggle is mainly *commercial*, economic as a pay raise. The "Civil Rights Movement" is passé, hypocrisy or delusion. It has *been* over! (Remember that, and you can make some money!)

African Kings and Queens can be put to work for Budweiser. Martin Luther King for McDonald's and Malcolm X for Warner Brothers. ABC makes millions from our *Roots*.

The Sowells, Walter Williams, Crouches, Playtoy Beenyesman, Glenn Lourys, Roy Innises, Melvin Williams, Juan Williams, and Tom Ass Clarences tell us the same things white racists told us earlier. Their employment is how the bourgeoisie adapts to our past victories. These racists camouflage themselves as backward Negroes, who during the '60s upsurge of the Black Liberation Movement were pods growing in the cellars of our politics.

Skip Gates and the Negro deconstructionists actually re-raise the reaction of the backward white Southern agrarian so-called "New Critics" of the '40s and '50s. The attempted disconnection of literature from real life. To render beauty and intelligence neuter and abstract. To make truth mysterious and an individual perception; and society metaphor and metaphysical.

So we begin to understand if we analyze this retrograde trend, these bought-and-paid-for Negro white supremacist "intellectuals" and academics, these petty surrogate racist Negro politicians, as mayors, congress- or councilpersons, corporate figureheads, institutional jigaboos, these eurocentricoon "happen-to-be-Negro" artists whose notoriety is that now their confessions of submission can be included in the curricula.

After any social-political upsurge by the people, it is necessary for the rulers to, as quickly as possible, cover, obscure, distort, reverse, outlaw any trace of the entire epoch, its meaning, its victims, its ideas, its victories, and its material human life.

Just as the two other previous epochs of Black American social-political upsurges are now obscured: the nineteenth-century antislavery movement including the Civil War and Reconstruction, and the early twentieth-century social insurgency, including the sharpened Afro-American and international Black democratic struggle, Pan Africanism and its Anti-Colonialism, the Harlem Renaissance and Garvey movement. These were initially resisted by the continuing slave society, then obstructed, then distorted, then "deconstructed" and made obscure. So the most recent upsurge of the '60s has likewise suffered the same overall attack. The Black retrograde trend of diverse new and long-in-the-tooth "buppie" spokespersons is one leading edge of this attack. Confirming not only a pattern of slave master to imperialist repression and suppression of African Americans, but of the post-'60s consolidation of an expanded Black petty bourgeoisie with an expanded and more powerful conservative sector, including a more powerful comprador sector.

It is a bitter irony that this expansion of the Black petty bourgeois was created by the struggle, victories, and impact of the '50s and '60s Black national democratic civil rights and liberation movement. The expansion of the Black petty bourgeoisie was an expression, supposedly, of the expanded power (socio-pol-eco) of the Afro-American people and the fruits of their victory over formal American apartheid.

But within that movement, the objective Black United Front, like the whole people, is divided into classes whose internal class struggle is only obscured by the struggle of the whole people against white supremacy and imperialism.

Since the '50s-'60s upsurge, the Afro-American people's movement has been co-opted by the Black bourgeoisie. But since they only "represent" Black people but are not organically or ideologically connected to the people, they do not *actually* have power. So they become expressions of betrayal, collaboration, co-optation, of the need for actual power, democracy, and self-determination.

Jesse Jackson, one of the best-known and articulate spokespersons for what purports to be a progressive sector of the Black petty bourgeoisie, demonstrated the final sterility of even these "well-meaning" folks, viz., Jesse's open capitulation to the Democratic party, even after the insulting Dukakis lie about offering the VP nomination to him.

The question of self-determination, once the mainstream of the Black petty bourgeoisie feels they are in a position to compete for or contest "space in America," becomes more or less irrelevant. They see it as "separatism" or, from farther right, the very reason for our "failing to make progress."

They see the historical struggle for Afro-American Self-Determination useful only to pimp, as a cosmetic political device, hence the publicly "powerful" Blacks in society who should by their own declarations be leading Black struggle for self-determination, who betray and disclaim it hourly.

They tell us, "Our struggle is best handled by the electoral system, by electing Black elected officials, so that Black Power becomes a reality. Didn't Malcolm say 'The ballot or the bullet'?"

But these officials in most cases become colored "public servants" controlled by big business and big politics. Like the Black police we struggled for in the '50s and '60s. Now they become mercenaries of white supremacy and Black national oppression. They keep it manageable under imperialism!

In too many of the schools, Black teachers are entirely part of the racist superstructure. Poison Negroes poisoning our children with submission and self-hate. We see the more known of these backward academics. Along with them, the retrograde Negro body-snatchers who cavort as critics, journalists, media personalities, spokespersons, who are responsible to vilify, defame, and frame Black people, in order to work out their own opportunism and self-hate as profitably as possible.

Ngugi (*Petals of Blood*)[2] has told how in the neo-colonial development of Kenya, after the Mau Mau drove out the British, international imperialism raised up many traitor Negroes to assume the bureaucratic formalities of running the neo-colonial state to keep real power from the Kenyan people.

Many of the reactionary and conservative Negro voices now being pumped up by imperialism in the U.S. were on the defensive, under attack, obscure, in the '50s to '70s. Now they have become "prominent," inflated by white supremacy resurgent in the '90s.

There is even a sector of the newer generation of this backward Negro petty bourgeoisie that has never even lived with Black people, never lived in the ghetto. Children of Negroes the anti-us apartheid movement of the '50s and '60s allowed to move to the suburbs and be the token. Black people would not move forward, only a small sector of a class as "role models."

But now there are more Negroes for whom "Black culture" is abstract or theoretical or a *style*. These last are the pop-bup Negroes, whose soi disant "new Black aesthetic" or "blues aesthetic" seeks to disconnect Black culture and art from its material history and revolutionary essence.

Like Spike Lee's, their opportunistic use of Black culture is exploitative, a form of "economism" (as Lenin called it), replacing the political struggle for self-determination with a superficial rhetoric aimed at gaining economic concessions under imperialism. Some even put out the line that "racism will always exist."

In essence, this is ideological, in form, often a crass commercialism crossing many times over into straight-out mercenary comprador betrayal. Spike's cry of "independent" Black filmmaker has very quickly revealed itself as a marketing device, like the "Blackness" of his movies.

Also, there is another historically verifiable pattern of imperialist repression that mandates that after every period of Black militance, not only must this be "covered" (like Elvis P covered Big Mama Thornton, etc.) but also caricatured and distorted. One constant method has been minstrelsy, whether it is *Birth of a Nation*, Al Jolson, *Gone With the Wind*, Step 'n Fetchit, Elvis, Playtoy Beenyesman, or Vanilla Ice.

So that the militant post–Civil War folk must be replaced with Griffith's eye-rolling blackface whites. Consider the connection between ideology and social organization, when the white Rice Minstrels, performing a blackface skit called *Jim Crow*, should be used to title the continuation of the slave society as segregation and discrimination. Or the apparent self-mockery of the Black performers using blackface who continued the slander.

All this is necessary to understand not only the historical impact and significance of Malcolm X, but the need imperialism has now to cover, distort, and caricature his historical factual existence. Particularly as ideological.

Malcolm's real life, from his childhood, intersected American social reality and was shaped by it. Not only as a Black youth, whose life must invariably be formed by the American system of Black national oppression, but in its internal development, which is always principal; his father, a Garvey preacher and organizer, his mother, a Grenadan nationalist, gave the initial direction to his early growth.

It cannot be mere coincidence, for example, that Malcolm's father's Garveyism, so critical as an early twentieth-century expression of Black struggle for self-determination, should be renewed through the Black nationalist teaching of Elijah Muhammad.

His father's murder, and the subsequent destruction of his family by the white supremacist state organs, including the intense psychological terror that drove his mother to a nervous breakdown, directed Malcolm's life into America as a *conscious* victim.

The fact that Michigan presented a superficial integration to the American society Malcolm X grew in adds the ironic summation of Black rejection as the essence of U.S. social organization. The much-referenced rejection of Malcolm's dream to become a lawyer is met, even in the "integrated" classroom, with an enforced continuation of slave status that blocks Malcolm's youthful aspirations *to be* in America. Malcolm's reaction to this rejection, his eventual emergence in urban ghetto society as an "outlaw," is classic, even predictable.

Malcolm's father was a working-class Black whose "vocation" as preacher provided a lower-middle-class field of proposed social mobility for the family, but his father's murder quickly threw the family back into a constantly diminishing status as impoverished working class.

From here, racist social barriers and his own sense of rebellion threw Malcolm into the criminal world as he became partially "lumpenized" i.e., broken, by imperialism.

Spike's focus on the Detroit Red personality and social world as the basis of Malcolm's development is, for instance, a form of commercialism and ideological belittling of the personal, political, and social factors that helped create Detroit Red. Malcolm's early life is not just disconnected "memory," as Spike would have it, but a catalyst for his real life and ideological "Journey." Malcolm's life is consistently, in overview, a struggle for Self-Determination. A material base for his expressed consciousness.

It is his consciousness, and its meaning and development, that is the most critical to an understanding of Malcolm. Why and to what does it change? And how is it reflected in the masses of the Afro-American people?

When Malcolm goes to prison, a prisoner so opposed to the social life and philosophical "status quo" of U.S. society he is called SATAN, he is seen as opposed even to the American (Xtian) "God." He is insisting that he exists outside of "the given." That he is not the submissive Negro, the Black victim, or the nigger cipher.

His prison education, including Elijah Muhammad, gives him the form with which overtly to combine consciousness with his actual life. Or at least more so than ever before. As a function of experience and maturity, but also of philosophical revelation.

From his father's Garveyism to the revelations of Elijah Muhammad, Malcolm is still actually on a continuous line of *nationalist development* and expanding consciousness. The entrance into the Nation of Islam gives total expression to this historical ideological continuum!

But compare Malcolm's early tenure as the Messenger's messenger, the chief spokesman for the "Honorable Elijah Muhammad," and his last years when he had developed a clearly political nationalist line, in open contrast to the more metaphysical cultural and economic nationalism of Elijah Muhammad.

What changed is that as Malcolm gained more of an overview of American society and the forces at work within it, and the alignment of these forces, even internationally, he diminished his "White Devil-Mothership," "nonpolitical" metaphysical rhetoric and began to speak to the specific character of the Black Liberation Movement as a struggle for political self-determination.

The Civil Rights Movement has as one element of its total political thrust the struggle for democracy. Even in the "nonviolent" expression posited by Martin Luther King, there was an activist aspect that made Elijah Muhammad's "noninvolvement" in politics seem openly conservative. No matter the metaphysical rhetoric of white society's divine doom!

Malcolm was moved by the political force inherent in Elijah Muhammad's teaching, though his Detroit Red life had made the "religious atonement" and conversion aspect of it relevant, as if they were one and the same.

But this "conversion" was at base political, like his philosophically enhanced nationalism. Malcolm eventually saw that it was revolution that made change in the here and the now more directly than "Allah," that it was Black revolution that was needed, which was political, not metaphysical and religious.

Elijah Muhammad's call for Black separation from the U.S. and five Southern "Black belt" states as the landbase of the Black nation (also expressed, in various ways, by the old African Blood Brotherhood, late-1920s Communist Party USA, the '60s African Peoples' Party, and some of the organizations of the so-called New Left of that same period, including the still-existent Republic of New Africa) becomes more and more subsumed in Malcolm's "Message to the Grass Roots" and "Ballot or the Bullet" into a call for Black unity against white supremacy and Black national oppression. It becomes a call for Self-Determination, as a function of unified Black political struggle, rather than the "independence" Elijah Muhammad preached, which implied the existence of a Black state within the boundaries of an imperalist USA.

It was not a Bantustan Malcolm X called for but mobilization against national oppression. In the '60s we summed up Malcolm as calling for Self-Determination, Self-Respect, and Self-Defense. The act of struggle was itself an act of Self-Determination, expressing and the expression of Self-Respect, the "true Self-Consciousness" Du Bois called for.

Imperalism and its spokespersons always try to make Malcolm's call for "Self-Defense" a call for violence. But in reality it is a call for a force that will stop the wanton violence against the Afro-American people. In the backward corridors of today's political climate, where violent physical (and verbal) attacks on Black people have accelerated, Malcolm's call takes on an enhanced relevance.

"If the federal government won't protect us then we will do it ourselves." Against the Howard Beach, Yusef Hawkins, Tawana Brawley, Philip Pannel, new Klan attacks, this call reverberates in and reignites the Black consciousness.

Malcolm's "separatism" became the call for a Black national revolutionary unity to struggle for Self-Determination. Black people would be served by their own struggle, the catalyst being their own consciousness and historical will.

Malcolm's split with Elijah Muhammad and the Nation of Islam was another example of how "one splits into two." That is, how entities are transformed by the dialectical motion of their internal contradictions.

Malcolm's call for Self-Determination was revolutionary in the sense that it saw Black Self-Determination coming only as the result of the political confrontation with and destruction of the continuing slave society. Elijah Muhammad's "separate states" theoretically could be accomplished under existing U.S. imperialism. Not too different from Buthelezi's projection of a "cultural autonomy" for South African Blacks, postapartheid apartheid.

Malcolm's last years, the whole of his overtly political years, are a casebook of ideological change, of social cause and effect. From cultural and religious nationalism, he moves through expansion and clarification of the political dimension into a more politically defined Black nationalism.

The religious and metaphysical trappings of his nationalism were shredded by the real-life politics of the insurgent Black national united front as well as by the revelation of Elijah Muhammad's personal sexual corruption and the petty obstructions of his Nation of Islam theocrat "rivals."

What is so telling is that JFK's assassination, which is the context for the confirmation of Malcolm's call for Black political Self-Determination, corresponds to Black perception that Kennedy's murder removes the "helping hand" of white liberalism from Black people, forcing them to go it alone!

It is now that Malcolm becomes the principal spokesman for the Black struggle for Self-Determination and so is doomed himself to assassination. At this point the Black Liberation Movement emerges as the raised voice of Black struggle. The Civil Rights Movement is transformed into the Black Liberation Movement. "Separation," Self-Defense, and Black Consciousness (Self-Respect) become the dynamic interior of Afro-American struggle.

For Malcolm, Self-Respect was a call to "Black consciousness." In the "true self-consciousness" that W. E. B. Du Bois called for, which opposed the "double consciousness" of the Black-hating, white-submitting schizophrenic "house Negro." This Self-Respect would best be served through organizational and institutional development.

SNCC (Student Non-Violent Coordinating Committee), at first shaped by SCLC (Southern Christian Leadership Conference) and its "Christian nonviolence" à la Dr. King, not only splits between "separatists" and "integrationists" but is changed by the exit of many of the white student activists, ultimately into the antiwar movement.

Jimmy Baldwin's Blues for Mr. Charlie[3] characterizes the class struggle for influence over the student movement. So that now the

A. J. Muste pacifist type leadership, such as Bob Moses, gave way to the more militant Stokely Carmichaels and H. Rap Browns. Where the struggle for democracy and self-determination is unified in Malcolm X's catalyzed militance.

Malcolm's trip to Mecca, and subsequently to Africa, was the further expansion and consolidation of an ideology of Black revolutionary self-determination, plus now with an added universalism—actually, internationalism. The recognition of "white Muslims" was, objectively, an expression of Malcolm's recognition of internationalism and the worldwide antiimperialist struggle.

Yet Malcolm's close-up on the Bandung conference of Third World nations, his exposure to the Organization of African Unity (OAU), his meetings with the great African (including Arab) leaders as a Black national (Pan Africanist) front provided a practical clarification of the need for such a front in the U.S., the OAAU.

In my meeting with Malcolm in January 1965, in Muhammad Babu's hotel room at the Waldorf-Astoria, one month before his murder, Malcolm stressed the need for political activists, including myself, to animate and make politically viable a Black united front in the U.S. He insisted that we must move the whole people into a live revolutionary unity.

This is the opposite of the religious sectarianism of the Nation of Islam. It is an admission that Islam is not the only road to revolutionary consciousness and that Muslims, Christians, Nationalists, and Socialists can be joined together as an antiimperialist force in the U.S.

Malcolm had made the connection between Black struggle for democracy and Self-Determination, between white supremacy and its political economic base, imperialism.

Malcolm's Oxford speech (January '65), during the same period he was expelled from France, where he predicted white uprising as a collateral development to Black revolution, indicated an even more advanced internationalist rationale to substantiate a victorious struggle for Black Self-Determination.

The Nation of Islam justified Malcolm's murder, and the government even placed his assassins within the Nation of Islam. But the Nation of Islam and Elijah Muhammad were not the assassins, it was the U.S. government! The same murderers of JFK, RFK, and MLK. The same forces who currently inhabit the *white house.*

And even at the pit of current social backwardness in the U.S.

and the world created by the elimination and co-optation of people's revolutionary forces, there is a visible rise in the reforming revolutionary movement. There is a "fight back," a resistance, especially among the young, and in some quarters of the Black "intelligentsia." Black people in Louisiana unified to spank David Duke. Howard students rejected Bush's Atwater. Political rap artists carry a sharp and aggressive attack on white supremacy. The Black studies and multicultural forces reflect Malcolm's call for Self-Determination, Self-Respect, and Self-Defense.

The ideological struggle and development of Black Self-Determination begins with Malcolm's OAAU and proceeds past the general United Front to a political party. A party created to struggle for total U.S. social transformation, based on the call and mobilization for Black Self-Determination. An independent U.S. party, probably formed and, in the main, led by Afro-Americans, but open to the whole of the U.S. people.

Malcolm X, in essence, is a figure representing struggle and Black Self-Determination. Attention to his life and teachings will show immediately how the co-optation of the Black Liberation Movement by the Black bourgeoisie must be resisted and exposed.

His "House Negro" vs. "Field Negro" example of class struggle among the Afro-American people analyzes and exposes Black liberals and conservatives and describes the whole backward sector of the Black petty bourgeoisie.

Part of the Black bourgeoisie's attack on Malcolm X will be to make him their spokesperson. To render Malcolm's embrace of "internationalism" (i.e., the "revelation" that revolution is a worldwide process, in which Black people are not only included but required to make alliances and coalitions as confirmation of this fact and as the concrete furthering of their own struggle) as the abandoning of Elijah Muhammad's separatism and a militant and acceptable form of "integration," actually submission to U.S. imperialism and white supremacy.

Malcolm's fundamental ideological stance to white supremacy is opposition and an attempt to destroy it. Not coexistence as employment. Like Spike's waving of the red, black, and green in opposing a white director for the Malcolm film is the transparent nationalism of any bourgeoisie trying to secure its market. In effect, it's Spike saying "Only Black me truly can sell y'all these swine foots . . . no whitey can sell authentic swine foots." Hey, they still swine foots! Afro Sheen vs. Vaseline. Securing an economic concession under imperialism, not attempting to destroy it.

And even though the Black national bourgeoisie must be included in the broad Afro-American United Front against imperialism (national bourgeoisie, the sector that still does serve a Black market, as opposed to the compradors, that sector whose market is imperialism), we must still understand the essential *shallowness* of the Black bourgeoisie's commitment to actual Black Self-Determination. They are not there for the long haul, and ours is a protracted struggle.

So Spike's swine foot declaration is the narrowest (i.e., almost wholly economic) claiming of "Black." The removing of the political essence of such "independence" makes it more an attempt at inclusion in imperialism than a point of departure for Black Self-Determination. Indeed, Spike's much-touted call for Black "independence" has vanished quickly right before our eyes, and with 25 million Warner Brothers' dollars on the line, he has already moved to the point where he must answer to imperialism and he now publicly dismisses as "repression" any question of him "answering" to Black people.

Malcolm's last ideological disposition was, again, a movement toward internationalism. After the Mecca and Africa trips, Malcolm used orthodox (Sunni) Islam to disassociate himself from Elijah Muhammad and the Nation of Islam. The trips themselves better familiarized him with international third-world leadership and streams of revolutionary thought inside the third world.

His statement on forming the Organization of Afro-American Unity shows he still identified publicly as a "Black Nationalist" ("Black control of the politics and economics of the Black community . . .") for whom religion had become a "personal" matter.

The political faces of the Black movement must now be formed as a united front of the entire community. This was certainly the essence of what we discussed those several hours at the Waldorf a month before his murder.

But even earlier, Malcolm had said in a speech, "find a capitalist and you find a bloodsucker!" And then in that stunning bit of recorded history, during his Oxford speech, Malcolm chided the mostly white students that "when Black people make revolution, the majority of white folks will rise up with us."

The specter of Malcolm no longer limited by the ideological parameters of the Nation of Islam, possibly giving leadership to a broad Black united front and able to make international alliances and coalitions (in the whole sense and meaning of that world) could not be tolerated by imperialism.

Recent and proposed attacks on Malcolm X by the bourgeoisie (including Spike's film) seem to indicate that they do not intend for Malcolm's image to survive either. No accurate historical portrait can be drawn of Malcolm without some ideological precision, rendering each of his changes, his stages, in exact dimension. But the bourgeoisie's intentions are not clarity of image, but the exact opposite.

To distort Malcolm so that, like most of Black history, there will be no trace of the actual Malcolm, no trace of his struggle for Self-Determination or our own.

Just as today Spike Lee and others lead a trend of *real* Black exploitation flicks, made by Black reactionaries, while any real analysis of those '60s films media "gofers" call "Black Exploitation films" (e.g., *The Education of Sonny Carson*, *Superfly*, *The Mack*, *Buck and the Preacher*, *Across 110th Street*, even *Shaft*) will find them much more progressive, even much more pro-Black Self-Determination than the "She's Gotta Have It," "In Living Color," "House Party" syndrome of neo-Step 'n Fetchit derogations and caricatures of Black life, which completely eliminate even the slightest discussion of Black Self-Determination. (Except, perhaps the twisted superficial backwardness of *Do the Right Thing* where Black struggle is perverted to mean photos in a pizza parlor.)

But since these pictures are made by Black reactionaries, as the expression of our domestic neo-colonialism—"imperialism ruling through native agents," Cabral called it—those of us unused to "close reading" of films (or anything else, for that matter) or educated analysis are "chumped off" by the color trick and absorb even larger doses of "double consciousness" Negro antiblackness than we would ever accept from white folks.

Spike Lee's general "dis" of the Black Liberation Movement including his treatment of Elijah Muhammad in the film, his dismissal of Malcolm's political meaning, will be seen very shortly. Let us hope it will be understood for what it is and widely opposed.

The main focus of these attempts (with more sighted coming up every day) to distort Malcolm's life is the youth and the future generations more than those of us who lived through that period when he was alive and leading the Black Liberation Movement. The widespread signs that Black youth are not content to be set up as confused and essentially self-destructive targets of white supremacy, uninformed "public enemies" as a result of their miseducation by imperialism and the co-optation of the leadership of the Black Liberation Movement by the Black bourgeoisie, has made the twisting of Malcolm's image a priority in the official U.S. disinformation bureaus and businesses.

Du Bois not only said the problem of the twentieth century is the color line, but he also said that the twentieth century was the epoch of propaganda, since we (human beings) had already formally and legally obtained human rights and now the rulers had to convince us not to make use of them. Malcolm's life, in its real dimension, is a resource and an instrument to be used by all progressive people, but certainly the Afro-American and Pan African peoples for Self-Determination.

Malcolm's very ideological movement, his groping and seeking, his stumbling and continuous rising from confusion to partial clarity and on, are something that should be taught and studied and widely understood by all of us who would make sweeping social transformation and revolution.

The very struggle for multicultural and Black studies courses in schools is part of that struggle for clarity, and against the masters of propaganda. This must be part of an even broader cultural revolution, where revolutionary politics are struggled for in the area of the superstructure, those ideas and institutions created to forward those ideas created by the economic base of the society. Since this is a society with an imperialist economic base, the main superstructural ideas and institutions that carry them are imperialist, which means economically exploitative, politically oppressive, socially racist, and male chauvinist.

It was Mao who pointed out the importance of Class Struggle, elaborating on what Lenin had said about the need to destroy the state apparatus of imperialism; otherwise it would retard the building of socialism even after the military victory of the proletariat. It is the need to continue the class struggle, the revolutionary struggle in the sphere of culture, the arts, education, otherwise even though we win a revolutionary battle by force of arms, our enemies will reverse that victory if they maintain control of the superstructure.

This has been shown to be viciously, tragically true in both the USSR and People's China, where now we see the Soviet Union itself overthrown and capitalism restored. In China, where Mao said if the people did not continue the Cultural Revolution, the party would "change colors" and become a party controlled by capitalist roaders, maybe even a fascist party. This is exactly what has happened. The grim events in Tiananmen Square a few years ago, where Deng (pronounced Dung) Tsiao Peng, a reactionary Mao once made to wear a dunce hat during the Cultural Revolution, has now killed more communists than Ronald Reagan.

In the U.S.—though we are not defending a socialist state—the gains that we made in the '50s and '60s, not only the outright defeat of American apartheid, but the advance of the Afro American peoples' struggle for Self-Determination, must be protected at all costs.

In the dimensions of the Sisyphus Syndrome I described earlier, we are now at a downward stroke. The whole host of progressive leaders that were murdered, the aggressive disruption of the movement by government counterinsurgency forces such as KAOS and Cointelpro, added to the principal negative, which was *inside* the Black Liberation Movement, i.e., the absence of a scientific revolutionary party, plus the co-optation of the movement by the Black bourgeoisie (principally through electoral politics, and more recently through the arts). These are the factors that left us open to the dogged and continuous decline in the focus and mobilized militancy of the movement.

The covering and distortion of Malcolm X is just another technique to disrupt the "orderly" passage of revolution from one generation to another. Now that the younger generation is looking for more profound reasons for our lives, naturally they turn to the most profound struggle in this society, the most profound confirmation of the nobility of their lives. So they must turn to the Black Liberation Movement, they must inevitably turn to Malcolm, who ultimately will be revealed as the most profound figure of the '50s–'60s black political upsurge.

Part of our cultural revolution must be to protect the reality of Malcolm's life, because that is the only way we will protect the reality of our own, and the actual historical gravity and meaning of our struggle. This is the reason we ourselves must take our struggle into the schools, into the movie studios, the theaters, the concert halls and nightclubs. It is why we must build cultural and educational and arts institutions to provide an alternative to the poisonous fruits of the American superstructure, even though we must not abandon our struggle for influence and control over those sectors of the superstructure where such relationship is possible.

This is why we are in contention about Malcolm's life and image and history. This is why imperialism and white supremacy and their little running dogs are too.

The editor of this collection said to the writers he wanted no essays celebrating Malcolm. This, he has been made to think, will make such essays "objective." But Malcolm X, *objectively*, was a leading force of struggle for Afro-American Self-Determination. That this is a *fact*, whether it is praiseworthy or to be condemned, is a matter of ideology.

NOTES

1. Bruce Perry, *Malcolm: The Life of a Man Who Changed Black America* (New York: Station Hill Press, 1991).
2. Ngugi Wa Thiong 'O, *Petals of Blood* (New York: NAL, 1978).
3. James Baldwin, *Blues for Mr. Charlie* (New York: Dial Press, 1964).

Meditations on the Legacy
of Malcolm X*

≡

ANGELA Y. DAVIS

Malcolm had said to . . . black women earlier in December, 1964
that we were the real educators. We were the setter of fires that
would burn until our people set themselves free.
—Patricia Robinson

Patricia Robinson's engaging account of Malcolm X's political bequest to and acknowledgment of African-American women has been all but eclipsed by representations in contemporary Black popular culture that tend to portray Malcolm as the quintessential "Black man," as that historical figure whose style and rhetoric are the measure by which the revolutionary potential of African-American youth in the 1990s should be judged. "On Sunday afternoon, February 21, 1965," Robinson mused, "all of us, who had waited for centuries for that revolutionary son and brother to be reborn, gratefully and humbly accepted the revolutionary responsibility as it passed out of Malcolm's slowly descending body."[1] She contended that after Malcolm's disillusionment with the Nation of Islam, he began to turn toward and to listen to Black women in a way that had not been possible as long as he functioned under the ideological tutelage of a man—Elijah Muhammad—whose political/religious vision and whose personal life

*This essay is based on speeches delivered at Michigan State, Columbia, and Syracuse University.

were thoroughly shaped by male supremacy. Relying on the paradigm of the family, she interpreted his legacy as that of the "Black revolutionary son" driven by a new historical impulse to recognize and assist in a process of empowering the "mother" and the "sister." As problematic as this model might be, with its unavoidable masculinist implications, it seems to me that Robinson was calling for a feminist appreciation of Malcolm's political contributions.

In 1992, within a context constructed by ubiquitous images of Malcolm as the *essential Black man*, the juxtaposition of the words "Malcolm" and "feminist" rings strange and oxymoronic. Yet this is precisely why I feel compelled—using Patricia Robinson's analysis as a point of departure—to formulate a number of questions regarding some possible feminist implications of his legacy. I will not presume to answer all the questions I pose. Indeed, many of them are speculative in the Socratic sense, designed more to shift the focus of the popular discourse on Malcolm X rather than guide a substantive inquiry into his political history.

The first set of questions: Is it possible that if Malcolm had not been shot down on February 21, 1965, he might be identifying with the global feminist movement today? Would he have allowed his vision to be disrupted and revolutionized by the intervention of feminism? Or, in order to discuss the feminist implications of his legacy, is it even necessary to argue about the positions Malcolm X, the man, might have assumed?

Rather than directly address these questions, I want to parenthetically evoke my own recent experience with one of the persisting themes in Malcolm's political discourse—South African apartheid. When I visited South Africa in September 1991, political consciousness regarding the marginalization and oppression of women appeared to be transforming the character of the battle for democracy there. Not only were women in the various organizations of the Liberation Alliance—the African National Congress (ANC), the South African Communist Party (SACP), Congress of South African Trades Unions (COSATU), and so on—developing creative strategies for involving masses of women in the revolutionary process, they were also challenging the entrenched male dominance in the leadership of their organizations. Although a proposed affirmative action plan for women within the African National Congress was not accepted at the last convention, it was clearly gaining support as a legitimate means of reversing the decades-old assumptions that men deserved the preponderance of leadership positions.

Women in South Africa were also redefining the pervasive political violence (perpetrated by Black organizations such as Buthelezi's Inkatha, but supported by the white government) in terms that included the violence they suffered at the hands of their husbands at home. The women activists whom I encountered spoke of the futility of seeking to eradicate this epidemic public violence while their bodies continued to be battered by the violence defiling their private lives.

Feminist consciousness like this disrupts traditional modes of struggle, and many—men and women alike—in yearning for the simplicity of the "good old days" would wish it away, if such magical solutions were possible. In light of the misogynist attitudes often represented in the media (particularly in film and in the music videos and rap lyrics associated with hip-hop) as the consensus of contemporary young Black men, for whom Malcolm is the ultimate hero, I am led to pose another set of speculative questions that preempts the first, since what matters is not the "good old days," or what Malcolm might have become—what matters is what Malcolm's legacy means today. And so, is it the legacy of Malcolm X to wish such a feminist consciousness away? Is it his legacy to long for simple formulations and simple answers? Is it the legacy of Malcolm X to ignore the radical reconceptualization of the struggle for democracy urged by South African women?

Having posed these questions, I want to make a case for the possibility of responding to them in the negative—or, at the very least, for the importance of asking them. I will develop an argument based on the critical connotations of Malcolm's own eventual interrogation of his philosophical adherence to Black nationalism.

On January 23, 1963, Malcolm X delivered an address sponsored by the African Students Association and the campus NAACP at Michigan State University and later published under the title "Twenty Million Black People in a Political, Economic and Mental Prison." He prefaced his speech with words of thanks to the two sponsoring organizations "for displaying the unity necessary to bring a very controversial issue before the students here on campus. The unity of Africans abroad and the unity of Africans here in this country can bring about practically any kind of achievement or accomplishment that black people want today."[2] On the eve of his assassination two years later, Malcolm seemed to be deeply interrogating the nationalist philosophical grounds that had led him to use racialized metaphors of imprisonment at the core of his analysis of the African-American predicament and to advocate an exclusively Black unity as the strategic basis for emancipatory practice. While the thematic content of his speeches retained previous invocations of Black imprisonment—the dialectics of social and psychological incarceration—what was different about his approach two years later was a more flexible construction of the unity he proposed as a strategy for escape. At what was no doubt a tentative moment in the process of questioning his previous philosophy, a moment never fully developed because of his premature death, Malcolm appeared to be seeking an approach that would allow him to preserve the practice of Black Unity—his organization was called the Organization for Afro-American Unity—while simultaneously moving beyond the geopolitical borders of Africa and the African diaspora.

Because Malcolm was in the process of articulating the pitfalls and limitations of nationalism, I want to suggest that implied in that critical revisiting of his Black nationalist philosophy might be a similar revisiting of the male supremacist ramifications of Black nationalism. This is what he said about Black nationalism:

> I used to define black nationalism as the idea that the black man should control the economy of his community, the politics of his community and so forth. But, when I was in Africa in May, in Ghana, I was speaking with the Algerian ambassador who is extremely militant and is a revolutionary in the true sense of the word. . . . When I told him that my political, social and economic philosophy was black nationalism, he asked me very frankly, well, where did that leave him. Because he was white. He was an African, but he was Algerian, and to all appearances he was a white man. And he said if I define my objective as the victory of black nationalism, where does that leave him? Where does that leave revolutionaries in Morocco, Egypt, Iraq, Mauritania? . . .[3]

While acknowledging the problematic racialization of the North African man whose questioning caused Malcolm to interrogate his own position as a Black nationalist, I would point out that nonetheless, his internationalist recontextualization of the liberation struggle as a "Third World" struggle revealed and accentuated the narrowness and provincial character of the nationalism Malcolm had espoused before that time.

So I had to do a lot of thinking and reappraising of my definition of black nationalism. Can we sum up the solution to the problems confronting our people as black nationalism? And if you notice, I haven't been using the expression for several months. But I still would be hard pressed to give a specific definition of the over-all philosophy which I think is necessary for the liberation of black people in this country.[4]

These remarks, made in an interview with the *Young Socialist* shortly before his assassination (published in the March–April 1965 issue), indicate that even at a mature stage of the development of his philosophical position, Malcolm did not hesitate to reexamine his ideas and consider the possibility of radical shifts in that position. He was not afraid to explore the likelihood that his ideas could not stand the test of the complexities he encountered in his political travels. During the same international travels, he discovered that in a number of African countries and African liberation movements, women were becoming visible in new and important ways.[5] While I do not wish to appear to ignore the extremely complicated and often contradictory position in which women find themselves within processes of dismantling colonial systems, I do want to suggest that it is appropriate to speculate about a philosophical shift in Malcolm's thinking with respect to the place, position, and empowerment of women—specifically but not exclusively about African women and women in the African diaspora.

I am not certain about the political path Malcolm himself might have taken if he had not been assassinated at such an apparently critical juncture in the evolution of his political philosophy and practice. My meditations on Malcolm X are not necessarily about the ideas a dead man might have arrived at if his life had been spared; what concerns me more is what I would call the "progressive philosophical space" that can be discovered within the legacy of Malcolm X.

In 1992 Malcolm's legacy is being contested within the realm of popular culture. A number of major battles are currently unfolding, whose aim is to capture this legacy and fix it once and for all. There is the debate around the film on Malcolm directed by Spike Lee. Initially, Spike Lee's argument for replacing the original director, Norman Jewison, with himself, was based on the claim that a white director could never do justice to Malcolm's legacy. Once the film was in progress, Amiri Baraka claimed that Lee himself could not do justice to Malcolm's legacy. What is so striking about the debate is its anchoring point: the very conception of Black nationalism—with its conservative racializing limitations and strong masculinist implications—that Malcolm problematized at the end of his life.

Popular representations of Malcolm's "legacy" abound in contemporary youth culture. As Nick Charles has pointed out, "In death, the X has become ubiquitous, seen mainly on baseball and knit caps. The face, handsome and goateed, peers sternly from T-shirts, jackets and bags. His slogans, 'No Sellout' and 'By Any Means Necessary,' have taken on the dimensions of commandments."[6] This is Malcolm's commodified "legacy," as conjured and evoked in wearable images, flashed in music videos, and sampled in rap songs. Who or what is this commodified Malcolm, the seller of T-shirts and jackets and caps? What does the mark of the X mean to those who mark themselves with this sign that signifies everything and nothing? How is the legacy of Malcolm perceived by those who locate him as a movable image, a wandering voice traveling in and out of music videos and rap tunes such as Public Enemy's "Welcome to the Terrordome?" and Paris's "Brutal" and "Break the Grip of Shame"? What does it mean to the youth who catch a glimpse of Malcolm speaking and Malcolm dead, lying in his coffin in Prince Akeem and Chuck D's "Time to Come Correct"? How is Malcolm's legacy constructed in Def Jef's "Black to the Future," in Public Enemy's "Shut 'Em Down"? What is the meaning of the words "By Any Means Necessary," as flashed in bold letters across the screen in the last video?

In assuming a critical attitude vis-à-vis this iconization and, because of its commodified character, this reification of Malcolm's legacy, I do not thereby dismiss my own emotional response of enthusiasm about the sense of closeness the younger generation has for this African-American historical figure. And I do not wish to belittle the sense of pride young people express in Malcolm as an ancestral champion of our rights as African Americans. Young people feel connected to Malcolm in a way I could not have even begun to envision experiencing in my own youth, for example, in a sense of familiarity with Ida B. Wells. (In fact, when I was a teenager, I didn't even know she existed.) From this position of ambivalence, I express my anxiety in the face of the one-dimensional iconization of Malcolm X, because the iconization tends to close out possibilities of exploring other implications of Malcolm's legacy that are not heroic, nationalist, and masculinist.

From the vantage point of an African-American feminist, with revolutionary aspirations toward socialism that refuse to go away, I experience myself as, in part, a product of that historical moment informed, in part, by Malcolm's discourse, his oratory, and his organizing. Hearing him speak as an undergraduate at Brandeis University before an audience composed of the almost entirely white student population had a profound effect on my own political development. No one could have convinced me then that Malcolm had not come to Brandeis to give expression to my own inarticulate rage and awaken me to possibilities of militant practice. I therefore feel repelled by the strong resonances of unquestioned and dehistoricized notions of male dominance in this contemporary iconization of Malcolm X. This is not to imply that Malcolm was not as much a perpetrator of masculinist ideas as were others—men and women alike—of his era. What disturbs me today is the propensity to cloak Malcolm's politics with insinuations of intransigent and ahistorical male supremacy that bolster the contemporary equation of nationalism and male dominance as representative of progressive politics in Black popular culture.

Such slogans associated with Malcolm X as "The Ballot or the Bullet" are accorded a significance that overlooks the fact that the rhetorical brandishing of guns served a very specific purpose with respect to the 1960s mass movement for Black liberation. Not one to resort to circumvention and euphemism, Malcolm certainly meant what he said. Malcolm did not oratorically invoke the bullet for the primary purpose of shaping a romantic, masculinist image of "the Black Man"—which is not to say that this notion of "the Black Man" was not implied in his words—but rather to emphasize the Black community's determined quest for political power. Likewise, "Revolution By Any Means Necessary," another slogan through which Malcolm is evoked within a contemporary context, is used by some Black youth today to exalt abstract masculinist notions of political activism, with little or no reference to such indispensable aspects of revolutionary politics as strategies and tactics of organizing. In this sense, the slogans become anchoring points for surrogate "revolutionism" that denies access to new ways of organizing contemporary political movements.

I am not suggesting that we leave historical figures, phrases, and images in their original contextualization. What I am saying is that it becomes rather dangerous to project such one-dimensional appropriations on our past history and to establish them as standards for contemporary political consciousness. This kind of process flattens history to a video image that deflects rather than summons more complex efforts at comprehension. With respect to Malcolm X in particular, his pervasive presence in the lives of young Black people today has begun to be reduced to the letter he chose to replace "Little," his last name. The "X" was a sign indicating refusal to accept names accorded to Africans by the white families (although there were a few Black ones as well) who asserted ownership of our ancestors as slaves. Now, it seems, the X etched on baseball caps, jackets, and medallions strives to represent the essence of Malcolm X, the quintessential X. It is no longer necessary to include the "Malcolm" in Malcolm X, for the sign is the X and that X is invested with an abstract affirmation of Black identity, Black dignity, Black resistance, Black rage. I wonder whether young people feel that by wearing the X, they are participating in the experience of something that cannot be defined and fixed once and for all: freedom—the freedom of African Americans and, thus, human freedom.

A question often posed in connection with the exaltation of Malcolm: "Are you Black enough?" Can this question be posed in relation to Latinos/Latinas or Native Americans or Asians or Pacific Islanders or European Americans or indeed in relation to African-American women who wear the X? Another question: "Are you revolutionary enough?" Are you willing to fight, to die? Can this question be posed in relation to women who wear images of Malcolm?

Thus, my third set of questions: Does the passive reception of Malcolm—adorning one's body with his images and consuming movable video images and voice samples of the hero—fix male supremacy as it appears (and perhaps only appears) to challenge white supremacy? Does the contextualization of bits—infobytes—of Malcolm's body, voice, and political wit amid references to women as bitches, groupies, and hoes invest our historical memory of Malcolm with a kind of vicious putdown of women that contradicts a possible turn toward feminism that some of us might associate with his legacy?

Again, instead of directly addressing the questions, I turn to Malcolm, the man—and more specifically, Malcolm the husband and father as represented by his wife, Betty Shabazz. In the February 1992 issue of *Essence*, Betty Shabazz reflects on her life with Malcolm—on her love for him and on some of the conflicts in their marriage arising out of the prevailing acceptance of patterns of male dominance in heterosexual partnerships and marriage. "I shared Malcolm," she says, but I don't know if he could have shared me to the same extent. He was possessive from the beginning to the end, though I think he learned to control it. . . . All my stress was over the fact that I wanted to work and he wouldn't even entertain the idea. He didn't want anybody to have any influence over me that would in any way compete with his. Each time I left him, that's why I left. . . .[7]

Shabazz says that she left Malcolm three times—after each of their first three children were born.

Like all of us from that generation, Shabazz has been affected by the changing economic roles of women as well as by the rise and circulation of feminist ideas. As she reflects upon her own personal transformation, she does not find it difficult to say: ". . . I think Malcolm probably needed me more than I needed him—to support his life's mission. But I don't think that what I would look for in a man today would be what I looked for in a man then. I was very accepting. I just wanted love. I found a sharing and mature man—and I was lucky."[8]

I want to engage for a moment in some speculative reflection, pausing on the question of whether Malcolm might have sufficiently transformed with respect to his personal relations in order to fulfill the contemporary hopes of his wife Betty Shabazz. My purpose is to try to begin to liberate his legacy from the rigid notions of male dominance that were a part of the ideological climate in which Malcolm grew to personal and political maturity. Considering the willingness of Malcolm to reevaluate his political positions, I would like to think that under new ideological circumstances he might have also reconfigured his relationship with his family—and that if Betty Shabazz were hypothetically to reencounter Malcolm during these contemporary times, she might find more of what she seeks today in the man than the historical Malcolm was capable of providing.

But again I am indulging in speculations about what a dead man—a man who has been dead for almost three decades—might be like today, if he were not dead, when I have repeatedly insisted that I do not intend to suggest that definitive statements may be made regarding what Malcolm X might or might not have been. So, once more I remind myself that I am really concerned with the continuing influence of both those who see themselves as the political descendants of Malcolm and our historical memory of this man as shaped by social and technological forces that have frozen this memory, transforming it into a backward and imprisoning memory rather than a forward-looking impetus for creative political thinking and organizing. It is highly ironic that Malcolm's admonition regarding the "mental prison" in which Black people were incarcerated can be evoked today with respect to the way his own legacy has been constructed.

How, then, *do* we contest the historical memory of Malcolm invoked by Clarence Thomas, who did not hesitate to name Malcolm as one of his role models and heroes? Is it not possible to argue that Anita Hill, in challenging the widespread presumption that male public figures—or any man, for that matter—can continue to harass women sexually with impunity, has situated herself within a complex tradition of resistance? Such a tradition would bring together the historical movements for Black liberation and for women's liberation, drawing, for example, both on Malcolm's legacy and on the legacy of Ida B. Wells, whose antilynching efforts also challenged the sexual violence inflicted on Black women's bodies. This tradition can be claimed and further developed not only by African-American women such as Anita Hill and those women among us who, like myself, identify with feminist political positions, but also by our brothers—as well as by progressive women and men of other cultures and ethnicities.

My interrogation of Malcolm X's contemporary legacy means to encourage discussion of some of the urgent contemporary political issues that some who claim to be Malcolm's descendants are reluctant to recognize. Thus my final set of questions: How do we challenge the police violence inflicted on untold numbers of Black men, such as Rodney King, and at the same time organize against the pervasive sexual violence that continues to be perpetrated by men who claim to be actual or potential revolutionaries? How do we challenge the increasingly intense assault on women's reproductive rights initiated by the Reagan and Bush administrations? How do we bring into our political consciousness feminist concerns—the corporate destruction of the environment, for example—that have been historically constructed as "white people's issues"?[9] How do we halt the growing tendency toward violence perpetrated by African Americans against Asians? How do we reverse established attitudes within the African-American community—and especially in popular youth culture, as nourished by the iconization of Malcolm X—that encourage homophobia, sometimes even to the point of violence, associating such backward positions with the exaltation of the Black man? How do we criticize Magic Johnson's compulsion to distinguish himself as a heterosexual who contracted HIV through heterosexual relations, thereby declaring his own innocence, which effectively condemns gay men with HIV? How can we speak out against racist hate crimes, while simultaneously breaking the silence about antigay hate crimes that occur within the Black community, perpetuated by Black homophobes against Black or Latino/Latina or white gay men and lesbians?

More generally, how do we live and act at this juncture of history— in the five hundredth year since Columbus's invasion of the Americas? What are our responsibilities to the indigenous people of this land where we all now live? To Leonard Peltier, who remains a political prisoner, as Assata Shakur remains in exile? How do we make it forever impossible for sports teams to bear such racist, derogatory names as the Washington "Redskins" and the Atlanta "Braves"?

If in 1992 we talk about the necessary means, as in "Revolution By Any Means Necessary," it might make more sense to figure out the means necessary to rethink and reshape the contours of our political activism. I have a fantasy; I sometimes daydream about masses of Black men in front of the Supreme Court chanting "End sexual harassment by any means necessary," "Protect women's reproductive rights, by any means necessary." And we women are there too, saying "Right on!"

NOTES

1. Patricia Robinson, "Malcolm X, Our Revolutionary Son and Brother," in John Henrik Clarke, ed., *Malcolm X: The Man and His Times* (Trenton, NJ: Africa World Press, 1990), 63.

2. Bruce Perry, ed. *Malcolm X: The Last Speeches* (New York: Pathfinder Press, 1989), 25.

3. Interview in *Young Socialist* (March–April 1965), excerpted in George Breitman, ed., *Malcolm X Speaks* (New York: Grove Weidenfeld, 1990), 212.

4. Ibid., 212–213.

5. In an interview conducted by Bernice Bass on December 27, 1964, Malcolm made the following comment: "One thing I noticed in both the Middle East and Africa, in every country that was progressive the women were progressive. In every country that was underdeveloped and backward, it was to the same degree that the women were undeveloped or underdeveloped and backward."

(Perry, ed., *Malcolm X: The Last Speeches*, 98). During the same interview, he spoke of his meeting with Shirley Graham Du Bois, who at that time was the national director of television in Ghana: "She's a woman, and she's an Afro-American, and I think that should make Afro-American women mighty proud" (96).

6. Nick Charles, "Malcolm X The Myth and the Man," *Cleveland Plain Dealer Magazine*, February 2, 1992.

7. Betty Shabazz (as told to Susan Taylor and Audrey Edwards), "Loving and Losing Malcolm," *Essence* 22, no. 10 (February 1992): 50.

8. Ibid.

9. Three out of five African Americans live in communities with abandoned toxic waste sites. Three of the five largest commercial hazardous waste landfills (that is, 40 percent of the nation's landfill capacity) are located in predominantly African-American communities. In Los Angeles, 71 percent of African Americans and 50 percent of Latinos live in areas with the most polluted air—as compared to 34 percent of white people. See Robert D. Bullard, "Urban Infrastructure: Social, Environmental, and Health Risks to African Americans," in Billy Tidwell, ed., *The State of Black America, 1992* (Washington, D.C.: National Urban League, 1992), 185, 190.

Malcolm X and Black Rage

CORNEL WEST

You don't stick a knife in a man's back nine inches and then pull it out six inches and say you're making progress.
—Malcolm X

No matter how much respect, no matter how much recognition, whites show towards me, as far as I'm concerned, as long as it is not shown to every one of our people in this country, it doesn't exist for me.
—Malcolm X

Malcolm X articulated Black rage in a manner unprecedented in American history. His style of communicating this rage bespoke a boiling urgency and an audacious sincerity; the substance of what he said highlighted the chronic refusal of most Americans to acknowledge the sheer absurdity that confronts human beings of African descent in this country—the incessant assaults on Black intelligence, beauty, character, and possibility. His profound commitment to affirm Black humanity at any cost and his tremendous courage to accent the hypocrisy of American society made Malcolm X the prophet of Black rage—then and now.

Malcolm X was the prophet of Black rage primarily because of his great love for Black people. His love was neither abstract nor ephemeral. Rather, it represented a concrete connection with a degraded and devalued people in need of *psychic conversion*. This connection is why Malcolm X's articulation of Black rage was not directed first and foremost at white America. Malcolm spoke love to Black people; he believed the love that motivated Black rage had to be felt by Black people in order for the rage to take on institutional forms. This love would produce a psychic conversion in Black people in that they would affirm themselves as human beings, no longer viewing their bodies, minds, and souls through white lenses, but believing themselves capable of taking control of their own destinies.

In American society—especially during Malcolm X's life in the 1950s and early '60s—such a psychic conversion could easily result in death. A proud, self-affirming Black person who truly believed in the capacity of Black people to throw off the yoke of white racist oppression and control their own destiny usually ended up as one of those strange fruit that Southern trees bore, about which the great Billie Holiday poignantly sang. So when Malcolm X articulated Black rage, he knew he also had to exemplify in his own life the courage and sacrifice that any truly self-loving Black person needs in order to confront the frightening consequences of being self-loving in American society. In other words, Malcolm X crystallized sharply the relation of Black affirmation of self, Black desire for freedom, Black rage against American society, and the likelihood of early Black death. Black psychic conversion—the decolonization of the mind, body, and soul that strips white supremacist lies of their authority, legitimacy, and efficacy—begins with a bold and defiant rejection of Black degradation and is sustained by urgent efforts to expand those spaces wherein Black humanity is affirmed; it often ends with early death owing to both white contempt for such a subversive sensibility and, among those captive to Black self-contempt and self-doubt, a Black disbelief.

Malcolm X's notion of psychic conversion holds that Black people must no longer view themselves through white lenses. His claim is that Black people will never value themselves as long as they subscribe to a standard of valuation that devalues them. For example, Michael Jackson may rightly wish to be viewed as a person, not a color (neither black nor white), but his facial revisions reveal a self-measurement based on a white yardstick. Despite the fact that Jackson is one of the greatest entertainers who has ever lived, he still views himself, at least in part, through white aesthetic lenses that devalue some of his African characteristics. Needless to say, Michael Jackson's example is but the more honest and visible instance of a rather pervasive self-loathing among many wealthy and professional-class Black people. Malcolm

X's call for psychic conversion often strikes horror into this privileged group because so much of who they are and what they do is evaluated in terms of their wealth, status, and prestige in American society. On the other hand, this group often understands Malcolm X's claim more than others precisely because they have lived so intimately in a white world in which the devaluation of Black people is so often taken for granted or unconsciously assumed. It is no accident that the Black middle class has always had an ambivalent relation to Malcolm X— an open rejection of his militant strategy of wholesale defiance of American society and a secret embrace of his bold truth-telling about the depths of racism in American society. One rarely encounters a picture of Malcolm X (as one does Martin Luther King, Jr.) in the office of a Black professional, but there is no doubt that he dangles as the skeleton in the closet lodged in the racial memory of most Black professionals.

In short, Malcolm X's notion of psychic conversion is an implicit critique of W. E. B. Du Bois's idea of "double-consciousness." From Malcolm X's viewpoint, double-consciousness pertains more to those Black people who live "betwixt and between" the Black and white worlds—traversing and crisscrossing these worlds yet never settled in either. Hence, they crave peer acceptance in both, receive genuine approval from neither, yet persist in viewing themselves through the lenses of the dominant white society. For Malcolm X, this "double-consciousness" is less a description of the Black mode of being in America than a particular kind of colonized mind-set of a special group in Black America. Psychic conversion calls for not simply a rejection of the white lenses through which one sees oneself but, more specifically, a refusal to measure one's humanity by appealing to any white supremacist standard. Du Bois's double-consciousness seems to lock Black people into the quest for white approval and disappointment due mainly to white racist assessment, whereas Malcolm X suggests that this tragic syndrome can be broken. But how?

Malcolm X does not put forward a direct answer to this question. First, his well-known distinction between "house negroes" (who love and protect the white master) and "field negroes" (who hate and resist the white master) suggests that the masses of Black people are more likely to acquire decolonized sensibilities and hence less likely to be "co-opted" by the white status quo. Yet this rhetorical device, though insightful in highlighting different perspectives among Black people, fails as a persuasive description of the behavior of "well-to-do" Black folk and "poor" Black folk. In other words, there are numerous instances of "field negroes" with "house negro" mentalities and "house negroes" with "field negro" mentalities. Malcolm X's often-quoted distinction rightly highlights the propensity among highly assimilated Black professionals to put "whiteness" (in all its various forms) on a pedestal, but it also tends to depict "poor" Black people's notions and enactments of "blackness" in an uncritical manner. Hence his implicit critique of Du Bois's idea of double-consciousness contains some truth yet offers an inadequate alternative.

Second, Malcolm X's Black nationalist viewpoint claims that the only legitimate response to white supremacist ideology and practice is Black self-love and Black self-determination free of the tension generated by double-consciousness. This claim is both subtle and problematic. It is subtle in that every Black Freedom Movement is predicated on an affirmation of African humanity and a quest for Black control over the destinies of Black people. Yet not every form of Black self-love affirms African humanity. Furthermore, not every project of Black self-determination consists of a serious quest for Black control over the destinies of Black people. Malcolm's claim tends to assume that Black nationalisms have a monopoly on Black self-love and Black self-determination. This fallacious assumption confuses the issues highlighted by Black nationalisms with the various ways in which Black nationalists and others understand these issues.

For example, the grand legacy of Marcus Garvey forces us never to forget that Black self-love and Black self-respect sit at the center of any possible Black Freedom Movement. Yet this does not mean that we must talk about Black self-love and Black self-respect in the way in which Garvey did, that is, on an imperial model in which Black armies and navies signify Black power. Similarly, the tradition of Elijah Muhammad compels us to acknowledge the centrality of Black self-regard and Black self-esteem, yet that does not entail an acceptance of how Elijah Muhammad talked about achieving this aim—by playing a game of Black supremacy that awakens us from our captivity to white supremacy. My point here is that a focus on the issues rightly targeted by Black nationalists and an openness to the insights of Black nationalists does not necessarily result in an acceptance of Black nationalist ideology. Malcolm X tended to make such an unwarranted move.

* * *

Malcolm X's notion of psychic conversion is based on the idea of Black spaces in American society in which Black community, humanity, love, care, concern, and support flourish. He sees this Black coming-together as the offspring of the recognition of a boiling Black rage. Facilitating this coming-together is where Malcolm X's project really falters. The fundamental challenge is: How can the boiling Black rage be contained and channeled in the Black spaces such that destructive and self-destructive consequences are abated? The greatness of Malcolm X is, in part, that he raises this question with a sharpness and urgency never before posed in Black America. Unfortunately, in his short life he never had a chance to grapple with it or solve it in idea and deed. Instead, until 1964, he adopted Elijah Muhammad's response to this challenge and castigated Martin Luther King, Jr.'s response to it.

In contrast to Malcolm X, Elijah Muhammad and Martin Luther King, Jr., understood one fundamental truth about Black rage: It must neither be ignored nor ignited. Both leaders, in their own ways, knew how to work with Black rage in a constructive manner, shape it through moral discipline, channel it into political organization, and guide it by charismatic leadership. Malcolm X could articulate Black rage much better than Elijah Muhammad or Martin Luther King, Jr.—but for most of his public life he tended to ignite Black rage and harness it for the Nation of Islam. Hence Malcolm's grappling with how to understand Black rage and what to do with it was subordinate to Elijah Muhammad's project of Black separate spaces for Black community, humanity, love, care, concern, and support. Malcolm X, however, did have two psychic conversions—the first was to the Nation of Islam, but the second, in 1964, was to orthodox Islam that rejected any form of racial supremacy.

The project of Black separatism—to which Malcolm X was beholden for most of his life after his first psychic conversion—suffered from deep intellectual and organizational problems. Unlike Malcolm X's notion of psychic conversion, Elijah Muhammad's idea of religious conversion was predicated on an obsession with white supremacy. The basic aim of Black Muslim theology—with its distinct Black supremacist account of the origins of white people—was to counter white supremacy. Yet this preoccupation with white supremacy still allowed white people to serve as the principal point of reference. That which fundamentally motivates one still dictates the terms of what one thinks and does—so the motivation of a Black supremacist doctrine reveals how obsessed one is with white supremacy. This is understandable in a white racist society—but it is crippling for a despised people struggling for freedom, in that one's eyes should be on the prize, not the perpetuator of one's oppression. In short, Elijah Muhammad's project remained captive to the supremacy game—a game mastered by the white racists he opposed and imitated with his *Black* supremacy doctrine.

Malcolm X's notion of psychic conversion can be understood and used such that it does not necessarily *entail* Black supremacy; it simply rejects Black captivity to white supremacist ideology and practice. Hence, as the major Black Muslim spokesperson, he had many sympathizers, though few of them actually became Muslim members. Why did Malcolm X permit his notion of psychic conversion to serve the Black supremacist claims of the Nation of Islam—claims that undermine much of the best of his call for psychic conversion? Malcolm X remained a devoted follower of Elijah Muhammad until 1964 partly because he believed the other major constructive channels of Black rage in America—the Black church and Black music—were less effective in producing and sustaining psychic conversion than the Nation of Islam. He knew that the electoral political system could never address the existential dimension of Black rage—hence he, like Elijah, shunned it. Malcolm X also recognized, as do too few Black leaders today, that the Black encounter with the absurd in racist American society yields a profound spiritual need for human affirmation and recognition. Hence the centrality of religion and music—those most spiritual of human activities—in Black life.

Yet, for Malcolm, much of Black religion and Black music had directed Black rage away from white racism and toward another world of heaven and sentimental romance. Needless to say, Malcolm's conception of Black Christianity as a white man's religion of pie-in-the-sky and Black music as soupy "I Love You B-a-b-y" romance is wrong. While it's true that most—but not all—of the Black music of Malcolm's day shunned Black rage, the case of the church-based Civil Rights movement would seem to counter his charge that Black Christianity serves as a sedative to put people to sleep rather than to ignite them to action. Like Elijah Muhammad (and unlike Malcolm X), Martin Luther King, Jr., concluded that Black rage was so destructive and self-destructive that without a moral theology and political organization, it would wreak havoc on Black America. His project of nonviolent resistance to white racism was an attempt to channel Black rage in political directions that preserved Black dignity and changed American society. But his despair at the sight of Watts in 1965 or Detroit and Newark in 1967 left him more and more pessimistic about the moral channeling of Black rage in America. To King, it looked as if cycles of chaos and destruction loomed on the horizon if these moral channels were ineffective or unappealing to the coming generation. For Malcolm, however, the Civil Rights movement was not militant enough. It failed to speak clearly and directly to and about Black rage.

Malcolm X also seems to have had almost no intellectual interest in dealing with what is distinctive about the Black church and Black music: *their cultural hybrid character in which the complex mixture of African, European, and Amerindian elements are constitutive of something that is new and Black in the modern world*. Like most Black nationalists, Malcolm X feared the culturally hybrid character of Black life. This fear resulted in the dependence on Manichean (black-and-white or male/female) channels for the direction of Black rage— forms characterized by charismatic leaders, patriarchal structures, and dogmatic pronouncements. The Manichean theology kept the white world at bay even as it heralded dominant white notions such as racial supremacy per se or the nation-state per se. The authoritarian arrangements imposed a top-down disciplined corps of devoted followers who contained their rage in an atmosphere of cultural repression (regulation of clothing worn, books and records consumed, sexual desire, etc.) and paternalistic protection of women.

The complex relation of cultural hybridity and critical sensibility (or jazz and democracy) evident here raises interesting questions. If Malcolm X feared cultural hybridity, to what degree or in what sense was he a serious democrat? Did he believe that the cure to the egregious ills of a racist American "democracy" was more democracy that included Black people? Did his relative silence regarding the monarchies he visited in the Middle East bespeak a downplaying of the role of democratic practices in empowering oppressed peoples? Was his fear of cultural hybridity partly rooted in his own reluctance to come to terms with his own personal hybridity, for example, his "redness," light skin, close white friends, and so on?

Malcolm X's fear of cultural hybridity rested on two political claims: that cultural hybridity downplayed the vicious character of white supremacy and that it so intimately linked the destinies of

Black and white people that the possibility of Black freedom was unimaginable. Malcolm's fundamental focus on the varieties, subtleties, and cruelties of white racism made him suspicious of any discourse about cultural hybridity. Those figures who were most eloquent and illuminating about Black cultural hybridity in the 1950s and early '60s, such as Ralph Ellison and Albert Murray, were, in fact, political integrationists. Their position seemed to pass over too quickly the physical terror and psychic horror of being Black in America. To put it bluntly, Malcolm X identified much more with the mind-set of Richard Wright's Bigger Thomas in *Native Son* than with that of Ralph Ellison's protagonist in *Invisible Man*.

Malcolm X's deep pessimism about the capacity and possibility of white Americans to shed their racism led him, ironically, to downplay the past and present bonds between Blacks and whites. For if the two groups were, as Martin Luther King, Jr., put it, locked into "one garment of destiny," then the very chances for Black freedom were nil. Malcolm X's pessimism also kept him ambivalent about American democracy—for if the majority were racist, how could the Black minority ever be free? His definition of a "nigger" was "a victim of American democracy"—had not the *Herrenvolk* democracy of the United States made Black people noncitizens or anticitizens of the republic? Of course, the aim of a constitutional democracy is to safeguard the rights of the minority and avoid the tyranny of the majority. Yet the concrete practice of the U.S. legal system from 1883 to 1964 promoted a tyranny of the white majority much more than a safeguarding of the rights of Black Americans. In fact, these tragic facts drove Malcolm X to look elsewhere for the promotion and protection of Black people's rights—to institutions such as the United Nations and the Organization of African Unity. One impulse behind his internalization of the Black Freedom struggle in the United States was a deep pessimism about America's will to racial justice, no matter how democratic the nation was or is.

Malcolm X's fear of cultural hybridity also rested on a third concern: his own personal hybridity as the grandson of a white man, which blurred the very boundaries so rigidly policed by white supremacist authorities. For Malcolm X, the distinctive feature of American culture was not its cross-cultural syncretism but rather its enforcement of a racial caste system that defined any product of this syncretism as abnormal, alien, and other to both Black and white communities. Like Garvey, Malcolm X saw such hybridity—for examples, mulattoes—

as symbols of weakness and confusion. The very idea of not "fitting in" the U.S. discourse of whiteness and blackness meant one was subject to exclusion and marginalization by both whites and Blacks. For Malcolm X, in a racist society, this was a form of social death.

One would think that Malcolm X's second conversion, in 1964, might have allayed his fear of cultural hybridity. Yet there seems to be little evidence that he revised his understanding of the radically culturally hybrid character of Black life. Furthermore, his deep pessimism toward American democracy continued after his second conversion—though no longer on mythological grounds but solely on the historical experiences of Africans in the modern world. It is no accident that the non-Black persons Malcolm X encountered who helped change his mind about the capacity of white people to be human were outside of America and Europe—Muslims in the Middle East. Needless to say, Malcolm found the most striking feature of the Islamic regimes not to be their undemocratic practices but their acceptance of his Black humanity. This great prophet of Black rage—with all his brilliance, courage, and conviction—remained blind to basic structures of domination based on class, gender, and sexual orientation in the Middle East.

The contemporary focus on Malcolm X, especially among Black youth, can be understood as both the open articulation of Black rage (as in film videos and on tapes targeted at whites, Jews, Koreans, Black women, Black men, and others), and desperate attempts to channel this rage into something more than a marketable commodity for the culture industry. The young Black generation is up against forces of death, destruction, and disease unprecedented in the everyday life of Black urban people. This raw reality of drugs and guns, despair and decrepitude generates a raw rage that, among past Black spokespersons, only Malcolm X was able to approximate. The issues of psychic conversion, cultural hybridity, Black supremacy, authoritarian organization, borders and boundaries in sexuality, and other matters all loom large at present—the same issues Malcolm X left dangling at the end of the short life in which he articulated Black rage and affirmed Black humanity.

If we are to build on the best of Malcolm X, we must preserve and expand his notion of psychic conversion (best seen in the works of bell hooks) that cements networks and groups in which Black community, humanity, love, care, and concern can take root and grow. These spaces—beyond Black music and Black religion—reject Manichean ideologies and authoritarian arrangements in the name of moral visions, subtle analyses of wealth and power, and concrete strategies of principled coalitions and democratic alliances. These visions, analyses, and strategies never lose sight of Black rage, yet they focus this rage where it belongs: on any form of racism, patriarchy, homophobia, or economic injustice that impedes the opportunities of people to live lives of dignity and decency. Poverty is as much a target of rage as degraded identity.

Furthermore, the cultural hybrid character of Black life leads us to highlight a metaphor alien to Malcolm X's theology—yet consonant with his performances to audiences—namely, the metaphor of jazz. I use the term "jazz" here not so much as a term for a musical art-form as for a mode of being in the world, an improvisational mode of protean, fluid, and flexible dispositions toward reality suspicious of either/or viewpoints, dogmatic pronouncements, and supremacist ideologies. To be a jazz freedom fighter is to attempt to galvanize and energize world-weary people into forms of organization with accountable leadership that promotes critical exchange and broad reflection. The interplay of individuality and unity is not one of uniformity and unanimity imposed from above but rather of conflict among diverse groupings that reach a dynamic consensus subject to questioning and criticism. As with a soloist in a jazz quartet, quintet, or band, individuality is promoted in order to sustain and increase the *creative* tension with the group—a tension that yields higher levels of performance to achieve the aim of the collective project. This kind of critical and democratic sensibility flies in the face of any policing of borders and boundaries of "blackness," "maleness," "femaleness," or "whiteness." Black people's rage ought to target white supremacy but also realize that maleness can encompass feminists such as Frederick Douglass or W. E. B. Du Bois. Black people's rage should not overlook homophobia; it also should acknowledge that heterosexuality can be associated with so-called straight antihomophobes—just as the struggle against Black poverty can be supported by progressive elements of the well-to-do regardless of race, gender, or sexual orientation.

Malcolm X was the first great Black spokesperson who looked ferocious white racism in the eye, didn't blink, and lived long enough to tell America the truth about this glaring hypocrisy in a bold and defiant manner. Unlike Elijah Muhammad and Martin Luther King, Jr., he did not live long enough to forge his own distinctive ideas and ways of channeling Black rage in constructive channels to change American society. Only if we are as willing as Malcolm X to grow and confront the new challenges posed by the Black rage of our day will we take the Black freedom struggle to a new and higher level.

Learning to Think for Ourselves: Malcolm X's Black Nationalism Reconsidered

PATRICIA HILL COLLINS

One of the first things I think young people, especially nowadays, should learn is how to see for yourself and listen for yourself and think for yourself. . . . this generation, especially of our people, has a burden, more so than any other time in history. The most important thing that we can learn to do today is think for ourselves.
—*Malcolm X*

In 1991 Clarence Thomas, an African American and grandson of sharecroppers, was confirmed as the 106th justice on the Supreme Court. In 1990 a twelve-year-old African-American girl dumped her unwanted newborn son down a garbage chute in New York City. These two events point to the unsettling contradictions that characterize contemporary racial politics in the United States. African-American men are incarcerated at a rate higher than Black South African men, African-American women and men both confront unemployment rates twice that of whites, one-half of all Black children live in poverty, and Black babies are still twice as likely to die during the first year of life than are white babies. At the same time, high school graduation rates for African-American youth are higher than they've been at any time, *Black Enterprise* and *Ebony* magazines vigorously tout the successes of African-American professionals and managers, the faces of Bill

Cosby, Oprah Winfrey, Arsenio Hall, and other African Americans smile out at us on television and in film, and basic civil rights remain codified in federal law.[1]

The magnitude of these contradictions and the complexity of the problems confronting all African Americans suggest that Malcolm X's insistence that we learn to think for ourselves is especially pertinent today. But the urgency of people's search for solutions often results in a tendency to avoid complex thinking in favor of one-dimensional heroes and catchy slogans. Ironically, the memory of Malcolm X himself appears caught in the crossfire of simplistic analyses. For example, when asked what they know about Malcolm X, the undergraduates in my African-American Studies classes easily recite the slogan "by any means necessary." But when pushed to explain what this means, few can do so. Similarly, many Black urban youths wear hats and T-shirts emblazoned with a symbolic X. For many, Malcolm X has become a fashion statement, reduced merely to his X.

Current attempts to refashion Malcolm X into a larger-than-life, heroic figure are troublesome because such efforts can easily lead us away from the types of self-critical analysis demanded by the seriousness of our times. Malcolm X was an astute, caring, charismatic leader from 1952 through 1965, the thirteen-year period in which he was active in African-American politics. He remains one of the few Black leaders chosen by African Americans ourselves, and not by dominant institutions such as the press, political parties, or universities. But despite his impressive achievements in the context of his own times, glorifying and canonizing Malcolm X will not tell us all that we need to know for today.

Malcolm X's extraordinary ability to think for himself leaves us with a complicated legacy. While the ideas he expressed during the three major periods of his life remain controversial and contradictory, they simultaneously indicate the magnitude of growth he achieved through sustained intellectual struggle with complex, important questions.[2] Malcolm Little, from his birth in 1925 to his conversion to the Nation of Islam in the late 1940s, demonstrated minimal interest in political issues. This is the Malcolm most easily overlooked, because many of Malcolm Little's actions and ideas directly contradict the main ideas of a more mature Malcolm's Black nationalism. There appears to be no Black nationalist philosophy from this period, not even an incipient one.

In contrast, the years spent with the Nation of Islam prior to his break with Elijah Muhammad in 1964 mark Little's transformation into Malcolm X and his development of a Black nationalism characterized by intense race pride. This Malcolm stands squarely in the Black nationalist tradition, one stretching from the words of nineteenth-century Black activist Alexander Crummell, through the one-million-person strong movement led by Marcus Garvey in the 1920s, and into the variations of Black nationalism expressed in the 1960s.[3] Like most Black nationalist thinkers, Malcolm X identified three components of a Black nationalist philosophy—the political, economic, and social—all designed to bring about Black control of Black communities. But at the same time, Malcolm's Black nationalist philosophy from this period can be distinguished from other types of Black nationalism that many would see as being more radical or progressive.[4]

Malcolm X's emerging politics during the fourteen months preceding his assassination, a period in which he remained a Muslim but broke from Elijah Muhammad's Nation of Islam, offer yet another much-needed and often contradictory perspective on Black nationalist philosophy. During this period, Malcolm X began to broaden three areas of his own thinking that had immediate and potential implications for his and our interpretation of Black nationalism.

First, Malcolm X's definition of race and his perceptions of the connections among race, color, and political consciousness changed. During most of his time with the Nation of Islam, Malcolm X saw race as a biological reality instead of a socially constructed, historical phenomenon. This assumption of biological essentialism colored his Black nationalist philosophy. Relinquishing this biological essentialism in the last year of his life opened the doors for a greatly reformulated Black nationalism, one encompassing different notions of Black political consciousness and the types of political coalitions that Blacks might forge with other groups. The importance of being able to distinguish worthwhile political coalitions from dangerous ones becomes increasingly important to an African-American community situated in today's complex multiethnic, multinational political economy.

Second, Malcolm X's emerging social class analysis also led to changes in his Black nationalist philosophy. Malcolm's increasing attention to global structures of colonialism and imperialism led him to begin to consider the influence of global capitalism as a major structure affecting African Americans. The principal Black struggles of Malcolm's time were against colonialism. But in our postcolonial era, the need to incorporate analyses of global capitalism in any Black nationalist philosophy becomes not only more noticeable but more important.

Finally, because Malcolm X was assassinated before Black feminist politics were articulated in the 1970s and 1980s, his Black nationalism projects an implicit and highly problematic gender analysis. Given today's understanding of the gender-specific structures of Black oppression, if unexamined, his ideas about gender may be interpreted in ways detrimental not only to both African-American women and men but to policies of Black community development.

RACE, COLOR, AND POLITICAL CONSCIOUSNESS

Malcolm X's perceptions about skin color are one avenue to understanding his underlying perspective on race and racism. In his autobiography, he uses skin color to construct a particular philosophy on race. Compare his description of his father as a "big, six-foot-four, very black man" to that of his mother, a woman who "looked like a white woman" because her father was white (*Autobiography*, 2). While Malcolm X portrays both of his parents as being heroic figures—he describes his father as risking his life to spread the philosophy of Marcus Garvey and his mother as engaging in a tireless yet unsuccessful battle with the welfare bureaucracy of her time—some subtle yet significant differences exist. Invoking a version of Black manhood that informed his own nationalist politics, he presents his father as a strong figure who dies under mysterious circumstances. In contrast, he depicts his mother as always working, as occasionally abusive to her children, and as beaten down to the point where she was confined to a mental hospital. Rather than dying in heroic fashion, she chooses to live by cooperating with the system as a victim. Where his father was strong, dark-skinned, manly, and nationalist, his mother was weak, light-skinned, feminine, and "mixed up." He should be admired, she should be pitied. Where he was racially pure, she was racially mixed or integrated.[5]

The emphasis placed on skin color in Malcolm X's autobiography must be seen in the context of the color politics of the 1940s and 1950s and corresponding social constructions of race and class based on such classifications. Malcolm's views on skin color preceded the growth of a multicolored Black middle class resulting from social mobility in the 1960s and 1970s. This new Black middle class was distinct from the longstanding Black bourgeoisie of Malcolm's time, and the politics of the new Black middle class deviated from the color politics of a much smaller, much more homogenous, light-skinned Black middle class in pre-1960s African-American communities.[6] Prior to the 1960s, bourgeois, light-skinned Blacks were thought to be more refined, intelligent, and beautiful, at least by each other, while darker-skinned Blacks were portrayed as lesser. Black cultural nationalism in the late 1960s, with its slogan "Black Is Beautiful," aimed at reversing this longstanding glorification of lighter skin within African-American communities. Malcolm X's linking of skin color and political consciousness must be assessed in the precultural nationalist context.[7]

The depiction of skin color in Malcolm X's autobiography serves as a metaphor for his perspective on race.[8] Prior to his pilgrimage to Mecca in 1963, Malcolm X forwarded a definition of race that saw race as rooted in biology and not constructed by society.[9] Within Malcolm X's Black nationalist philosophy, people are born pure "black" like his father, pure "white," or "mixed" like his mother. Blackness itself consisted of an essence possessed by so-called pure or darker-skinned Black people or those lighter-skinned Black people who, like himself, consciously rejected their European ancestors. This perspective on skin color and Blackness results in a view of race as a fixed, essentialist biological category.[10]

Malcolm X's perspective on race while he was a Muslim minister leads him to present Blacks as being superior to whites because whites "don't know what morals are. They don't try and eliminate an evil because it's . . . immoral; they eliminate it only when it threatens their existence."[11] While he never explicitly claims that Blacks and whites are biologically different and unequal, he sees whites as being hopelessly immoral and unlikely to change. Whiteness by its very presence becomes a badge of immorality and whites become racist by virtue of being biologically "white." Such thinking closely parallels core themes in racist biology that historically viewed Blackness as a biological marker indicating intellectual inferiority and sexual immorality.[12] Because they are allegedly more racially "pure" and allegedly possess more of the good qualities attached to Blackness, Malcolm X frequently describes darker-skinned Blacks as being the antithesis of immoral whites.[13] Consider Malcolm X's description of his sister Ella's physical appearance and why he admired her: "Ella wasn't just black, but like our father, she was jet black. The way she sat, moved, talked, did everything, bespoke somebody who did and got exactly what she wanted" (*Autobiography*, 33). By emphasizing not what Ella thought and did, but who she was physically, Malcolm X presents Ella as the embodied version of the essence of Blackness. In contrast, because they possess more "white blood," lighter-skinned Blacks either lack these qualities or must work hard to overcome their inherent deficiencies.[14]

Malcolm X's ideas about skin color frame his views on racism as well. For Malcolm, racism is a political, economic, and social system, and it rests on the foundation of a biological definition of race. Malcolm's notion of the "nation" also depends on biologically essentialist definitions of race. Given these assumptions, it is only logical that Malcolm chose "Black nationalism" or building one's own "Black nation" to confront the "white nationalism" of an immoral "white nation."

But there are two problematic dimensions to Malcolm X's pre-1964 perceptions of race and racism. First, seeing race as rooted in nature suggests that solutions to racism can be found only by manipulating existing "biological groups"; in this case, by finding ways to survive as a black nation within global racist institutions without challenging them directly. This approach implies that racism is timeless, inevitable, and resistant to human action. Designing effective strategies to confront racism, particularly institutional racism, becomes difficult if racism itself is seen as resistant to change. Moreover, this approach to race overlooks some important strengths within Black communities that could be used to forge effective alliances among African Americans. While Malcolm X consistently spoke about unity, the way he fostered unity was based less on pointing out internal factors, such as a common culture that pulled Blacks together, and more upon a common enemy that pushed Blacks of all persuasions together. Consider the following passage from "Message to the Grassroots," one of his better-known speeches: "We have a common enemy. We have this in common. We have a common oppressor, a common exploiter, and a common discriminator. But once we all realize that we have a common enemy, then we unite—on the basis of what we have in common. And what we have foremost in common is that enemy—the white man."[15] Defining Blacks as being held together solely by a common enemy means that Blackness can be defined only in relation to whiteness, and not in terms of other factors, such as a common African philosophical tradition shaping religious beliefs, family structure, and gender roles.[16] Blackness defined solely in terms of an oppositional identity becomes problematic when the face of the "enemy" appears to change, as it has in our own times.

Second, seeing race as rooted in nature leads to the related assumption that biological "Blackness" automatically provides a particular perspective that is antiracist. Such thinking can easily lead to political actions such as supporting African-American officials solely because they are Black, even if these individuals demonstrate little understanding of or fail to act to help resolve pressing Black problems. For example, consider the support given to Clarence Thomas by many African Americans solely because he is "biologically" Black. Despite his record of insensitivity to African Americans, many African Americans felt that his early poverty and continuing Blackness somehow would provide him with a particular pro-Black political consciousness. Such thinking made many African Americans unable to look beyond Clarence Thomas's skin color to critique his political consciousness. The Bush administration knew this fact and exploited it. Thus, using skin color as a superficial proxy for political consciousness can have disastrous results.

I stress Malcolm X's early ideas about race because they are the ideas with which he remains most closely associated. However, during the two years preceding his assassination, Malcolm X appeared to be rethinking his perceptions on race. After landing in Cairo while on a pilgrimage to Mecca, Malcolm X observed a crowd of Muslims from different countries, hugging and embracing. "They were of all complexions, the whole atmosphere was of warmth and friendliness," he observed. "The feeling hit me that there really wasn't any color problem here. The effect was as though I had just stepped out of a prison" (*Autobiography*, 321). In an interview published in the *Young Socialist* in 1965, Malcolm X reported how his thinking about Black nationalism had shifted after meeting an Algerian ambassador who Malcolm X considered to be "militant" and a "revolutionary in the true sense of the word." "When I told him that my political, social and economic philosophy was black nationalism," reported Malcolm X, "he asked me very frankly, well, where did that leave him? Because he was white. He was an African, but he was Algerian, and to all appearances he was a white man."[17] This experience jarred Malcolm X, who reports thinking that he began to see how he was "alienating people who were true revolutionaries, dedicated to overturning the system of exploitation that exists on earth by any means necessary."[18] While he remained committed to a belief in Black self-determination, he became less convinced of the utility of seeing the world in oppositional racial categories rooted in nature.

Malcolm X's views on race apparently were shifting to more closely approximate social constructionist approaches. On the same trip, Malcolm X was warmly received by an Arab whom he had been taught to see as a "white man." By critically examining his own reactions to this "white" man who wasn't "acting white," Malcolm X began to reject biological perspectives on race.

> That morning was when I first began to reappraise the "white man."
> It was when I first began to perceive that "white man," as commonly used, means complexion only secondarily; primarily it described attitudes and actions. In America, "white man" meant specific attitudes and actions toward the black man, and toward all other non-white men . . . That morning was the start of a radical alteration in my whole outlook about "white" men. (*Autobiography*, 333)

As the trip unfolded, Malcolm X compared the differences in the use of color in the Muslim world to his prior experiences with color in the United States. Malcolm X recounts a discussion he had with an ambassador on one of his internationl trips:

> I told him, "what you are telling me is that it isn't the American white man who is a racist, but it's the American political, economic, and social atmosphere that automatically nourishes a racist psychology in the white man." . . . That discussion with the ambassador gave me a new insight—one which I like: that the white man is not inherently evil, but America's racist society influences him to act evilly. The society has produced and nourishes a psychology which brings out the lowest, most base part of human beings. (*Autobiography*, 371)

Seeing race as socially constructed rather than as a biologically essentialist category opens up new possibilities for Black nationalist philosophy that frees it from the politics of oppositional identity that plagued much of Malcolm's earlier writings. A Black nation can be constructed on shared internal values, on a shared agenda that, while stemming from common experiences with racist institutions and individuals, is not confined to this. Clarity about such shared values and the agenda that it generates positions African-American communities or "nations" to know what is in our own best interests.

THE CHANGING SIGNIFICANCE OF SOCIAL CLASS

A second problematic feature of Malcolm X's Black nationalism is its failure to include a social class analysis that specifically addresses African-American impoverishment. Instead, Malcolm X's adherence to a definition of race and racism as rooted in nature limited his view of social class to one where the "white man" controls everything and the "Black man" suffers because of it. Malcolm X was acutely aware of the abysmal conditions facing many African Americans because he himself had grown up in poverty. But describing Black poverty and attributing its cause to a "white devil" who exploits African Americans because of his psychological and/or moral bankruptcy differs substantially from explaining poverty by examining trends in American and global capitalism. Missing from Malcolm X's analysis is a structural analysis of social class that addresses those features of capitalist political economies that profoundly shape both Black and white social class dynamics. The discriminatory investment policies of banks, the role of the real estate industry in controlling property in African-American neighborhoods, the culpability of existing approaches to school financing in fostering Black educational impoverishment, the employment and investment policies of major international corporations, all remain largely ignored and unanalyzed. Only in the year preceding his death did he acknowledge capitalism as a system that requires exploitation and poverty in order to maintain wealth.

In most of his speeches, Malcolm X uses social class as a descriptive attribute that people possess, and not as a social structural category of analysis that explains the racial patterns of wealth and poverty in the United States and across the globe. Moreover, in Malcolm's work only Blacks appear to possess social class; throughout his speeches and writings, Malcolm X alludes to the differences between working-class and middle-class Blacks. No such distinction is made for whites. They remain part of an undifferentiated mass lumped together under the label "the white man." The result is that Malcolm X castigates the flawed politics of the Black middle class of his era and spends remarkably little time pointing out the differences between the racism of the elite "white man" and the working-class "white man." This approach is consistent with the Black nationalist philosophy of concentrating on dynamics internal to African-American communities. However, the absence of a comprehensive class analysis fosters the disquieting assumption that the true enemies of working-class Blacks are the "white man" and his faithful sidekicks—middle-class Blacks.

Malcolm X constructs this notion of social class in many ways. Invoking a powerful metaphor of the "house Negroes" who protected the master's property as if it were their own and the "field Negroes" who felt no such allegiance, Malcolm X proclaimed, "I'm a field Negro. The masses are the field Negroes."[19] Using his own experiences with poverty to legitimize his philosophy, Malcolm X intimates that social class differences within African-American communities are of greater importance than those outside. Consider the following passage from one of the last speeches he gave before leaving the Nation of Islam, "Message to the Grassroots," delivered in 1963 to a virtually all-Black audience.

> Just as the slavemaster of that day used Tom, the house Negro, to keep the field Negroes in check, the same old slavemaster today has Negroes who are nothing but modern Uncle Toms, twentieth-century Uncle Toms, to keep you and me in check, to keep us under control, keep us passive and peaceful and nonviolent. . . . It's like when you go to the dentist, and the man's going to take your tooth. You're going to fight him when he starts pulling. So he squirts some stuff in your jaw called novocaine, to make you think they're not doing anything to you. So you sit there and because you've got all of that novocaine in your jaw . . . and you don't know what's happening. Because someone has taught you to suffer—peacefully.[20]

This passage eloquently captures the process by which white institutions aim to co-opt a segment of the Black community in order to control the rest of that community. Yet the passage simultaneously forwards the simplistic view that middle-class blacks are all sellouts while the masses remain racially pure and uncompromised. When combined with preexisting views of race proclaiming that those likely to be "house Negroes" are light-skinned, the potential political polarization within African-American communities becomes counterproductive. In actuality, Blacks of all social classes, skin colors, and genders can be compromised in this way. For example, drug dealers, as was Malcolm X himself, can be seen as "house Negroes" who implement a pacification program for masses of Black people. The power to Malcolm X's analysis is compromised by this strategy of tying the metaphor of the house and field Negroes so closely to social class. But could the idea of co-optation have been presented as powerfully if the "house" and "field" Negroes had been removed from the story? Probably not. This type of contradiction makes Malcolm X's work simultaneously compelling and disturbing.

Malcolm X apparently was unaware of or suspicious of a longstanding Black progressive tradition concerning social class. As early as the turn of the century, African-American thinkers such as William E. B. Du Bois and Ida Wells Barnett forwarded sophisticated analyses of capitalism as a system of global economic exploitation. They argued that social class dynamics both within Black communities and between Black and white communities were influenced by a global political economy. Identifying the interconnections of global capitalism, its domestic corporate structure, and domestic and global racism, scholar/activists such as these analyzed the causal effects larger structures had on high rates of poverty in African-American communities. Black intellectuals such as Oliver Cox, E. Franklin Frazier, Paul Robeson, Pauli Murray, and Richard Wright all participated in a Black progressive tradition of the 1930s and 1940s in which race and class analyses were closely linked. Stands against racism meant simultaneously seeing the effects of social class as an analytical versus a descriptive category. While this Black progressive tradition on social class was largely silenced by the McCarthyism of the early 1950s, the tradition never disappeared entirely.[21]

Malcolm X either never connected with the Black progressive tradition concerning social class or explicitly rejected it. Prior to his incarceration, the poverty of his childhood and adolescent years meant that he was denied basic literacy and probably lacked access to ideas like these. While being in prison enabled him to study and read for the first time, incarceration also isolated Malcolm X from African American communities and the everyday contexts in which ideas are developed and shared. His conversion to the Nation of Islam while in prison probably provided him not only with his first comprehensive analysis of race and racism, but with his first formal introduction to social class theory. While Malcolm X traveled widely as a representative of the Nation of Islam, membership in the Nation came at a cost. In order to belong, Malcolm X simultaneously had to embrace the Nation's perspective on social class for those twelve years in which he was a minister.

The Nation of Islam's perspective on social class was largely divorced from the Black progressive tradition. The Nation advocated Black ownership of a separate Black economy—in essence, a separate Black capitalism—that would provide African Americans with financial independence from whites. In other words, Blacks as a social class should rise up and create a separate Black-controlled economy. Those individuals who entertained aspirations outside of this class were labeled "house Negroes" and became problems to the Nation. "Why should white people be running all the stores in our community? Why should white people be running the banks of our community? Why should the economy of our community be in the hands of the white man?" asked Malcolm.[22] This approach fails to challenge the institutional structures, such as global corporate capitalism and nondemocratic governments, that support whites to keep African Americans impoverished. It aims to replace white faces with Black ones. Moreover, the question of how a separate Black economy would be maintained in the context of global capitalism was never directly addressed.

In essence, the Muslims advocated a philosophy for racial uplift paralleling that of white ethnics. But rather than using the economic base developed by buying Black and supporting Black institutions to empower African Americans in American political structures—white ethnic groups such as Italian Americans, Irish Americans, and Jews all used their group clout to gain control of mainstream political and social institutions—the Muslims had little interest in capturing positions of power in the wider political economy. Their economic philosophy aimed for Black self-determination within the system without Black people becoming a part of it.[23]

Malcolm X's beliefs about Black intellectuals may have been another contributing factor to how he treated social class in his Black

nationalism. "In the past," Malcolm X claimed in a 1964 Paris interview, "the Afro-American or American Negro intellectual perhaps
permitted himself to be used in a way that wasn't really beneficial to
the overall Afro-American struggle."[24] Because Malcolm seemingly
harbored a deep-seated distrust for Black intellectuals as being potential "house Negroes," he also found their philosophies suspect. In
describing white intellectuals, he pointed out, "They remind me of so
many of the Negro 'intellectuals,' so-called, with whom I have come
in contact—they are always arguing about something useless" (*Autobiography*, 180). Malcolm X was understandably wary of theories developed outside of the Black experience, such as social class analysis,
applied unthinkingly to Black people's situation. But he also entertained the potential importance of such theories when mined for ideas
useful for Black concerns.

> You take African socialism. Many of the African intellectuals that
> have analyzed the approach of socialism are beginning to see where
> the African has to use a form of socialism that fits into the African
> context; whereas the form that is used in the European country
> might be good for that particular European country it doesn't fit as
> well into the African context.[25]

If African intellectuals could engage in such thinking, why not African-
American "house Negroes"?

The checkered record of white progressives on matters of race may
also have contributed to Malcolm X's basic mistrust of social class as
a structural category of analysis essential to African-American social
struggle. Embracing social class as a primary category of analysis
meant that Malcolm X would have to reconcile the differences between
the words and deeds of whites who allegedly were also working for
social change, but whose actions indicated otherwise. His experiences
living and working in Michigan certainly exposed him to the racial
politics of a largely conservative American labor movement (when it
came to Blacks) in the automobile industry. While travel had broadening effects on his thinking, it simultaneously exposed him to the
limitations of allegedly progressive white groups. For example, he
recounts the case of communist trade union workers in France who
prevented Africans from renting a hall in which he could speak.[26]

Malcolm X's analysis of the connection between race and social
class could never be fully developed while he was a member of the

Nation of Islam because the class politics of the Nation both fueled his preexisting view of social class and forwarded a specific notion of social class.[27] Once freed from the constraints of being a Muslim minister, Malcolm X could more freely pursue his own ideas about social class and the workings of global capitalism. But did he?

Malcolm X's Black nationalism was undergoing some modification when he was suspended from the Nation of Islam on December 4, 1963, by Elijah Muhammad. During the next year, the last year of his life, Malcolm X remained firmly committed to Black nationalist philosophy, but indicated an increasing respect both for participating in electoral politics and for entertaining the possibility of forging useful coalitions with whites and other people of color. Both of these shifts represent an increased openness not only to doing reformist political work within African-American communities but to fostering institutional transformation of the political institutions in which Black communities were housed.

Malcolm X's well-known speech "The Ballot or the Bullet," delivered in the spring of 1964, projects the shifting contours of his Black nationalism. "The political philosophy of black nationalism means that the black man should control the politics and the politicians in his own community; no more," claimed Malcolm X.[28] This statement can be read to mean that the Black community should turn inward and develop its own political structure. But in the same speech, Malcolm compared the ballot to a bullet and argued that united ballots would bring about political self-determination if strategically aimed like bullets at the proper "targets." We can only wonder what those "targets" might have been.

Malcolm's growing interest in forging political coalitions also appears in the last year of his life. He remained staunchly nationalist in that he had little interest in integrating existing organizations or in creating new multiethnic ones. But his nationalism did shift with an increasing willingness to consider the potential importance of well-chosen coalitions. In a March 12, 1964, statement delivered during a formal press conference, Malcolm outlined the contours of his newly emerging position. He announced the formation of the Muslim Mosque, Inc., which would "remain wide open for ideas and financial aid from all quarters." While Malcolm X reaffirmed the basic tenets of community self-development, he hinted at a different role for the community:

Whites can help us, but they can't join us. There can be no black-white unity until there is first some black unity. There can be no worker's solidarity until there is first some racial solidarity. We cannot think of uniting with others, until after we have first united among ourselves.[29]

But a more important coalition lay ahead for Malcolm X. During his last year, he began to promote coalitions among people of color who shared a similar location in an "international power structure." In one of his last speeches, he spelled out the contours of his deepening analysis of the interconnections of global capitalism and racism.

Colonialism or imperialism, as the slave system of the West is called, is not something that is just confined to England or France or the United States. . . . It's one huge complex or combine, and it creates what's known not as the American power structure or the French power structure, but an international power structure. This international power structure is used to suppress the masses of dark-skinned people all over the world and exploit them of their natural resources.[30]

Calling for coalitions among African Americans, Africans, Asians, and other people of color can be seen as a widening of his earlier essentialist stance concerning Blacks and whites in the United States. But it might also signal the initial emergence of a truly class-conscious analysis.

Part of the problem in deciding which interpretation is more valid stems from the context in which Malcolm was operating. Malcolm X was shaping his Black nationalism during a time of extreme anti-colonial struggle in Africa. Prior to the mid-1950s, the vast majority of what are now independent African nations were colonies. In 1956 and 1957 the Sudan and Ghana respectively gained their independence. Nigeria, the Ivory Coast, Niger, Zaire, Benin, and a host of other countries joined them in 1960. In the middle of the dismantling of colonialism, it seemed logical to think that political independence would bring much-needed economic development or, in social class terms, a reduction of Black poverty. Malcolm X's lack of attention to structures of global capitalism that represent the political arm of colonialism is somewhat understandable in the context of his times, and his intellectual life. But in the contemporary postcolonial situation of African independence, and the contemporary domestic situation where African Americans have gained political power yet remain disproportionately impoverished, it becomes more difficult to overlook the importance of a social class analysis.

THE UNANSWERED GENDER QUESTION

In his many speeches, Malcolm X had relatively little to say about gender oppression and its effects on African-American men and women. Though Malcolm X changed his ideas on race and increased his attention to social class, he overlooked gender as a comparable category of analysis. And, in addition to his silence on the issue of gender, masculinist assumptions pervaded Malcolm X's thinking, and these beliefs in turn impoverished his version of Black nationalism.

It would be nice to think that Malcolm X simply left women out of his analysis. But he didn't. His comments about women, especially those contained in his *Autobiography*, offer one avenue to uncovering his underlying views on gender. Taking his cues from the dominant gender ideology of his times, Malcolm X's views on women reflected dominant views of white manhood and womanhood applied uncritically to the situation of African Americans. "All women, by their nature, are fragile and weak: they are attracted to the male in whom they see strength," Malcolm X claimed (*Autobiography*, 93). But, according to Malcolm, women were not all the same in their ways of dealing with male strength.

Much of Malcolm X's thinking classified women into two opposing categories. Some women were Eves—deceptive temptresses who challenged male authority, often by using their sexuality for their own gain. These were the women who could not be trusted. From Malcolm X's perspective, Black and white women both fell into this category. For example, consider Malcolm X's description of the actions of women during World War II. "Many of the black ones in those wartime days were right in step with the white ones in having husbands fighting overseas while they were laying up with other men, even giving them their husbands' money. And many women just faked as mothers and wives, while playing the field as hard as prostitutes—with their husbands and children right there in New York" (*Autobiography*, 91).

Malcolm X claimed to have learned about the true nature of women from prostitutes, themselves archetypal Eves, who schooled him to "things that every wife and every husband should know" (*Autobiography*, 91). But most of his advice was directed not to wives but to husbands, and much of that advice concerned how men should handle the potential "Eve" in every woman. According to Malcolm X, Islam's laws and teachings posit that the "true nature of a man is to be strong, and a woman's true nature is to be weak, and while a man must at all times respect his woman, at the same time he needs to understand that he must control her if he expects to get her respect" (*Autobiography*, 226). To him, women needed and admired a man who was strong. He forwarded a version of strength grounded in control and domination, even though it often came masked by love. "A woman should occasionally be babied enough to show her the man had affection, but beyond that she should be treated firmly," suggests Malcolm X (*Autobiography*, 92–93). Consider Malcolm X's description of Mamie, his Black dancing partner:

> She was a big, rough, strong gal, and she lindied like a bucking horse. . . . A band was screaming when she kicked off her shoes and got barefooted, and shouted, and shook herself as if she were in some African jungle frenzy, and then she let loose with some dancing, shouting with every step, until the guy that was out there with her nearly had to fight her to control her. . . . I started driving her like a horse, the way she liked. (*Autobiography*, 64)[31]

Numerous stereotypes of Black women pervade this passage. In contrast to white women who are stereotyped as being "fragile and weak," Malcolm X admired Black women who were strong, who shouted and shook themselves as if they were in "African jungle frenzies." While Mamie's skin color is not described, Malcolm calls her "big, rough, and strong," euphemisms often applied to darker-skinned African-American women. Like all women, Mamie possessed a disorderly "nature" that could emerge at any moment, a nature that needed controlling by a man stronger than her. Malcolm X describes Mamie as being "like a bucking horse," as an animal that needed to be tamed. Portrayed as wild and animallike, Mamie's dancing symbolizes her sexuality. Her need to be "driven like a horse" parallels Malcolm X's view that a woman needs to be "controlled" by a good man. Moreover, Mamie "liked" being "driven" and thus is portrayed as welcoming her own subordination.[32]

In contrast to Eve, other women were Madonnas—archetypal wives and mothers who sacrifice everything for their husbands and children. Malcolm X's description of the Muslim women he observed during his pilgrimage to Mecca indicates that, while his views on race and social class underwent revision, his basic classificatory scheme for women remained intact. He describes the women in the Holy Land as "modest" and "feminine." In contrast, he found the "half-French, half-Arab Lebanese women" projecting in their dress and street manners more "liberty" and "boldness," traits that reflected the influence of European culture, traits coincidentally reserved for men. "It showed me how any country's moral strength, or its moral weakness, is quickly measurable by the street attire and attitude of its women. . . . Witness the women, both young and old, in America—where scarcely any moral values are left" (*Autobiography*, 349). The Eves of the West are contrasted to the Madonnas of the East—with the major difference being that men in the East know how to control their women, while white men in the West not only fail to control their women but have set a bad example for Black men who are consequently losing the ability to control theirs.

The gender ideology reflected in Malcolm X's perspectives on women was influenced by and in turn influenced his Black nationalism. It is important to remember that the Nation of Islam was a heavily male-dominated organization during the time Malcolm was a member. The typical congregation of the 1950s was predominantly male (up to 80 percent), ranging in age from seventeen to thirty-five. Men assumed the dominant roles in the affairs of the temples, with women holding honored but secondary roles.[33] Like other leaders in the 1950s and 1960s, Malcolm X included Black women's issues and the question of gender under the generic phrase "the black man." Occasionally the "black man" actually meant Black *men* and the ways in which racial oppression is structured for Black men because of their gender. But more often the term was intended to stand for Black *people*. Malcolm X's overall approach was to allow the term "the black man" to serve as proxy for the "nation" and for African Americans of both genders. The resulting conflation of Blackness, masculinity, and political astuteness sets the stage for some of the main ideas of Malcolm X's Black nationalism.

Much of Malcolm X's symbolism and many of the metaphors he used to describe Black oppression were derived from the experiences of Black men. Malcolm X typically described political struggles confronting Black people as confrontations between the "white man" and the "black man." In describing the reasons why African Americans had rioted in Harlem, Malcolm X observed, "It's a corrupt, vicious, hypocritical system that has castrated the black man, and the only way the black man can get back at it is to strike it in the only way he knows how."[34] We might ask whether the metaphor of male castration works as well at explaining women's involvement in urban insurrections. We might also question what version of Black community control Malcolm X had in mind for the economic, political, and social development of African-American communities. Would the vision of "strong" Black men offering benign leadership to Black women who willingly accepted their gender subordination be part of the separate Black nation? Equating Black oppression with the state of Black masculinity is in effect offering a masculinist analysis of Black oppression.

The potential resurgence of Black nationalism in contemporary African-American communities mandates that we take a closer look at Black nationalist philosophies like Malcolm X's, particularly concerning their gender ideology. Two issues in his work are relevant to contemporary Black sexual politics.

First, omitting Black women from analysis gives the impression that African-American women's experiences with racism differ little from those of African-American men. Most African-American men do not confront issues such as sexual harassment in the workplace, sterilization abuse, being single mothers, domestic violence, and rape. Yet these issues profoundly affect African-American community development and the ability of Black people to exercise self-determination. The invisibility of Black women in Malcolm X's Black nationalist philosophy fosters the view that issues unique to Black women will be addressed by strategies aimed solely at black men.

Second, conflating the experiences of Black women with those of Black men leads to the trivialization, distortion, and denial of issues that Black women confront because they are both Black and women. Consider, for example, Malcolm X's discussion in a speech delivered six days before his assassination of his views concerning Elijah Muhammad's sexual harassment of teenage women in the Nation of Islam. "You can't take nine teenaged women and seduce them and give them babies and not tell me you're—and then tell me you're moral. You do it if you admitted you did it and admitted that the babies were yours. I'd shake your hand and call you a man. A good one too. [Laughter.]"[35] By today's standards, Elijah Muhammad's actions would constitute sexual harassment and, depending on the age of the women, statutory rape. To Malcolm, the immorality of Muhammad's acts hinged not on his immoral treatment of women but on his not acting like a "man" and owning up to his actions. Moreover, by saying that he would "shake the hand" of a man who fathered many children, Malcolm unwittingly fosters a view of Black manhood based on biological reproduction. A "good man" is one who gives women as many babies as he can. This approach clearly fails to appreciate the situation of women raising unplanned children, with partners who do or do not admit to the paternity. In essence, this passage trivializes a very important issue facing African-American communities, namely, Black male accountability in the growth of impoverished female-headed households.

It is important to remember that when it comes to gender, Malcolm X's philosophy was virtually indistinguishable from that of his contemporaries, both Black and white. Malcolm X's gender ideology was entirely consistent with the treatment of gender generally in African-American social and political thought and activism in the 1950s and 1960s. Malcolm X did not have access to Black feminist writings of the 1970s and 1980s—such as those by Toni Cade Bambara, Barbara Smith, Alice Walker, Audre Lorde, Toni Morrison, Ntozake Shange, Angela Davis, or bell hooks—where gender emerges as a major category of analysis in explaining Black women's oppression.[36]

Malcolm X's treatment of gender reflected the widespread belief of his time that, like race, men's and women's roles were "natural" and were rooted in biological difference. Like his essentialist definition of race, Malcolm X held equally essentialist notions about gender. Women did not learn to be a certain way—their actions were part of their "nature." Despite the limitations of Malcolm X's philosophy on gender, it's also true that his work, especially his speeches after the break with the Nation of Islam, contains a nascent philosophy on gender that was leading him away from essentialist notions. Just as he learned to see racial categories as socially constructed, Malcolm may have been learning to see gender categories as socially constructed categories of analysis.

But his later work goes both ways. There are instances of his growing ability to distinguish between the ways in which particular issues impacted differently on African-American men and women. He began to sense that ignoring this differential impact on and contributions by women would weaken the goal of Black self-determination. Consider the following segment from a November 1964 Paris interview.

> One thing that I became aware of in my traveling recently through Africa and the Middle East, in every country you go to, usually the degree of progress can never be separated from the woman. If you're in a country that's progressive, the woman is progressive. If you're in a country that reflects the consciousness toward the importance of education, it's because the woman is aware of the importance of education. But in every backward country you'll find the women are backward, and in every country where education is not stressed it's because the women don't have education.[37]

This passage reflects Malcolm X's recognition that the status of women is indicative of the status of a nation. However, while Malcolm in this passage appears to be for women's equality, by limiting women to the traditionally feminine spheres of family and education, he continues to see women in circumscribed albeit potentially political roles. Malcolm continues: "So one of the things I became thoroughly convinced of in my recent travels is the importance of giving freedom to the woman, giving her education, and giving her the incentive to get out there and put that same spirit and understanding in her children."[38] Women do not earn freedom or fight for it like men—they have it given to them, supposedly by Black men who have earned theirs and who maintain control over women, however much it is done with respect. Moreover, this newfound freedom is to be used to instill the value of education in children, again a reiteration of the revered Madonna role. Despite its limitations, this passage does demonstrate that just prior to his assassination, Malcolm X was beginning to grapple with issues of how strategies for the development of Black communities might need to be gender specific.

The logic Malcolm X followed in thinking about other issues might have led him to Black feminist analysis of Black oppression and liberation. For example, his perspective on violence seems contradictory: He apparently accepted male violence against women in order to control them but opposed white violence against African Americans for the same purpose. In describing how his father beat his mother, Malcolm X blamed the victim. "It might have had something to do with the fact that my mother had a pretty good education. . . . But an educated woman, I suppose, can't resist the temptation to correct an uneducated man. Every now and then, when she put those smooth words on him, he would grab her" (*Autobiography*, 4). Here, Malcolm condones the use of male violence against women who refuse to stay in their subordinate place, in this case, an educated Black woman who allegedly reminds a less educated African-American man of his educational inferiority. In another situation, Malcolm X described how he had to fend off a "hot-headed Spanish Negro" girlfriend of a friend. "Not able to figure out why Sammy didn't shut her up, I did . . . and from the corner of my eye, I saw Sammy going for his gun. Sammy's reaction that way to my hitting his woman—close as he and I were— was the only weak spot I'd ever glimpsed" (*Autobiography*, 115). For this experience, the major problem Malcolm X seemed to have with striking his friend's girlfriend was that Sammy demonstrated weakness by letting a woman interfere with male bonding. Both beatings were designed to ensure male dominance. Moreover, Malcolm X's unquestioned acceptance of Black male violence against Black women is not only unsettling but, accepted uncritically, could be used as an endorsement of such behavior.

Contrast these beliefs concerning violence against women to Malcolm X's analysis of the interconnectedness of global violence and violence in the United States. In the following passage from "Message to the Grassroots" Malcolm contends:

If violence is wrong in America, violence is wrong abroad. If it is wrong to be violent defending black women and children and black babies and black men, then it is wrong for America to draft us and make us violent abroad in defense of her. And if it is right for America to draft us, and teach us how to be violent in defense of her, then it is right for you and me to do whatever is necessary to defend our own people right here in this country.[39]

Taken together, these examples suggest that Malcolm X accepted male violence against other males if it was used to enforce legitimate male authority. Because he views racism as granting white men illegitimate or immoral authority, white male violence in defense of white supremacy cannot be condoned, and he encourages African-American men facing such illegitimate violence to defend themselves "by any means necessary," including violence. Violence used by oppressed groups such as Black men becomes legitimate if it is used to resist the illegitimate violence of dominant groups such as white men. But because Malcolm X has not yet come to see gender oppression as being comparable to racial oppression, he correspondingly fails to see the ways in which sexism grants men a similar illegitimate or immoral authority to engage in violence against women. Thus, the logic of his own arguments concerning racism would, over time, lead him to see that his endorsement of the model of the strong Black man controlling his woman, respectfully if possible, but through force if needed, was unacceptable.

Developing a Black feminist analysis would broaden these contradictory perspectives on violence in order to reveal the interconnectedness and immorality of all types of violence used to defend domination and oppression. Whether police brutality in African-American communities, the more hidden yet pervasive family violence directed toward African-American women and children by their husbands and fathers, or the illegitimate violence used to support South African apartheid, if all victims of violence were encouraged to protect themselves against illegitimate uses of force, Malcolm X's much-quoted phrase "by any means necessary" would acquire a whole new meaning.

LEARNING TO THINK FOR OURSELVES

The growing tendency to celebrate Malcolm X's well-earned achievements without critically evaluating how his ideas address contemporary issues is problematic because it limits our ability to be politically effective in the context of our own times. While studying Malcolm X's legacy is important, we must be careful not to refashion his image to suit our own purposes. Cookbook formulas gleaned from superficial understandings of past philosophies, even those as widely respected among African Americans as that of Malcolm X, offer a weak substitute for original, analytical thinking that takes on contemporary issues.

African Americans must take the lead in addressing problems facing Black communities. But these problems are unlikely to be solved without highly developed theories that address the interconnectedness of race, class, and gender in structuring the African-American experience. Comprehensive strategies for Black community development must deal with the embeddedness of African-American communities in global structures of postcolonial racism, capitalism, and male domination.

Malcolm X's later work certainly pointed in the direction of this type of comprehensive theorizing, but it does not contain a fully articulated theory that embraces such complexity. For example, Malcolm X was moving toward a socially constructed theory of race and racism. But much of his work did remain rooted in biologically essentialist notions of race and the limited political vision that can accompany this perspective. Similarly, while Malcolm X did broaden his perspective on social class, he never fully articulated a comprehensive social class analysis that took capitalist development into account. Malcolm X's position on gender was also highly problematic. As a result, while his version of Black nationalism contains many groundbreaking insights germane to the context of his times, his overall analysis remains limited in its ability to address the complexity of contemporary Black issues. He points us in the right direction on race and class but was not able to pursue the logic of his own arguments to their own conclusions.

Malcolm X's work is a major contribution; it is a model of an important sort of intellectual struggle—the kind that remains tied to ongoing political activism. The type of leadership that Malcolm offered may prove to be far more valuable to African-American communities than any specific idea he embraced or action he took. Malcolm X was not exclusively either a scholar or a political activist. He managed to combine the best of both—he was an individual who was able to think for himself and act upon the strength of his convictions.

NOTES

1. Manning Marable, *Race, Reform, Rebellion: The Second Reconstruction in Black America, 1945–1990, Second Edition* (Jackson: University Press of Mississippi, 1991); and William Julius Wilson, *The Truly Disadvantaged: The Inner City, the Underclass, and Public Policy* (Chicago: University of Chicago Press, 1987).

2. Malcolm X describes these different phases of his political development in his

autobiography, Malcolm X with Alex Haley, *The Autobiography of Malcolm X* (New York: Ballantine Books, 1964).

3. For basic introductions to Black nationalism, see: Alphonso Pinkney, *Red, Black, and Green: Black Nationalism in the United States* (New York: Cambridge University Press, 1976); Jeremiah Moses Wilson, *The Golden Age of Black Nationalism, 1850–1925* (New York: Oxford University Press, 1988); and Marable, *Race, Reform, Rebellion*, 86–113.

4. Pinkney, *Red, Black, and Green*, discusses the differences between revolutionary nationalism as practiced by the Black Panther Party, cultural nationalism as expressed in the Black Arts Movement of the 1960s and 1970s, and religious nationalism as practiced by the Nation of Islam. While Malcolm X's nationalism emerged in the context of religious nationalism, his thinking during the final year of his life began to broaden to incorporate other types.

5. Malcolm X also measured other people in his life using the yardstick of skin color. When adolescent Malcolm first met his adult sister Ella, she had a major impact on him because she was the "first really proud black woman I had ever seen in my life. She was plainly proud of her very dark skin" (*Autobiography*, 32). Skin color apparently played an important role in his dealings with a range of people. As the lightest child in his family, Malcolm remembers that "just as my father favored me for being lighter than the other children, my mother gave me more hell for the same reason" (*Autobiography*, 7).

6. William A. Sampson and Vera Milam, "The Interracial Attitudes of the Black Middle Class: Have They Changed?" *Social Problems* 23, no. 2 (1975): 153–165.

7. For a highly critical analysis of the Black middle class, see E. Franklin Frazier's *Black Bourgeoisie* (New York: Free Press, 1957).

8. Bruce Perry's recently published biography, *Malcolm: The Life of a Man Who Changed Black America* (New York: Station Hill Press, 1991), refers to the importance of skin color in Malcolm X's childhood and young adulthood. Although Perry places far too much emphasis on this theme in explaining Malcolm X's psychological profile, the color politics of the 1940s and 1950s and corresponding social constructions of race based on skin color were important factors in Malcolm's thinking.

9. The *Autobiography* was finished after Malcolm's pilgrimage to Mecca. One interpretation of the *Autobiography* is to see it as Malcolm's efforts to describe his former thinking as it actually was rather than trying to reinterpret his own past in a more favorable light.

10. Unlike today where analyses of race and racism emphasize their social construction, Malcolm X's definition of race was highly consistent with the thinking of his times. For an overview of scholarship on race and racism, see Michael Omi and Howard Winant, *Racial Formation in the United States: From the 1960s to the 1980s* (New York: Routledge, 1986). Winthrop Jordan, *White Over Black: American Attitudes toward the Negro, 1550–1812* (Chapel Hill: University of North Carolina Press, 1968), offers a historical overview of race in the United States. A historical treatment of race and its connections

to science can be found in Stephen Jay Gould, *The Mismeasure of Man* (New York: W.W. Norton, 1981). Recent works that aim to reformulate our thinking about race include Robert Miles, *Racism* (New York: Routledge, 1989); and David Theo Goldberg, ed., *Anatomy of Racism* (Minneapolis: University of Minnesota Press, 1990).

11. George Breitman, ed., *Malcolm X Speaks* (New York: Grove Press, 1965), 5.

12. Jordan, *White Over Black.*

13. The issue of what these "good qualities" are remains germane in our own times. Efforts to structure a positive Afrocentric past in opposition to an oppressive Eurocentric past can result in defining Blackness as being the opposite of what whiteness is thought to be. The result is that Blackness or Afrocentricity is not defined on its own terms but becomes a residual category that can be defined only in relation to whiteness. Malcolm X's views on race illustrate this issue. Typically, he spends far more time identifying what is wrong with whiteness and Eurocentricity and far less time on explaining what is positive and affirming about Afrocentricity.

14. This view of race as a biological category parallels biologically deterministic definitions of race first forwarded by scientific racism in the 1800s. For a discussion of scientific racism, see Gould, *The Mismeasure of Man.*

15. Breitman, *Malcolm X Speaks*, 5.

16. For efforts to specify this Afrocentric tradition, see Molefi Kete Asante, *The Afrocentric Idea* (Philadelphia: Temple University Press, 1987); Dominique Zahan, *The Religion, Spirituality, and Thought of Traditional Africa* (Chicago: University of Chicago Press, 1979); John Mbiti, *African Religions and Philosophies* (London: Heinemann, 1969); Tsenay Serequeberhan, *African Philosophy: The Essential Readings* (New York: Paragon House, 1991); and Norm R. Allen, *African-American Humanism: An Anthology* (Buffalo, NY: Prometheus Books, 1991).

17. Breitman, *Malcolm X Speaks*, 212.

18. Ibid.

19. Ibid., 11.

20. Ibid., 12.

21. Marable, *Race, Reform, Rebellion*; and Cedric J. Robinson, *Black Marxism: The Making of the Black Radical Tradition* (London: Zed Press, 1983).

22. Breitman, *Malcolm X Speaks*, 39.

23. The membership of the Nation of Islam may offer another clue concerning Malcolm X's perspective on social class. While the Civil Rights establishment was primarily led by middle-class African Americans, its rank-and-file membership reflected much more social class diversity. In contrast, the Nation of Islam drew most of its membership at that time from working-class Black people, many of whom moved in and out of poverty. Like Malcolm, this group was disenfranchised, and was often treated badly not only by the white establishment but by Blacks who seemed to be doing well in white institutions. See Pinkney, *Red, Black, and Green*, 160.

24. Malcolm X, *By Any Means Necessary: Speeches, Interviews, and a Letter by Malcolm X* (New York: Pathfinder Press, 1970), 180.

25. Ibid., 181.

26. Bruce Perry, ed. *Malcolm X: The Last Speeches* (New York: Pathfinder Press, 1989), 113.

27. Malcolm's break with the Nation of Islam in 1964 marked the beginning of a transformation of his views on a number of issues, among them his definitions of who are the racist oppressors, a broadening of his growing international orientation, and more generous appraisals of civil rights struggles in the United States (Perry, *Malcolm X: The Last Speeches*, 14).

28. Breitman, *Malcolm X Speaks*, 38.

29. Ibid., 21.

30. Ibid., 160.

31. This passage describes a dance from his adolescence. In order to give readers a sense of his mindset, Malcolm X might have deliberately chosen to describe Mamie using the terminology and ideology that he possessed at that time in his life. Or this passage might have accurately expressed his views on Black women like Mamie at the time the *Autobiography* was written.

32. The linking of darker-skinned peoples with animals remains a familiar tenet of racist thinking. See Gould, *Mismeasure of Man*, and Jordan, *White Over Black*. For an analysis of Black women's images and their connection to systems of race, class, and gender oppression, see Patricia Hill Collins, *Black Feminist Thought: Knowledge, Consciousness, and the Politics of Empowerment* (New York: Routledge, 1990), 67–90 and 163–180.

33. Pinkney, *Red, Black, and Green*, 160.

34. Breitman, *Malcolm X Speaks*, 167.

35. Perry, *Malcolm X: The Last Speeches*, 121–22.

36. Collins, *Black Feminist Thought*.

37. Malcolm X, *By Any Means Necessary*, 179.

38. Ibid.

39. Breitman, *Malcolm X Speaks*, 8.

Philosopher or Dog?

HILTON ALS

for Darryl A. Turner and Kenneth E. Silver

I should like so much to begin with an idea, would you mind? This idea—it concerns the definition of one or two words. Some words—they are defined by the exigencies of time, right? And generally words defined by their epoch become very stupid words. The words currently defining our epoch are "otherness" and "difference." Appropriate definitions of these words are "beside the point" and "never mind." Those definitions—they must stick. And why? Because writers of a color who find their expression—so called—in their "otherness" and "difference" do so in a manner comfortable to the legions who buy their work not to read them, oh no, but because these writers confirm the nonideas stupid people assume about "otherness" and "differ-ence"—two words that define privilege in the epoch of some.

If pressed by the thumb of thought, where does the idea of this "otherness" and "difference" come from? It is an acquired habit really. One learns it in infancy, sitting on the knee of someone—perhaps Mom—who may not be unlike oneself in a respect: her appearance. Appearances speak not of themselves but of preceding generations and the haunting of each subsequent one with: Because I appear not unlike you, we are each other. What folly! The belief that the dimen-sions of some mother's mask, say, fitting—becoming—one's physiog-nomy is oneself. What manipulation! To appropriate her mask of a different sex (if you are a boy), a different generation (if you are a child), so experientially different (if you are a person), because experience is an awful thing. Truly, who "loves" it? In order not to have it—experience—we do a number of things, chief among them speaking to stupid people who cannot possibly understand us. How slimily we creep toward them—on our bellies, masks intact, the better to make our way toward the inconvenient places their ignorant experience hides—in their armpit, in their speech, in their sex, the last being, for many, experience in toto.

The cowardly experience described previously—applying that mother's mask, say, to protect oneself. How easily this is done! How easily this is done! We apply her mask to get us through a world we do not understand wherein we embrace the experience of people who cannot understand us. We accomplish this brand of retarded experience by nursing her words through the tit of her experience. Are we less lonely because of it? In X situation, Mother does exactly as I would have done. Mother says. And I am so much like her, et cetera. What if all this were simply untrue? What if one were to remove oneself from the lap of comfort—the comfort of identification with Mom? It is never done. One fears the isolation of one's own language so much one upholsters Mom and others like her in the blind fabric of others-like-myself.

These others like myself. What does their mask of piety yield? For those who write but do not care to dissect the mask—let alone its expression of piety—it yields a career. This career is celebrated by very stupid people who define an epoch with one or two words. Their world comprised of one or two words—in it they support writers of a color who do not challenge their privilege by writing against it. These writers are limited to becoming those one or two words—"other" and "different." What can this mean? It does not mean writing. These writers are killed by stupid people and their acceptance. Their acceptance is a form of control, as it has always been, and for generations.

When these writers of a color are embraced—it is wrong. The world is too quick to celebrate their wearing of the mask of piety, behind which they sit, writing nothing. These writers of a color often center on the figure of Mom, say, as a symbol of piety—she of an oppressed race, depressed sex, and the bad men who didn't love her and how meek and self-sacrificing she was and what shape her mask of piety took and just how big her lap was—which the child, the writer, knew the measure of because of crapping in it. Once Mom is crapped upon, she is never wondered about or cared for again because she's beside the point, she's Mom and a symbol of all one would like to get away from in this common world. Which is one reason a career is struggled for in the first place: to get away from all the true and infinitely more horrible stories Mom could tell about how she came to wear the mask of piety in the first place. The mask of piety—it is the one thing standing between her children and death. Yes, sir, Yes, ma'am, she says from behind the mask. And, with eyes lowered, Please, sir, do not kill my children. And with breasts exposed, We will not take too much. And in the bile of a tearful farewell: Children, please do not reach toward the world that despises you because it despises me.

Regardless of what Mother says, everyone reaches toward this world, everyone, and when it burns the only thing standing between you and this burning death is the idea of others like myself—a wall that protects. Writers of a color write stupidly on this wall of race for the approval of very stupid people who, in granting their approval, may decide not to kill you. If these stupid people decide not to kill you, something must be compromised, given up. Generally, what is compromised is one's voice. That voice—it is all a writer has. Stupid people do not ask to claim this voice outright—one way in which they are not stupid. They acquire it slowly: at drinking parties and over the telephone to discuss the drinking party of the night before and at dinner and the walk following dinner under the glare of gossip dinner chat generates, and in the feigned intimacy of shared experience. That experience—it is found in the armpit and has been described at length before. It is so dreary, the scenario people of a color follow as they live an experience they believe to be intimate. This experience generally amounts to: Let me wear the mask of my mother, the mask of piety, generosity, and forbearance, for you. The "you" to whom all this is addressed—it is almost never to another person of a color. That would be too much. If the mask of piety were understood, one would be forced to speak from behind it and the fake piety, generosity, and forbearance one has used to get what one needs: feigned intimacy, the armpit not of a color.

Perhaps Mom knows all of this. What Mom knows: In reaching toward the world, her child will eventually have to wear the mask of piety, too. What Mom knows: very stupid people look upon this mask with affection, especially as it stutters: Yes, sir, Yes, ma'am. This humiliation—it is so familiar and colored, one kills oneself in it, especially in the world of intimacy wherein we speak to people who cannot understand us, hoping they are not colored beneath all that ignorance.

Does Mom protect and nurture this child so that the child remains "open" to experience? Or to a career? Or to fill her lap? In the end, no one can say, but I should like to so much anyway: What Mom wants is for her child's life not to be loveless and to have some fortitude and be capable of calling a thing stupid if it is so, not behind a mask, oh no, and without fear of death.

But I digress.

Past the ostensible subject, Mrs. Louise Little.

In writing "Mrs. Louise Little," I digress even further. For in writing her name do you not see what I become? My intention? I become a writer of a color complicit with another—Malcolm X—who will compromise any understanding of her for a career. This career— it is a handful of dust in the end. One may fixate on it as if it were not. Presumably this career safeguards one from having to regard one's face and the mask behind it, which reveals, truly, what is in the mind and the quality of what is in the mind. When this mask cracks— underneath it, that is writing. How little it is done! Is *The Autobiography of Malcolm X* on Mrs. Little writing? "My mother, who was born in Grenada, in the British West Indies, looked like a white woman. Her father *was* white. She had straight black hair, and her accent did not sound like a Negro's" (*Autobiography*, 2). What beauty in the sentence "she had straight black hair and her accent did not sound like a Negro's"! Enough beauty undoubtedly to provoke nonthought in the mind of very stupid people: no complexity whatsoever, just Mom as the symbol of her son's career-to-be: reverence of people not of a color.

Could any critical analysis of Mrs. Little substantiated by biographical fact bear up to "My mother . . . looked like a white woman"? No, it could not. Unless one's sense of competition as a writer of a color in relation to another—Malcolm X—were very keen on representing Mrs. Little as something other than a nearly colorless vision. Since practically any audience will make me a writer of a color solely and, as such, I am meant to suffer, I will gladly undertake the gargantuan task of remaking Mrs. Little. But how? And according to whose specifications? Shall I begin with the hatred and self-hatred Malcolm projected onto his mother's face—"My mother . . . looked like a white woman. . . . I looked like my mother"—while remembering my own (at times) hatred toward Mother? How shall I "capture" Mrs. Little?

As an abhorrent phantom eventually driven mad by her ghostly, non-colored half? What if one were to write of her not as a mother at all, but as Louise, adrift in Grenada, in the then—British West Indies—a part of this common world my own mother knew well enough to escape. To write of Louise's crêpe de chine dress—her only one—limping as she eventually made her way to America—are these facts? Did she see her future in the stars—the murder of her husband by men not of a color; the murder of her son by men perhaps of a color; her not-gradual slide into madness following her husband's death and the removal of her children to one foster home or another? Why could she not save them? Didn't she know obeah? She was so alone. Was her life more horrible than Malcolm's? And if so, why did she not make the world pay for it, like Malcolm? Was she lonelier than Malcolm, living in this common world? She was not lonelier than Malcolm, living in this common world. Malcolm lived less for other people than he did for power. His mother had no choice but to live for other people, being first a woman and then a mother. She was not alone long enough to know herself, emigrating, as she did, from Grenada, in the then—British West Indies, to Canada, where she met Earl Little, "an itinerant minister," whom she married and settled with, finally, in Lansing, Michigan, in western America. No one knew just how young she was before she went to Canada. No one knew just how young she was before she met Earl Little. In Canada, what did Earl Little preach as an "itinerant" minister? Was Louise Little charmed by his speech? Was it as mad as Malcolm's? Was Earl Little charmed by Louise Little's crêpe de chine dress—her only one—as he limped through the provinces, preaching what? Did Louise Little have more language? No one knew what her presence would mean to the United States, its future. Her emigrating to the States—it is never explained let alone described in the *Autobiography*. She exists in the *Autobiography* to give birth to Malcolm, go mad, and look nearly colorless. What did Louise feel, growing up in Grenada? What did Louise feel in America? She came from Grenada, in the West Indies, and its green limes, subbitter people, the blue sea, and sense, garnered from her family, that the yellowness of her skin raised her above having to don the mask of piety. Being yellow in the West Indies—what does it mean? It is a kind of elevated status based on folly. This folly began in the minds of those who contributed to the creation of this yellow skin. It began: Those smart-mouthed coloreds who want to come into this house where they will learn to hate darkness and the dark ones who remain in the sun, please come in. The stupid people—no, the Masters—who offered this up: They created another race within the colored race when they invited those dark ones in: the Yellows. The meaning of the Yellows to people in the West Indies is this: Their external self calls up hatred, self-hatred, and contempt in the dark; pity and scorn in the nondark.

People not of a color who "loved" the *Autobiography*: In the main they are not different from the noncolored people Louise Little was born to. Since we know so little about these people, we have to assume what Bruce Perry's biography says about one pivotal person is true: Louise "had never seen her Scottish father."[1] Had Louise Little's father read his grandson's book, I am certain he would have loved it. I am certain of this because for someone neither Earl nor Malcolm knew, Mrs. Little's Scottish father commanded so much attention. The success of a thing is best measured by the attention men pay it. The noncolored ghost that is Louise Little's father hovers happily in the *Autobiography*. That is because he commands the attention of the living ghosts who read this book and love it, not knowing why. They love it because of Grandfather. He is what Malcolm's noncolored readers identify with—a power. Earl and Malcolm speak of no one else with such passion. Earl Little is reported to have said to his parents, on the occasion of Malcolm's birth: "It's a boy, . . . But he's white, just like mama!"[2] Malcolm is reported to have said to his collaborator, Alex Haley: "Of this white father of hers I know nothing except her shame about it" (*Autobiography*, 2). What is Louise reported to have said about her own father? I do not know. And of Louise's "shame"? Did she ever describe it as that? And to a child? Malcolm said: "I remember hearing her say she was glad that she had never seen him. It was, of course, because of him that I . . . was the lightest child in our family" (*Autobiography*, 2). Was Louise Little glad not to have seen her father for reasons other than his skin not of a color? Was she glad not to have seen him so as to imagine him as dead as her unfortunate mother who died "giving birth to the last of her three illegitimate children"?[3] Was Louise Little glad not to have seen him because she was frightened by Malcolm's more than physical resemblance to her father's side of the family? Did Malcolm want to be noncolored too? He had so much ambition—was it genetic? And his need for love on his own terms. From whom did he learn the need not ask for it? Grandfather? Grandfather did not wear the mask of piety. In order not to, one must believe in oneself to the exclusion of other people. Malcolm believed in the reality of his experience to the exclusion of all other reality except one: Grandfather, who was a ghost.

Earl and Malcolm attached themselves to Louise's male, noncolored half. Louise did not have to meet her father. Earl and Malcolm lived him by competing with his ghost at every turn. Is that why Earl loved Louise? Because she looked like the memory of someone he might have loved before her? Had Earl known noncolored people he thought beautiful at one time or another? As a preacher who "[roamed] about spreading the word of Marcus Garvey" (*Autobiography*, 3) in Omaha or one place and another, did Earl spot someone with Louise Little's father's red hair, blue eyes, and, long before knowing Louise, think that person beautiful? Was that person with red hair and blue eyes kind to Earl Little? Did she feed him a cool drink of water with her own hands by the side of some road time has forgotten? When he met Louise, did he find her to be the living embodiment of a memory, which is to say was Louise Little that cool drink of water in that noncolored hand which did not lie to Earl Little? Admittedly this cool water slipping through a noncolored hand past Earl Little's lips and onto the side of a side road—it would have been a remarkable thing to see outdoors in Omaha, Nebraska, in the late 1920s. It would not have been a remarkable thing to have happened secretly, in America, ever. Did Earl really want Louise's father? Malcolm holds Louise Little's father responsible for his mangled consciousness: ". . . I was among the millions of Negroes who were insane enough to feel that it was some kind of status symbol to be light-complexioned. . . . But . . . later, I learned to hate every drop of that white rapist's blood that is in me." (*Autobiography*, 2). I am sure Malcolm did not mean that literally. First of all, how do we know Louise Little's mother was raped? How do we know that Louise Little's mother—who is not mentioned in the *Autobiography* at all—did not love Louise's father? In my mind's eye I see Louise Little's parents meeting on the side of a road in Grenada. Mrs. Little's mother—she is on foot. Mrs. Little's father—he is not. What he is: red in the red sun and on a horse. There is the sound of crickets. There is the sound of a mongoose's stuttering run. In pausing to look at one another, they do not pause to consider the eventual outcome of their meeting: Louise Little, Louise Little in America, Louise Little in America with Malcolm.

Does history believe in itself even as it happens? Malcolm wrote, "I feel definitely that just as my father favored me for being lighter . . . my mother gave me more hell for the same reason. She was very

light herself. . . . I am sure that she treated me this way partly because
of how she came to be light herself." Which was? "Her father."
(*Autobiography*, 7–8). The judgmental air emanating from the above!
The judgmental air that comes with knowing nothing! If Malcolm were
in the least her mother's son, he would know that in the West Indies
a father is an immaterial thing—a scrap of man born as torment.
Louise Little knew that. Perhaps Louise Little's lack of interest in her
father was cultural. Malcolm knew nothing of his mother's culture.
Instead, Malcolm preferred to indulge in the fantasy of Grandfather,
his "rape." That is all Malcolm cared to know of his mother's past or
all that was useful to him about his mother's past. It is clear Malcolm
indulged in this potential fantasy of Grandfather as rapist because it
endowed Grandfather with the power Malcolm needed to emulate in
order to learn how to take and take in this common world.

   Mrs. Little was "smarter" than Mr. Little. How much did Malcolm
hate knowing that? He hated the fact of his mother's smartness because
he admired it. He admired his mother's mind in the way he admired
most things—with loathing and fear, if he couldn't control it. What
Mrs. Little is in the *Autobiography*: representative of Malcolm's fear
that because he and Mom shared a face, he and Mom shared intelligence. Was Louise Little's smartness the precursor of her madness?

   Malcolm felt envy for Mrs. Little's "smartness." Was his expression of this envy only for himself, or for his father too? "My father and
mother . . . seemed to be nearly always at odds. Sometimes my father
would beat her. It might have had something to do with the fact that
my mother had a pretty good education." (*Autobiography*, 4). Malcolm
said, "An educated woman, I suppose, can't resist the temptation to
correct an uneducated man. Every now and then, when she [my mother]
put those smooth words on him [my father], he would grab her."
(*Autobiography*, 4). Is this not mad? Being smart—it made Mrs. Little
feel so different. It made my mother silent so as not to feel different.
Did Mrs. Little ask, by speaking, to be punished? Is that how she lost
her mind, really? The famous photograph of Malcolm standing at a
window in his house with a gun looking out the window—I believe he
is on the lookout for his mother. What did he see, looking out that
window? Did he see his mother's quite appropriate anger? Based on
the fact that in the *Autobiography* he refers to her as Louise and in
Malcolm: The Life of a Man Who Changed Black America, Bruce Perry
refers to her as Louisa? What was her name? Her date of birth? What
parish was she born in in Grenada? When Malcolm looked out that

window, did he see his mother holding a diary? What was written in it? Mrs. Little (as I call her) did not write: He did not know my name. He could not bear my presence. What did Mrs. Little write? I had a son named Malcolm? Mrs. Little did not write anything. I am writing her anger for her and therefore myself since I hate the nonwriting I have done about my own mother. The fact is, my nonwriting couldn't contain my mother's presence. The fact is, Malcolm knew his nonwriting couldn't support Mrs. Little. My mother's presence showed my nonwriting up. I am writing the *idea* of Mrs. Little with, I hope, some authenticity, in the hope that every fake word, idea, gesture, lie I ever told about my mother and others like her will vanish.

Therein lies the paradox of trying to create an autobiography Mrs. Little can inhabit. Since I am not capable of writing about my mother, how can I honor Mrs. Little? I did not know her. How did I not know my mother? What I know: Malcolm's interest in his mother is evident in his avoidance. In one of his typically Johnsonian sentences, Malcolm writes of the effect his father's death had on her, but only as it affected him: "We began to go swiftly downhill. The physical downhill wasn't as quick as the psychological. My mother was, above everything else, a proud woman, and it took its toll on her that she was accepting charity. And her feelings were communicated to us" (*Autobiography*, 12). I cannot break Mrs. Little's heart by not at least trying to imagine what the emotional truth of the following might have meant to *her*. ". . . I remember waking up to the sound of my Mother's screaming again . . . My father's skull, on one side, was crushed in, I was told later. . . . Negroes in Lansing [the town they lived in then] have always whispered that he was attacked, and then laid across some tracks for a streetcar to run over him. His body was cut almost in half" (*Autobiography*, 10).

Mrs. Little was in her early thirties when her husband was murdered for "political" reasons. Earl Little was a Garveyite. Marcus Garvey was a native of Jamaica. Mrs. Little was a native of Grenada. I do not know what Mrs. Little's political beliefs were. Were they the same as Earl Little's? Earl Little's being a Garveyite—was this the result of Mrs. Little's political influence? Her being West Indian? This is just one more thing Malcolm did not speak of: Mrs. Little's politics.

Mrs. Little lost her mind for political reasons, in a sense. When Mrs. Little lost her mind, she was not quite ready not to believe in love, the bed empty of her mortal enemy (according to Malcolm), whom she loved (according to Malcolm), and with whom she lived first in

Canada and then Omaha and then Michigan. I am sure Mrs. Little was not quite ready for a space in her mind to be filled with unconquerable grief and madness. I am sure Mrs. Little did not want to see her children parceled off to one foster home or another. A young woman in her early thirties, her husband dead, with no means of support for herself and with eight children. What did Malcolm make of that? What do I make of that? I cannot bear to imagine unraveling my mother, her hair, her retribution. There is my mother—what to make of her? What to make of Mrs. Little? What to make of these questions? Will they always be at the fore of my consciousness? Is Mom all one will ever have to say who one is or care what one will become? It is difficult to forgive Mom for having to shoulder this responsibility alone as precious few pay attention to her language. It is difficult to forgive the world for not being a place conducive to this complexity. It is not difficult to produce nonwriting that rejects Mom as too great a reality.

American people of a color who "loved" the *Autobiography*. The *Autobiography* plays out the violence of their feelings toward the colored immigrant. Once Malcolm has identified his mother as an immigrant in his book, it is impossible not to see her at a remove. That is the true nature of difference: something stupidly defined so as to be controlled. When American people of a color look at this photograph of Malcolm, gun in hand, and cheer, it is because they believe he is looking for his mother, too. People like Mrs. Little only make Americans feel difference among themselves. Mrs. Little's appearance is not a comfort; her story is not a comfort; her place of birth is not a comfort: she is a woman of a color, but different. Malcolm represented an intolerance of this difference, and for a very long time. Malcolm says his mother was different at every turn: "She would go into Lansing and find different jobs—in housework, or sewing—for white people. They didn't realize, usually, that she was a Negro. . . . Once when one of us . . . had to go for something to where she was working, and the people saw us, and realized she was actually a Negro, she was fired on the spot, and she came home crying, this time not hiding it" (*Autobiography*, 12). And "Louise Little, my mother, who was born in Grenada, in the British West Indies, looked like a white woman."

In the countries they emigrate from, West Indians of a color are in the majority. They project the arrogance and despair that comes with this sense of being central but small onto everything and everyone else in the world. Everyone else in the world counters this arrogance by defining it as that—especially American people of a color. They do so because they are Americans first and prefer to exclude the complexity inherent in imagining what despair means to someone else and how that despair may shape arrogance. Arrogance is a theatrical device, and self-protective. The West Indians I grew up with employed this arrogance to mask their feeling less than most things and seeing this less feeling everywhere. This feeling does not exclude one's relationship to people of a color.

For example: Most West Indians regard most American people not of a color as ghosts. A ghost weighs on one's consciousness at times but is not a constant. West Indians are generally not ambivalent about the relationship one must establish with these ghosts: West Indians believe in ghosts. One takes from these ghosts what one must: warnings given in dreams and one's waking life, so as to live as profitably in the real world as possible. For American people of a color, these ghosts are made real through the renting of other people's blood—the blood, specifically, of American people of a color. This blood—it feeds their "double-consciousness," as Du Bois termed it. This double-consciousness is not so much the "two souls, two thoughts, two unreconciled strivings; two warring ideals in one dark body" Du Bois wrote of but, rather, hatred of people not of a color and their reverence for this hatred.

My grandmother, a native of Barbados, was a Royalist. She did not grow up in a "free" Barbados but in a Barbados not so different from the Grenada Louise Little emigrated from. Both islands were in the same commonwealth—British—which meant both islands were the province of Royals who sold their subjects the sense that wearing the mask of piety was identity.

My grandmother refused to accept that description of herself by believing she was not of any color. She was as wrong in this as she was in her belief that the world attempted to ignore the fact she was a woman. To forget herself and the hideousness of her reality, she attempted to ignore her children who were women, and their children, who were dark. Not unlike Louise Little, my grandmother was Yellow. In my mind's eye I can see my grandmother now. She is wearing her crêpe de chine dress—her only one—and sits, as she often did, with her legs spread, smelling not of limes but of something equally bitter. Because I am not Yellow, my grandmother encouraged me not to play in the sun; often she said I had the look of someone who had been covered in germs. My color—it was an illness to her. Was Malcolm's color an illness to his mother? "I feel definitely that just as my father favored me for being lighter . . . my mother gave me more hell for the same reason." My grandmother emulated so many Royalist tendencies. She had so little to rule, though. There were no mountains, colonies, or large groups of smart-mouthed coloreds to whom she could say shut up. There was just my little self who hated her for this so much I wrote this hatred down so as not to forget it. Like Malcolm. My version of an *Autobiography* would be just as mad as his, but more so, since it is difficult for me to speak this madness. Like my mother. Like Louise Little.

Most people from the island I know best—Barbados—believed in the attainment of property as a citadel against the influx of the ghosts and the memory of not being better than anyone—not the Yellows, not anyone except, they thought, most Americans of a color who did not believe in having anything because most things were so painfully real to them they were unreal. Like love and the cracking of the mask of piety.

Did Louise Little beg Mr. Little to work harder than was possible to attain property that might protect her children against the ghosts who eventually murdered him for his Garveyite preachings? Could Earl Little not attain this dream of protection? Theirs was a mixed marriage, in every sense. There was such a difference in their cultures. There is no photograph of that difference. There is just Malcolm's memory of it, which he hated—a hatred which became his career. Did Mr. Little wear a mask of piety familiar to Mrs. Little given her ghostly noncolored half? Did she pull rank with her yellow skin, which Malcolm hated as much as he hated his own? Mrs. Little is one long sentence that is a question.

For not writing any of that outright but sneaking in bits about his hatred of Mom just the same; for transferring his hatred of Mom's light skin onto a race of people he deemed mad because their skin was lighter than Mom's and, therefore, madder still, Malcolm was rewarded. He was rewarded by very stupid people who labeled his ideologically twisted tongue "marvelous."

Stupid Americans define their epoch and defend their privilege through one or two words. These words generally connote the sublime in order to bear the truth of what is being said. Americans distrust knowledge if it is presented as empirical—a fear of the "European." Since the root function of language is to control the world through describing it and most Americans are embarrassed by their will to do so, language is made palpable by being nice. Americans defend this niceness by declaring it makes language more social. Language, no matter how stupid, always leaves someone out. That is because an idea belongs first to an individual and not a public.

The word marvelous was popular in the 1930s through the early '70s, not least because of Diana Vreeland and Delmore Schwartz, and not least because Diana Vreeland and Delmore Schwartz were connected to two powerful industries that propagated the idea of the marvelous and "genius"—the fashion industry and the university. For Schwartz, the author who delineated manners in a book—say, Proust—was marvelous, or one should marvel at the author's ability to represent manners, regardless of class, as a way of describing a moral code in either decline or ascendence. For Vreeland the thought was the same but as it was expressed on the body, its look. Since Malcolm was lauded in *Vogue* for telling people not of a color that their faces and bodies were ugly, and since Malcolm was a treasured speaker at universities where he said he and others like himself would one day blow privilege out from between their student ears, he was taken by the marvelous, just as those people in fashion and at universities were taken by Malcolm's not tolerating their difference. They applauded and supported his "rage" because it reinforced their privilege.

As Malcolm became more famous, Mrs. Little was diminished by the loving glare of his publicity. That publicity—did it love him more than any mother could? In the *Autobiography*, he describes this love in great detail and more fervor than he ever describes Mrs. Little:

> *Life, Look, Newsweek* and *Time* reported us [the Nation of Islam]. Some newspaper chains began to run not one story but a series of three, four, or five "exposures" of the Nation of Islam. The *Reader's Digest*, with its worldwide circulation of twenty-four million copies in thirteen languages, carried an article titled "Mr. Muhammad Speaks," . . . and that led off other major monthly magazines' coverage of us. (*Autobiography*, 244)

Us against *them*. The them to whom Malcolm refers—that was Mrs. Little. She exists not at all during this period. Malcolm visited her from "time to time" in the state mental hospital at Kalamazoo, where she was committed—by whom?—for twenty-six years. She existed there, Malcolm says, in "a pitiful state" as her son became more and more famous. What was her bed like in that institution? What did

Malcolm speak of to this woman? Did other inmates call her Madame X or Mrs. Little? When he saw her face did he see his own? Did she slap him? "She didn't recognize me at all. . . . Her mind, when I tried to talk, to reach her, was somewhere else. . . . She said, staring, 'All the people have gone' " (*Autobiography*, 21). Gone where? Malcolm did not ask. Did he attempt to convert her? Was it too late? Had she become a Jehovah's Witness? She could not speak. Did anyone place a sheet of paper before her? A pencil? She did not write the book we need. This book—it is already forgotten. Mrs. Little survived her son—insane, by all accounts, but she survived him. Did she read his book? Did she find herself missing? Did she consider writing her own? Presumably, writers of a color have one story—the mask of piety, Mom, and what have you. Did Mrs. Little believe her son's book could not be surpassed? Did she ever possess the confidence to believe she could smash that piety by writing it down? She was a mother, and therefore responsible for the life of her children, one of whom did write her life down but for himself, not her, and in scraps, and incorrectly.

The *Autobiography* has everything very stupid people embrace— the mother driven mad by her husband's murder, the dust of patriarchy, religious conversion into the sublime—and yet it has nothing. The *Autobiography*—how can it be rewritten? This question—it must not be mistaken as a deconstructionist ploy, oh no. We mean to create an autobiography rich in emotional fiber, with a love of God and children and Mrs. Little and so forth.

As a model, the *Autobiography* can be used. Mrs. Little's autobiography has some potential for success if we use her son's book as a model. Think of *Manchild in the Promised Land*. That is the Autobiography of the Streets, but without the religious conversion. If the *Autobiography of Malcolm X* were written by Mrs. Little, it is certain it would not be the same book. Louise Little would not be capable of writing nothing. She was a mother. Consider Louise Little's story inside the model of the *Autobiography*, the book we need. In her son's book, the beginning is written this way:

Chapter One: Nightmare

When my mother was pregnant with me, she told me later, a party of hooded Ku Klux Klan riders galloped up one night. Surrounding the house, brandishing their shotguns and rifles, they shouted for my father to come out. My mother went to the front door and opened it. Standing where they could see her pregnant condition, she told them that she was alone with her three small children, and that my father was away. . . . (*Autobiography*, 1)

If Louise were to speak this, how would it be written? Must one remember one's own mother to reconstruct Louise Little's Chapter One: Nightmare, point by point? Would Louise Little write: Can you see me from a description? Was I fat? When I opened the door to those men, did it appear to them that I ate empty food? In a fat body—did I appear self-sufficient to some, a mountain of solace to my husband and children as they took and took? Did I require nothing? Will I go mad requiring nothing still?

To construct Mrs. Little point by point—would an "honest" approach be to transplant my mother's emotional history in her story? Speak for herself—that is what I mean Mrs. Little to do. Speaking for myself—that is what I can do. And in doing so, say: I am writing of Mrs. Little. What will this make of me? A boy who speaks (badly) for women—the too-familiar story? There is Mrs. Little in the British West Indies. There she is in hot sun. There she is before she became a mother driven partially mad with love for her children. There she is as a young girl with broad feet curled in gray or yellow sand. There she is in America with feet curled in bad shoes too small for her broad feet. There she is dead, lying upon the verbal catafalques created by her son Malcolm and me. There are Mrs. Little's sons, of which I am one, with their experience, wearing masks of piety as they sit in their mothers' death, resembling every inch of her face, speaking loudly, hating everything, writing nothing.

NOTES

1. Bruce Perry, *Malcolm: The Life of a Man Who Changed Black America* (New York: Station Hill Press, 1991), 2.

2. Ibid.

3. Ibid.

Malcolm X: The Art of Autobiography

JOHN EDGAR WIDEMAN

We urgently need to retrieve those past traditions that can become the source of reconciliation and wholeness, for it is more important to learn from those traditions than to dwell on pain and injustice.
—Francoise Lionnet,
"Autoethnography: Dust Tracks on a Road"

Sometimes the god wears a woman's face, sometimes a man's. Both suffer the same fate. Betrayal, dismemberment, the body pieces scattered, interred in a thousand thousand unknown places. Then she comes, always she, inconsolable, her tears a frozen rain drenching the land that has not cycled past winter since her lost one disappeared. She will scour the whole wide world until she finds every fragment of her beloved. And when she has gathered them and united them and breathed life again into the body, the earth too, as if it has been kissed, will begin softly to stir again, bud, bloom, warm as she does, her outstretched arms and smile open wide as a horizon in welcome.

Malcolm Martin, Martin Malcolm, the *m*s are some ancient sister in the amen corner *mmmmmm*, they are great mountains, cloud crowned, silhouetted against red dawn, as close to sky as solid earth ever reaches. They are men, mortals, mothers' sons; they were murdered, martyred, mirror our suffering, our history—betrayed, torn apart, dispersed. They wear the masks of men, of life or death, but it is not these accidental features we mourn. We are seeking always the body of our wholeness, what we once were and could be again, the promise of redemption Malcolm Martin Mandela seem to carry in their persons, a new day close enough to touch, to bestow a name upon—Malcolm, Martin, Mandela. What is snatched always just as it appears close enough to grasp.

For me writing about Malcolm is entering a space of myth and mourning. The way you enter an intense conversation, many voices that have been speaking to, at, and through one another for a very long time. In another way you are dreaming and responsible for every word you write, the words overheard and words not heard, words you say and words dismissed, echoed, repeated, inserted, quoted, paraphrased. Nothing escapes you. Everything does. *All stories are true*, as Achebe tells us the Igbo say. Reliable and unverifiable as dreams.

What could be viewed as a rather undignified squabble, an endless wrangling over our past, over what's dead and gone, bickering over the corpse of a dead man—who gets the head, the heart, the eyes, the penis, the gold teeth—is also a struggle to constitute the present, a present self and selves inseparable from the kind and quality of remembering we empower ourselves to imagine. In dreams responsibilities are assumed. A culture is a network of responsibilities, dynamic, willed, shared, sustained over time to create meaning, shape for individual lives. Du Bois said culture begins with a lie. A more benign word than lie, a word retaining the sense of illusion but emphasizing illusion's creativity, not its deceptive side, is artifice. Artifice (dreaming) makes artifacts: a self, a culture can begin with a vision of Malcolm as both seed and the fruit it wishes to produce.

This space of mourning and myth, then, is also and also and also (as Albert Murray might say) a magical space. A language appropriate to this terrain is required, language conducive, or at least not immune, to the conjuring properties words bear. Sound and sense. Sense and sound. What comes round goes round. Words spoken or written or said inside the mind have a life of their own, a history, a sensual reality. They are events in a specific time-space continuum, sense data, things perceived but also possessing properties beyond the penumbra of the perceiver. Qualities that allow them to be said or heard by others, simultaneously shared by the living and the dead, the writer and the reader, yesterday and tomorrow. We try to conventionalize words by embedding them in our discourse, attempt to tame them, make them conform, delimit, define. But words inherit minds and bodies of their own. Keep slipping and sliding away. Contain tensions, energies within themselves, that are volatile, contagious, responsive to conditions of extreme initial sensitivity the speaker/writer cannot predict or control. So utterance is compromise, approximation, and what a word brings to the dance often confounds its partner. Correspondences, dissonances, ruptures, healing, a primal, evocative power.

Metaphor, symbol, myth, rhythm, repetition, alliteration, rhyme that alludes to music's density and precision, are appropriate here in this space conjuring Malcolm. If these registers of language are absent in discussions of Malcolm, be suspicious, and doubly suspicious of languages and points of view that claim they don't speak in tongues. Such texts are not being candid, are engaging in misrepresentation, fashioning crude allegories even as they inveigh against those ways of writing they claim are unscientific. My goal is not the truth about Malcolm, but an understanding of how he has been used, could be used, and perhaps should be used to reconsider what passes for truth about him, ourselves, our culture, our country.

You are sitting in a room listening to a man talk and you wish to tell the story of the man's life, using as far as possible the words you are hearing to tell it. As writer you have multiple allegiances: to the man revealing himself to you; to the same man who will read and judge what you write; to an editor with an editor's agenda and maddening distance; to yourself, the demands of creating a text that meets your aesthetic standards, reflects your politics; to a potential publisher and reading public, etc., etc. You are serving many masters, and inevitably you are compromised. The man speaks and you listen but you also take notes, the first compromise and perhaps betrayal. Your notes are intended to capture the words you hear, but they are also designed to compress, select, filter, discard. A net, no matter how closely woven, holds some things and loses others. One crucial dimension lost, like water pouring through the finest seine, is the flow in time of the man's speech, the sensuous environment of orality that at best is crudely approximated by written words.

You may attempt through various stylistic conventions and devices to reconstitute for the reader your experience of hearing face to face the man's words. The sound of the man's narration may be represented by vocabulary, syntax, imagery, graphic devices of various sorts—

quotation marks, punctuation, line breaks, visual patterning of white space and black space, markers that encode print analogs to speech—vernacular interjections, parentheses, ellipses, asterisks, footnotes, italics, dashes . . . The drama of the encounter between yourself and the man may be enhanced by "stage directions" that set the scene and cue the reader to the hows and whys of what's being said.

> Visiting the Muslim restaurant in Harlem, I asked how I could meet Minister Malcolm X, who was pointed out talking in a telephone booth right behind me. Soon he came out, a gangling, tall reddish-brownskinned fellow, at that time thirty-five years old; when my purpose was made known, he bristled, his eyes skewering me from behind horn-rimmed glasses. "You're another one of the white man's tools sent to spy!" he accused me sharply. (*Autobiography*, 383)

Imagine yourself in a hotel room late at night listening to a man whose life story you wish to write and perhaps you'll invent other means serving the end of representing the man's voice, his presence, ultimately his *meaning* on the page. Perhaps you'll begin to appreciate how intimately truth and technique are entangled.

What's striking about Alex Haley's *Autobiography of Malcolm X* is the peculiar absence of the sorts of narrative strategies listed above. Haley presents a "talking head," first-person narration recorded from the fixed perspective of a single video camera. With a few small and one very large exception to this rule—the Epilogue from which the quote above is drawn—what we get from first to last page of the *Autobiography* is one voice addressing us, an extended monologue, sermon rap, recollection in tranquility of the awesome variety and precipitous turnabouts of Malcolm's life. The enormous popular success of the autobiography (millions of copies sold and selling), the power and persistence of the image of Malcolm it achieves, makes it worthwhile to investigate how Haley does so much with so little fuss, how an approach that appears rudimentary in fact conceals sophisticated choices, quiet mastery of a medium.

First, what does the exception tell us about the rules? Though the Epilogue was written after Malcolm's death and focuses upon his assassination and its aftermath, it remains a record of life as much as death, a concrete manifestation of how a spirit transcends the physical body's passing if the spirit's force continues to touch those who loved it, or those who didn't love but can't forget its impact, its continuing presence. Appended to the *Autobiography*, the Epilogue in many reader's minds blends with Malcolm's story, becomes part of the "as told to," a further conversation between the writer and Malcolm, Malcolm and the reader in spite of the attempt of Malcolm's enemies to silence him.

Several new, important subjects are introduced in the Epilogue: the writer of the *Autobiography*, the process of constructing the book, the relationship between writer and subject. Haley utilizes a variety of narrative modes and devices in the Epilogue. He inserts himself into the story, describes how, where, and why Malcolm is speaking, Malcolm's appearance, state of mind. Haley quotes, summarizes, cites other sources for points of view on Malcolm, ventures his own analysis and opinions explicitly in first person. This mixed form of narrative exposition is handled quite adroitly. The Epilogue becomes an eloquent extension of the *Autobiography*, a gripping, dramatically structured fugue that impels the reader toward the climax of assassination, the inevitable slow shock of recognition afterward as the world assesses the loss of Malcolm. Nearly one-sixth of the *Autobiography* (74 pages out of 456—a 4-page comment by Ossie Davis, a 6-page Introduction by M. S. Handler complete the volume), the Epilogue is proof positive that Haley's choice of a "talking head" for the body of his book was not chosen because he couldn't compose in another fashion.

"Nothing can be in this book's manuscript that I didn't say, and nothing can be left out that I want in" (*Autobiography*, 387). Malcolm insisted this guarantee be part of the contract between Haley and himself. In return Haley received a pledge from Malcolm to "give me a priority quota of his time for the planned 100,000 word 'as told to' book," and later Haley asked for and tells us he received from Malcolm permission to write "comments of my own about him which would not be subject to his review." How Malcolm's death affected this bargain, what kind of book his final cut of the manuscript might have produced, we can only guess. We could have posed this question to Haley, but now he's gone too. However, the nature of writing biography or autobiography or any kind of writing means that Haley's promise to Malcolm, his intent to be a "dispassionate chronicler," is a matter of disguising, not removing, his authorial presence.

Allowing Malcolm to speak for himself meant constructing a text that *seems* to have no author (in a first draft I slipped and wrote "*no other*"), that *seems* to speak for itself without mediation. I've encountered many readers who experienced the book in just such a fashion, who were surprised when reminded of Alex Haley's role. Calling the book an autobiography is of course an explicit denial of an authorial presence and encourages this reaction in readers. Yet as we should have learned from Afro-American folklore or from novelists such as James Joyce who confess the secrets of their craft, effacing the self is also a way of empowering, enabling the self. If you're skillful enough at the sleight-of-hand of storytelling (witness Charles Chesnut's "Uncle Julius"), you can disappear, charm your audience into forgetting you're there, behind and within the tale, manipulating your audience, silently paring your fingernails. Haley performs a double-dip, disappears twice. Once into Malcolm and again with Malcolm as Malcolm the monologist, oracular teacher/preacher, the bardic bluesman who knows there because he goes there, Malcolm the storyteller collapses distance between teller and tale, tale and audience.

In the *Autobiography* Malcolm's voice issues from no particular place, no particular body, no particular time. The locus of the voice is his mind, and of course the mind can routinely accomplish what the most sophisticated experiments in written narrative can only suggest and mimic: flashback, flashforward, a seamless flow/exchange between inner and outer worlds, great leaps from location to location, lightning switches between levels of diction and discourse, switches in verb tense, grammatical person, time-space elisions, characters bursting into a scene full blown, announcing, establishing their intricate histories, their physical appearance with a single word. So it's not exactly as if Haley has narrowed his options by situating and representing the *Autobiography* as the first-person flow of Malcolm's speech and thought. Haley grants Malcolm the tyrannical authority of an author, a disembodied speaker whose implied presence blends into the reader's imagining of the tale being told.

Physical descriptions the *Autobiography*'s speaker offers of himself are "time capsules" scattered through the narrative, snapshots of how he appeared at various periods in his life, the boy with "reddish brown mariny color" of skin and hair, the conked teenager in zoot suit and knobby-toed shoes. The voice presently speaking is as generic as the business suits Malcolm X wore as a minister delivering the Honorable Elijah Muhammad's message. Yet the voice also gains a larger-than-life status as it gradually usurps our attention. We make up a body to match the deeds being described, a body substantiated by our participation, identification. No actor could ever match the image of the Lone Ranger I conjured as a kid listening to the masked man's adventures on the radio (who knows, part of the attraction, part of me may have been seeing part of him as black) so I never cared much for the disappointing version of the masked rider that eventually appeared in a TV series.

Haley's disappearance into Malcolm's voice permits readers to accomplish an analogous disappearing act. We open the boundaries of our identities, we're suspended, taken up to the higher ground of Malcolm's voice as a congregation is drawn into the crystal-clear parables and anecdotes of a righteous sermon. We recognize ourselves in what's being said. We amen it. Speaking for us as well as to us, the voice attains the godlike veracity and authority conventionally attributed to the third-person omniscient mode of history texts. The story becomes our story; we manufacture a presence to fill the space Haley seems to have left undefined, unoccupied. Of course some readers, fewer and fewer now, would bring living memories of Malcolm to their reading, and many would have seen photos or films, but these fragments don't alter the rhetorical design of the book and may even enhance it because the *Autobiography*'s omnipresence, its compelling version of its subject, continues to influence images of Malcolm preserved in other media.

Haley's choice of standard English for Malcolm's voice sustains the identification, the exchange between speaker and audience. Vernacular expressions, idiomatic, traditional formulas of African-American speech, occur infrequently in the *Autobiography*, and usually appear within quotes, italics, marked explicitly to indicate that the speaker is abandoning his chosen register. Conservative as the device of a talking head, the strategy of mainstreaming Malcolm's voice is just as quietly effective. The blandness of the language of the *Autobiography* invites the reader not to perform it, but ignore it. The choice of a particular black vernacular would have raised questions of class, as well as race, potentially divisive issues. Would Malcolm be speaking only *for* and *to* those people who speak like him? Would a publisher try to sell to predominantly white readers a book in which one black man addresses other black people in terms only partially comprehensible to the white audience? (How gender is implicated raises further issues that won't be addressed here.) Haley finesses potential problems by sticking to transparent, colorless dialect. Words in the *Autobiography* are cloaked in the same sort of invisibility as its author. Haley signals us to read the text as the events of a life, directly told to us by the person who lived it. Someone is talking to us. When we listen, the writing, like the narrator, disappears into the seemingly unmediated report. Haley's genius is to convince us to hear, not read.

Another advantage Haley gains by his choice of the standard English of TV announcers, textbooks, cereal boxes, and most best-sellers is the conspicuous absence of all but the most commonplace, inert, rudimentary figurative language. Attention is drawn to action, to what's being represented, not how it's represented (unless you stubbornly, peevishly insist on asking the latter, often very relevant question). The "personality" of the narrative voice is minimalized, its role as camera eye, objective chronicler, window on reality is en-hanced. (Consider the reverse of this process, TV stations juicing up the inert "facts" of weather by foregrounding the "personality" of the weatherperson.) The narrator becomes an unintrusive "voice-over" in the movie the audience constructs from his relation of incidents. If not exactly infallible, the voice Haley fashions for Malcolm has the author-ity of a courtroom witness, well dressed, articulate, educated, intelli-gent, one whose account of his experience is seductive, can't be easily discredited or ignored. Another way of saying this is that particular registers of language contain very distinct shorthands or versions of reality, and what's being activated, confirmed when a speaker skillfully manipulates a given register is the world, the assumptions that con-senting adults have agreed in advance constitute what's real. Tit for tat the speaker becomes real as he or she verifies the unspoken compact.

Finally, Haley's choice of a voice for Malcolm (himself), because it's designed to transparently reveal what actually happened, can neatly accommodate an audience whose first language may not be standard English. Most African-American readers, whatever registers of English they commonly speak, can amen the familiar people, places, and events of Malcolm's story, can identify with the content of Mal-colm's experience, with someone who's been down and out, 'buked and scorned. Many would understand his immersion in the fast life, prison, his religious awakening, his outrage, his simmering frustration and anger toward the American way. The structure of Malcolm's dis-course complements its content. The ideological core of the *Autobiog-raphy*, the interpretation and analysis of Malcolm's life, would be familiar and convincing to African Americans whose primary mode of communication is oral, not written because in the culture of sermons, blues, street-corner raps, the speaker offers his or her life (our life) as parable, illustration, example, reasoning concretely, directly from the personal to the archetypal, from common nuggets of experience to general principles. Speakers share experiences you share with them. His or her conclusions are seldom surprises. You're taken where you've been. But because nothing is ever exactly repeated, return is not simply repetition, but sometimes often revelation.

That's me he's talking about, singing about, praying about, insulting. Yes. Yes. I was there. It happens just that way, every day. Tell the truth.

Malcolm in the *Autobiography*, like Richard Wright before him in *Black Boy* or Frederick Douglass in the *Narrative*, becomes representative in all the complex, exciting self-reflexive senses of that word. Microcosm paralleling macrocosm, laws governing the molecules in my body replicated in the movements of galaxies, ontogeny reproducing phylogeny, Picasso's art passing through stages that mirror the development of western art in the twentieth century, Du Bois embodying in *Souls of Black Folk* a multidisciplinary, multigenre, humanistic paradigm for African-American studies, a body dancing to the phases of the moon. Richard Wright was a black man born in rural Mississippi at the turn of the century who migrated to Chicago and learned the north was not the promised land. Wright's life reflects a people's passage from south to north, rural to urban, dependency to self-determination, illiteracy to literature, silence to assertion. The witness of Malcolm's life picks up and expands Wright's story, the terrible, destructive pressure of the industrial urban north on traditional black family life, the nearly inevitable adolescent rebellion and crime, imprisonment, the phoenix rise to consciousness, black consciousness, and political activity, discovery of spirituality in forms other than Christianity, the growing awareness of a larger context in which the oppression of African Americans is symptomatic of a global struggle, the struggle of the formerly enslaved, the colonized, the outcast, the dispossessed to seize responsibility, to forge personal identity and communal consciousness that will reverse centuries of subjugation, self-hate, a consciousness capable of opening doors through which healing, healthy people might walk unbowed. Richard Wright and El-Hajj Malik El-Shabazz, representative men whose lives recapitulate the general experience. Malcolm center stage at the podium, in charge of his story, proclaiming "I remember . . . I did thus and so . . .

nothing is lost." A Malcolm created and re-created in the space Alex Haley has vacated so the reader may step in, identify, become.

> I still can't quite conceive him dead. It still feels to me as if he
> has just gone into some next chapter, to be written by historians.
> (*Autobiography*, 456)

What you're reading is in a sense my autobiography: words on paper about my life I'm writing in the form of opinions, analysis, attitudes I've developed about the *Autobiography*. And you, as you read are constructing the continuing story, I almost said fiction, of your life. What I'm writing could be used as evidence against me in some book about me that most likely will never be written. But suppose it might. And suppose you too are a character in it. Maybe you're the star, the book's the story of your life, unauthorized version, and your biographer decides to reveal that on such and such a day you sat down and read a piece about Malcolm by a writer named Wideman, then goes on to quote one or two of these sentences to prove (a) they are pretty silly, (b) you were silly to read them, (c) similar instances of silliness pepper your life and characterize a significant portion of it. Suppose further that you are pissed off by these allegations (facts?) and decide to set the record straight. You engage yourself in doing what I'm doing and talking about doing. You write the story of your life.

Would you mention me in your book. Would you feel compelled to deny my influence or quote a passage or two to demonstrate how enlightening, how entertaining and accurate my portrait of Malcolm really is. Would you attack the writer who used me to make you look silly. Would your attack keep the allegations alive even if you discredited them. If you ignored the fabricated incident, would other future biographers discover it and accuse you of a coverup.

All the above, except you and me and Malcolm, of course, is a figment of my imagination. So nothing's really at stake. It's a dream. Except it's a dream that could happen, has happened already, as dreams have a funny way of happening, in spite of the fact they don't.

The words we use to express ourselves have a limited utility when it comes to distinguishing among levels of reality, between fact and fiction, because words themselves are carriers of disease as much as they are a cure. Each word has a story to tell and tells it autobiographically. Each word, like any autobiography, is an impenetrable network of commission and omission. From mist-shrouded myths of origin onward, a word, like an autobiography, is compounded of fact, fiction, dream, the product of every usage, utterance, transcription, misuse, thought, loving embrace it's been subject to. We never know a word. Only a partial collection of the uses it's been put to. Part of the story is silence. The times it wasn't said, or forgotten or censored or substituted for, the invisible, inaudible history in all the mind caves where it just might be lurking but no one will ever know for sure. Word. Malcolm.

The recent Bruce Perry biography of Malcolm needs to be read against this background. Read as a work of fiction whose every word is suspect. Word by word what Perry constructs is an autobiography, the tale of his own life fashioned from bits and pieces of Malcolm his research has uncovered, discarded, found usable. Perry does not enter my space of myth and mourning. He has no stake in closing the circle, assembling a body for Malcolm consubstantial with his own, that lives and breathes without his intervention. Perry's satisfied with grabbing a piece of Malcolm and pinning it on his wall like a trophy, the stuffed head glorifying the hunter. Perry neither acknowledges nor dreams the basic human connection between Malcolm and himself, except as one-way traffic that verifies Perry's authority, Perry's prerogatives, Malcolm's failure or success in living up to standards Perry concocts and imposes.

Not so much a matter of determining who's right and who's wrong about the facts of Malcolm's life, but asking, in response to Perry's mode of inquiry, his revisionist portrait, what are the potential benefits of his approach and who benefits? Perry uses Malcolm to authenticate a universe with Perry and others like Perry at the center. Recall the recent spate of movies that employ ostensibly "black" subjects to validate white humanity. *Cry Freedom, Mississippi Burning, A World Apart, Mean Season. (Dances with Wolves,* a red/white variant.)

Perry's biography is subtitled: *The Life of a Man Who Changed Black America.* You don't need to read any further to understand how Malcolm's life is going to be used—to drag him and us backward into an America that depends on discredited assumptions about race, class, and gender, a version of the world where black/white, male/female, separation/integration, and countless other either/ors act as fixed, essentialist categories into which people and experience must be sorted. Backward into the burning building. And sure enough, Perry asks if Malcolm is black or white, is he masculine or feminine, does he advocate integration or separation, love or hate, does he tell the truth or lie, are his eyes brown or green. The notion that white America and black America are separate places, the idea that a man could change one without changing the other, are variations of what Martin Bernal calls the Aryan Model, a nineteenth-century construct, romantic and racist, of the origins of Western Civilization that denies the African and Semitic roots of classic Greek culture and perpetuates the exclusion of blacks and Jews from full membership in the human family. Perry embeds Malcolm's life in historical and psychological fictions that smother felt life, reify the dead letter of theory, generate a fakelore to substantiate a cultural framework that simultaneously imprisons and excludes.

Malcolm bursts out of the frame, signals the failure of the frame to offer remedies for prejudice and oppression. Integration and segregation for instance are functionally equivalent options for Afro-American people since both concepts are hopelessly mired in, determined by bankrupt assumptions of race. Malcolm peeped the dominant group's hole card—in either a segregated or integrated society, the value of his life, African-American life, is decided by somebody else. If one group retains all political, economic, and myth-making power in its hands, those who live beside or among the dominant group have no rights the dominant group is bound to respect. In this context civil rights, equal opportunity, integration are empty formulations, illusions dependent on the same tired, twisted assumptions about race that created this mess we're in. Malcolm came to realize his life was always being measured against some other kind of life, and he understood the danger, the unmanliness, the hopelessness of such a no-win condition. So he burst the frame. Proclaimed: It's how I see them, not how they see me, that counts. I am viewer as well as viewed. Starting with myself at the center, I can generate a coherent, operative sense of being, of the world, at least as well, probably better than anybody else. I forfeit my life when I allow its value to be determined by somebody else, especially a somebody else motivated by their own interests, a somebody else (probably white) whose interests often conflict with mine, somebody not prepared to give up one iota for me to get my fair share, a somebody whose willingness to exercise any means possible, including enslavement and murder, to retain power has been conclusively documented for centuries.

What Malcolm is saying from the beginning to the end of his life, in ways progressively more conscious, humane, and sophisticated— rebel, outlaw, Muslim, Pan-Africanist, citizen of the world—is that he wants out. Out of the trick bag of dead-end ideas, a frame distorting and destroying the natural urge for self-determination, even as the urge is formulated in a language weighted to befuddle African-American aspirations. So he wants out. Forget integration or segregation. Out. And that's the freeing power of his example, its witness, its disruptive, revolutionary threat. Out. Out and gone. Malcolm delivers to the reigning elites of the sixties a message as absolute as the message runaway slaves delivered to Ole Massa. Except Malcolm wasn't running, and his direction was not "away" but toward a future, a center we're still struggling to glimpse.

The loss of Malcolm, his murder and martyrdom, our mourning clarify an emptiness at the center of my sense of myself as part of a culture. I belong to, belong with Malcolm wherever he was going. He never made it. Perhaps no one ever does. But he went on his way and left us behind. Words are one way of setting off to rediscover him, of picking up the pieces, of envisioning the myth, the mythical space engendered by identification, longing, the dream landscape the heart comprehends.

The work of Perry and others is to seal the rupture Malcolm created, restore business as usual. But the damage is past fixing, an emptiness remains in the center, an absence some of us are seeking not so much to fill as to understand. We know Malcolm is part of what we need to understand because through him we experience the bitter, bitter pain of loss, a personal loss and the hard recognition that the search for a center, for self-determination, requires a willingness to risk our lives, requires discipline, constant vigilance of body and spirit that exacts the best of us.

Bird man. Malcolm knew that much and not much more about the name. Audubon. All those years reading, reading, reading in his cell, then on the road, his briefcase stuffed with books. A hunger to know everything from A to Z and here he was, eyes bad, getting old already, and if the grim brothers and pale-faced spooks had their way, probably not going to grow much older and Audubon an A. Still at the beginning. Always starting over. If you knew the stories behind Harlem's place names, its people's names, you would understand its history better, yourself better. *Its*. Harlem's not an it. Surely a she. A sad-eyed, brown-skinned, big-breasted, skinny-ankled, hourglass-hipped woman who might be your elegant grandma, your tough baby sister, too much gold dangle and makeup and skirt way too tight for her own good dressed up and heading out to places where you both know she shouldn't be hanging. Would he have to rescue her. Would she come for him when he's cut down in some faraway land. In Africa would she gather you up in her arms and cradle your bloody head and sing you to the next place, *A* to *Z*. In Africa her name would not be Harlem. A blacker name like those carved in picture-writing on the jewelry of dead queens and kings, on the stones of the pyramids and temples, the statues of thick-lipped, snub-nosed gods. Would she go that far to find him and bring him home again. Home to these cities, to this wreckage of lives lost and torn apart and smoldering under tons of something too rotten, too evil to name. To this Audubon Ballroom on February 21, 1965, Harlem, New York. And if she found him and opened her arms to him would they really want to return. Here. The row of chairs he'd helped Sara Mitchell set out on stage. Empty chairs because the brothers he'd counted on to fill them had copped out. Was his brown-skinned Harlem angel already on stage, waiting invisible, occupying one of those chairs beside the microphone. Empty chairs an embarrassment, rebuke, warning, a reminder to the audience of what could have been, should be, the speaker flanked by stalwart brothers and sisters lending their weight, their support, putting their bodies on the line so he's not naked on the naked stage, so his body and theirs are one, clothing him, the flesh behind his words. But in less than a minute now, he'd leave the anteroom, face alone the ones who've come this Sunday afternoon to listen. Does he hear a whispering of wings out there. He smiles to himself thinking of the faces that will greet him on the other side of the flimsy anteroom door. He's proud and happy and gets the rise he always does, the charge of energy as he grows larger, fuller, wiser than himself, anticipating *As salaam alaikum, Wa alaikum as salaam,* the call and response, the chorus as excited as he is to begin, to transform what they feel, what they need him to say into a kind of chant, prayer, lesson, battlecry. And the bitter, galling ironic edge to his smile, the tight-lipped part that's steel and sneer and tastes like death, the knowledge that his enemies are sitting in the auditorium too, biding their time, waiting for him to slip, prepared to push him over the edge if he doesn't slip, cops in uniform, undercover cops, CIA, FBI, initials from *A* to *Z* standing for every nasty species of backalley, backstabbing surveillance and sabotage some smooth-faced, soft-handed assassin in a coat and tie in a clean office somewhere can dream up. Yes. They'll be out there to greet him too. His people. And he almost laughs out loud as he imagines the agent scared shitless who leaps out of his chair when the first shots are fired and hugs the Audubon's floorboards a million Harlem feet have danced smooth and black. The government agent who wastes the public's money filing his worm's-eye-view of what transpired on February 25, 1965:

> At this time a Negro male, wearing a three-quarter length black leather coat, pushed his chair back, stood up, and said to the Negro male sitting on his left "Get your hand out of my pocket."
> The Negro male who stood up was very dark complected, slender build, about 5'10" tall, weighing 160 pounds, age in the late twenties, lean face, with medium length straight hair.
> This man pushed his coat back and produced an object which looked to be metallic and raised his arm. At this point people from the audience, which consisted of about four hundred individuals, began jumping to their feet. Malcolm X told everyone to "take it easy."
> . . . four gunshots . . . were fired in rapid order.[1]

From that moment on the agent lying on the floor "could furnish no further information regarding the murder of Malcolm X." His view is restricted to what's below people's waists, undecipherable hieroglyphics, "the hands appeared to be those of a light-skinned Negro. This man wore brown or Cordovan-colored shoes and had medium-sized feet."[2]

The scene flashes across Malcolm's mind, consumes less than one of the seconds remaining before he leaves for the Audubon's stage. Benjamin X has primed the crowd. His voice rising and falling in those old-time religion cadences that summon spirits, harangue and levitate the congregation, a language Benjamin X will not permit his listeners to pretend they've forgotten.

Here is a man who would give his life for you.

Malcolm rubs his hands together. Color. Sweat. Blood. Pumps himself up again to answer the call. Words. Names. Audubon. Harlem. Malcolm Little. Detroit Red. Malcolm X. As he strides to the rostrum El-Hajj Malik El-Shabazz rehearses the greeting, natural to him now as the drawing in, the expelling of breath, *As salaam alaikum.*

EPILOGUE

Across the land X's are sprouting on people's caps. One hopes the X on the outside reflects activity inside the hats. When Alex Haley spoke for the time to the man who was born Malcolm Little, the man's name had become El-Hajj Malik El-Shabazz. The man had suffered the birth and death of Malcolm X, and had gone on to another name, another metamorphosis. X, after all, signified something lost, missing, mourned. Malcolm X was an identity the man had painfully wrought for himself and just as painfully unraveled and shed. And it's that story that Alex Haley presents to us, the story of Malcolm X who was shot dead in the Audubon Ballroom. El-Hajj Malik El-Shabazz had already split, left Malcolm X behind, was on his way somewhere else. A new story beginning . . .

Remember the movie *Viva Zapata*, the last scene when Zapata's horse, which has miraculously escaped an ambush, looks down from higher ground at the crowd gathering around its fallen rider. As government soldiers and their officers examine the rider they've shot to bloody pieces, the peasants whose rebellion Zapata led begin to quietly pass the word from mouth to ear to mouth, whispering, "That's not him, uh-uh, not our leader. No. Shit no. Not him they've shot. That bloody mess is not him."

Silhouetted against the sky the stallion rears up on its hind legs, then gallops off, bearing its invisible rider to the sanctity of the mountains, free, strong, always there when we need him, when we're ready to seek him out. El-Hajj Malik El-Shabazz.

NOTES

1. Clayborne Carson, ed., *Malcolm X: The FBI File* (New York: Carroll & Graf, 1991), 372.
2. Ibid., 373.

The Color of His Eyes: Bruce Perry's *Malcolm* and Malcolm's Malcolm

ARNOLD RAMPERSAD

You wouldn't believe my past.
—Malcolm to Alex Haley

In the fall of 1991, after a swirl of disconcerting rumors about the coming appearance of a biography of Malcolm that threatened to cast him in a new and highly unfavorable light, the obscure publishing house of Station Hill Press at last brought out Bruce Perry's *Malcolm: The Life of a Man Who Changed Black America*.[1] The major rumor hovering over the expected appearance of this volume was that the book undertook to show that in his lifetime, Malcolm had engaged in homosexual activity, and with several partners. This rumor caused some consternation among admirers of Malcolm, who has exemplified for them a quality of "manliness" or of "manhood"—loaded and controversial terms, to be sure—that had long been offered as a precondition for the ideal (male) African-American leader. No less a figure than W.E.B. Du Bois, as well as his brave colleagues in the Niagara Movement, as long ago as 1905 had insisted on the need for black Americans to demand and assert their "manhood rights."

Perry's volume was by no means the first study of Malcolm's life. After his death came a number of studies in a variety of forms, perhaps the most notable being George Breitman's *Malcolm X: The Man and*

His Ideas[2] and Peter Goldman's *The Death and Life of Malcolm X*.[3] Among less formal studies, more anecdotal in nature, was a book by a former colleague of Malcolm's, Hakim A. Jamal's *From the Dead Level: Malcolm X and Me* (1973).[4] But if autobiography can be considered a study of a life (and it should be so considered), then pride of place among studies of Malcolm must go to Alex Haley, who wrote *The Autobiography of Malcolm X* out of his interviews with Malcolm. This remains the central text about Malcolm's life, the rock on which the edifice of his reputation is supposed to rest.

Is Malcolm's mythic reputation really based on his autobiography? In some important ways, the answer is no. In the slightly more than twenty-five years since his death in 1965, Malcolm X has suffered the particular and sometimes cruel fate of certain men and women of genuine achievement. To paraphrase W. H. Auden in his famed elegy on the death of the poet William Butler Yeats, Malcolm has become his admirers. What these admirers "see" in Malcolm's legacy is what, more or less, he has become. In the process, the truth of his life, insofar as we can gauge the truth about an individual or recover it from history, is more or less immaterial. Malcolm has become the desires of his admirers, who have reshaped memory, historical record and the autobiography according to their wishes, which is to say, according to their needs as they perceive them.

This transformation, in the case of Malcolm as in the case of every other personage from the past similarly adapted, is both understandable and a violation. The transformation is understandable because the purpose of history is not to serve the past but above all to serve the present, to help us to understand ourselves and where we are going. The transformation is, at the same time, a violation to the extent that it deliberately obscures the reality of the life in question and thus denies us the full possible benefit of learning from the individual who has now passed into history.

Malcolm's transformation is solidly established. For many younger blacks, he has become the perfect icon of black humanity. He is admired, in particular, by many of the younger artists of the race, and especially those who work in the most influential of the media—in film and television, in music and videos. The gifted composer Anthony Davis has written an opera about Malcolm's life, and the acclaimed filmmaker Spike Lee has directed a motion picture about Malcolm's life. For many of Malcolm's admirers, figures as accomplished and admirable as W.E.B. Du Bois and Martin Luther King, Jr., are perceived as somehow inadequate to the full expression of black humanity in its struggle with white power, while Malcolm is seen as the apotheosis of black individual greatness. The black warrior-prince or warrior-king par excellence, he is a perfect hero—his wisdom is surpassing, his courage definitive, his sacrifice messianic.

In Malcolm's case, hero worship is accompanied by the contention that the process by which Malcolm has become a hero is irrelevant to his significance. But Malcolm's transformation from man to myth should not be held utterly beyond inquiry. Again, Malcolm's autobiography itself both fosters and contests the myth. In addition, scholarship and scholars still exist; the latter, encouraged in part by the example of Malcolm himself in his relentless, self-critical search for knowledge, insist on poring over the historical record. In his book, Malcolm advertised his faults for the world to see, and learn from. This purposeful advertising is Malcolm's tacit permission to us to dig deeper into his motives and his psychology. I believe that it amounts to his permission to us to "expose" the autobiography, to dig even deeper into the facts and forces of his life. If an autobiography that emphasizes moral change and growth, as this one emphasizes, does not give such permission, it is a document more of pride than of genuine spirituality. Malcolm's autobiography is, consciously, both a document about vulnerability and a vulnerable document—as all autobiographies are.

Already a master journalist, intelligent and well read, Alex Haley seems to have understood virtually all the key elements in the making of autobiography by the time he met Malcolm for the first time—"a gangling, tall, reddish-brownskinned fellow, at that time thirty-five years old" (*Autobiography*, 383). Haley took pains to append to the *Autobiography* a seventy-four–page essay on the writing of the book and his sense of Malcolm's motives, moods, and maneuverings as he negotiated the territory of autobiography. Haley understood that autobiographies are almost by definition projects in fiction, in which the autobiographer selects from memory such material as seems to him or her most alluringly totemic. He took pains to show how Malcolm dominated their relationship and tried to control the composition of their book, but Haley also knew that memory itself also selects, often in defiance of the autobiographer. And the autobiographer—in this case both Malcolm and Haley—is further guided by all the autobiographies he or she has ever read or heard about. The life, already distorted and diminished by the process of selection, thus acquires a narrative shape that may itself be its deepest meaning.

Looking over Haley's and Malcolm's shoulder, in this instance, is St. Augustine and his text *The Confessions of St. Augustine*, which is generally considered the primary text of Western autobiography. As in the case of Augustine, Malcolm's project was one of spiritual autobiography—the story of a sinner who, finding God, transforms his life in this way and writes the autobiography as a guide that may lead other sinners to God. Race and racism in America gave the narrative form yet another twist. Behind Malcolm stood many of the slave narrators, who themselves, in many instances, had St. Augustine behind *them* even as they, like Malcolm, knew that their narrative had to partake of the secular enterprise of describing the search for earthly freedom and earthly power.

Thus Malcolm's story is both about spirit and the flesh, about ideals and psychology, about disembodied impulses and the lures of the flesh and secular ambition. The *Autobiography* boldly concedes as much, for Malcolm inscribed in it the terms of his understanding of the form even as the unstable, even treacherous form concealed and distorted particular aspects of his quest. "I have since learned," he wrote in his book, "that the truth can be quickly received, or received at all, only by the sinner who knows and admits that he is guilty of having sinned much. . . . The very enormity of my previous life's guilt prepared me to accept the truth" (*Autobiography*, 163). Here the scholar is indispensable in helping us sort out the facts. But there is no Malcolm untouched by doubt or fiction. Malcolm's Malcolm is in itself a fabrication; the "truth" about him is impossible to know.

If Malcolm's autobiography is a license for further investigation of his life, how does Bruce Perry use, or possibly abuse, that license in his *Malcolm*? Perry's sense of responsibility may be inferred from his extreme dedication to the task of recovering the facts of Malcolm's life. In his search for evidence, he appears to have been relentless. Interviewing just about everyone who had information and would share it, he spoke to Malcolm's mother, his aunt Ella Little, his brothers, his friends, his acquaintances, and his enemies as well as other individuals with important information about this or that matter. He interviewed many people not once but repeatedly, as if he hoped to unearth further information by breaking down initial barriers.

He unearthed record after record—from prisons and courts of law, from schools and churches and the police, from the proverbial federal, state, and local authorities. He did so in the face of such difficulty, in many cases, that he could very well stand, on the matter of diligence, as the model of the biographer in quest of the most elusive subject. With about 380 pages of text come 125 densely packed pages of notes. And yet Perry's way of weighing and using information is sometimes questionable. Relentless in gathering hard evidence, Perry sometimes interweaves it with the soft in a disconcerting way. For example, the first page of his biography tells of a telegram sent at Malcolm's birth by Malcolm's father to his own parents: "It's a boy. . . . But he's white, just like mama!"[5] However, the source here is not the telegram itself or some other indisputable record but the memory of Ella Little, Malcolm's half sister, almost fifty years later. Ella Little is hardly unimpeachable as a source. (In fact, one of the major revelations in this biography is her extensive criminal record, never mentioned by Malcolm in his book.) And the question of Malcolm's skin color, and the attitude of others to it, is absolutely important to Perry's thesis.

Skepticism breeds further skepticism. Was any telegram approximately like this one sent? Was *any* telegram sent? The only matter about which readers cannot permit themselves to have any doubts is that Ella Little told Bruce Perry that a telegram, with these exact words, had been sent. But this fact is, by itself, an unimpeachable item in Ella Little's biography, not in Malcolm's. Perry had to use only four words to place the entire matter on a different footing: "According to Ella Little." Apparently, the temptation was too great. In biography, the temptation is strong to turn a report into a fact, and especially when the report so graphically illustrates a central element of one's thesis. But this is exactly the kind of temptation that has to be resisted.

Similarly, Perry not infrequently slides between the facts offered in the *Autobiography* and his own work. This procedure may be harmless when the borrowed matter is inconsequential, but it is dangerous on the whole given the fact that Perry's biography represents a major challenge to the autobiography. Having raised these points of criticism, however, one must insist that Perry's scholarly method is basically quite reliable. What about his analytical method, his overriding intellectual approach? His method is unquestionably psychoanalytical, or Freudian. "The reader will encounter in this biography," he writes in his introduction, "far more about the subject's childhood than one does in most biographies."[6] Perry does not so much believe, with Wordsworth, that the child is father to the man, as he believes, with Freud, that the man is a necessary extension of the child—that all truly important aspects of adult personality may be traced back to childhood events, especially to childhood traumas.

Facing the *Autobiography*, Perry sees both success and failure. The autobiography is "splendidly written" but with a method and a purpose that are illusory. "Its exaggerated portrayal of his youthful criminality enhanced [Malcolm's] tough image," writes Perry, "and dramatized the transformation of the pseudo-masculine, criminal Malcolm into the manly, political Malcolm. It inspired his followers to feel that, no matter how far they had fallen, they could still raise themselves up and surmount the handicaps that were largely due to the dreadful legacy of slavery."[7] And yet Perry sees it as his duty as a biographer to separate the facts from the manipulation of facts:

> Like many others . . . Malcolm coped with painful, youthful memories by forgetting or altering them. . . . Malcolm was a man in conflict—a living microcosm of the racial discord that corrodes American life. The story of his inner struggle to decide what color he wanted to "be" enables us to see beyond fashionable shibboleths about racism to bigotry's hidden roots.
>
> Malcolm was plagued by other, equally trying inner conflicts. He yearned for happiness and love, yet deprived himself of both. He craved success but courted failure. He longed for freedom but shunned it until it was too late. Deep down, he hungered for the approval of the very authority figures he defied. . . .
>
> Despite his efforts to attribute his unhappiness and his youthful delinquency solely to white "society," they originated largely in his loveless, conflict-ridden home. His subsequent moral, intellectual, and emotional growth was a triumphant victory over the ravages of a childhood that, until now, has been enshrouded in fiction and myth.[8]

One question immediately raised is whether any African-American life, much less Malcolm's, can be explained adequately in such psychoanalytical terms. I can only suggest that in the absence of some demonstrably superior mechanism for analyzing the individual mind, the insights of Freud and his followers, and in particular the psychologist-biographer Erik Erikson, are indispensable to our understanding of ourselves. Indeed, one can no more dismiss psychoanalysis as the basis of such investigation than one can dismiss the Augustinian model of confessional narrative on which the *Autobiography* is solidly based. Both forms may be inadequate to do justice to Malcolm's mind and meaning. Yet Malcolm cloaked himself in the latter and thus empowered himself as an autobiographer speaking to future generations. He must deal with the former—psychoanalysis—as those same future generations attempt to get a more full understanding of the life he offered in his book.

It goes without saying that such an investigation is difficult; the factors of race, sex, and gender, of violence, passivity, and fear, are intertwined in such a way as to be virtually inseparable. Let us begin where Malcolm began in his autobiography, with the matter of race. To Malcolm, race was not simply a matter of ideology but an intensely personal, deeply disturbing factor in his life. The notion of "racial purity" (Malcolm's words) within a specifically black context is raised on the first page of his autobiography, when Malcolm writes of his father's faith in Marcus Garvey, "the most controversial black man on earth" (*Autobiography*, 1). The declaration of Earl Little's skin color— "very black"—literally straddles the first two pages. And the color of his mother's skin—she "looked like a white woman"—appears on the second page. Malcolm's own skin color—"my reddish-brown 'mariny' color of skin"—is not only mentioned in the same paragraph but is brought up in a pathological or deviationist sense, as an affront to the notion of "racial purity" enshrined on the first page. The conclusion of that paragraph underscores the role of pathology here. Referring to his mother's father, a white man, Malcolm intones: "I learned to hate every drop of that white rapist's blood that is in me" (*Autobiography*, 2).

This last statement may be little more than a gorgeous lie. Malcolm offers no evidence that any rape had ever occurred. Perry himself finds none. Malcolm's mother, born on the island of Grenada in the West Indies, had been the last of three illegitimate children of a woman who had died giving birth to her. A Scotsman had fathered that last child, but whether he had fathered the two other illegitimate children is never raised by Perry; and Malcolm, of course, has no interest in such a matter—the Scotsman is "that white rapist." It is fashionable, at least in some circles, to think of every sexual act between a white man and a black woman—whatever her actual color—as a rape. But it is not clear that any violation occurred in the union of the Scotsman and Malcolm's maternal grandmother; indeed, Malcolm's mother appears to have boasted, at least during one period of her life, about her father and his people. By Malcolm's time, however, the idea of racial pollution and racial violation was profoundly important to him. Proud early in his life of his light skin, he came to hate the "blood" that had made it so; in short, he came to hate himself.

The idea of Malcolm's self-hatred or of his ambivalence about his skin color is unpalatable to some of his admirers. Spike Lee, casting his motion picture about Malcolm, wanted no such complication: to play the part of Malcolm he chose a richly brown-skinned actor, Denzel Washington. It may be that the peculiar focus of Lee's film makes it relatively unimportant what color the skin was; however, it is more likely that the colorization of Malcolm is designed for political ends. (One may point to a similar decision by the makers of a television film on Supreme Court justice Thurgood Marshall, a man of light complexion, to have him played by Sidney Poitier, whose skin color is quite close to black. On the other hand, although it is impossible to think that Marshall's color was not important to him as he grew up and even as he practiced law, there is little evidence that it impinged on much of the experiences involving his fight as an NAACP lawyer for Civil Rights.)

Malcolm himself could not pass for white—although one person in Perry's biography recalls mistaking him for a white man when he saw him for the first time, in Africa. But color appears to have played a vicious role in Malcolm's life. His father's mother, Southern-born, was virtually white but hated the white "blood" in her veins, if Perry is to be believed. Her husband had married her but apparently "hated" that same blood, so that he "wept" when he learned that his latest grandson (Malcolm), who was supposed to be named after him, was also born virtually white. "No 'albino' would be named after him," he vowed. Similarly, Malcolm's mother was often mistaken for white. "She was so light-skinned that she was frequently mistaken for white," Perry writes.[9] Her West Indian origin practically guaranteed, at least in those days, that she would be deeply ambivalent in her own response to black skin—yet she eventually married a dark-skinned man, Earl Little.

Malcolm was thus born utterly enmeshed in the most cruel of all the apparently "objective," as opposed to exclusively psychological, traps laid by slavery and its legacy. He was entranced by the pathologically unstable apprehension of skin color, with either demonic or angelic characteristics attached now to black, now to white skin, and with a maddening volatility marking his responses to permutations of black and white skin. Indeed, before he was four he seemed to embody this confusion, as Perry reports:

> His reddish-blonde hair was so close-cropped it gave his head a roundish, pumpkin-shaped appearance. Though his skin had grown darker, it was still fair. The other children teased him about his "high yellow" appearance. They called him "Chink" and made fun of his bluish eyes, which seemed to change color like his mother's. "We called him a freak of nature," Yvonne [Little, one of his sisters] recalled years later.[10]

Skin color drove a wedge between him and the other members of his family. At least one observer thought that Malcolm's mother favored him among her children because of his light complexion. And yet Malcolm believed differently, "partly because his mother bent over backward to make sure he would not think his fair skin made him superior." She liked to urge him to get out of the house and into the sunlight so that the sun would darken his skin. "He thought she favored the darker children, partly because his light skin, like hers, was a painful reminder of her illegitimacy. He felt he was her least favorite child." But there was no real solace in turning to his father. Malcolm "had neither parent's unqualified approval. And there was no way he could satisfy their irreconcilable demands."[11]

Perry understands that, by itself, skin color could have had no significant effect on Malcolm. But whatever Malcolm's admirers may think, the biographer is absolutely correct to probe the question of the consequences of the fetishization of skin color. To ignore its importance is to risk being guilty of willful blindness. After all, Malcolm himself openly introduces the topic of favoritism within his family based on color of skin, even if he does so mainly to appear to triumph over his father (a common characteristic of male autobiography). His father was "belligerent toward all of the children, except me. The older ones he would beat almost savagely if they broke any of his rules—and he had so many rules it was hard to know them all." Going further, Malcolm attributed his father's favoritism to the fact that "he was subconsciously so afflicted with the white man's brainwashing of Negroes that he inclined to favor the light ones, and I was his lightest child" (*Autobiography*, 4).

Malcolm's mother seemed herself to be afflicted with almost un-

speakably complicated attitudes to color, deriving from her own whiteness but complicated by the conflict between pride in it and shame
about illegitimacy and about not belonging, which was itself deepened
by the sometimes envious attitude of those about her in her youth
especially. Perry found people who remembered her as foolishly proud
of her color; yet she married dark-skinned Earl Little, who may have
been "marrying" his own near-white mother but could do so only with
feelings of guilt and shame. The result of their union was like the
cause: a mixture of sadism and masochism to go with the volatile
mixture of pride and shame that marked their psychologies. Malcolm's
mother committed her acts of sadism mainly on her children, and
Malcolm was not spared. "Nearly all my whippings came from my
mother," Malcolm remembered (*Autobiography*, 4). Perry declared
that she "ruled her children with an iron hand, without visible evidence
of affection. . . . She tyrannized them the way she had been tyrannized."[12]

One certain and deadly result was enmity among the children.
"Malcolm would later deny," Perry writes, citing the autobiography,
"that he had harbored negative feelings toward any of his brothers and
sisters. He asserted he was 'very close' to them. But Reginald, the
brother to whom he said he felt closest, did not feel close to him at
all; he said they communicated very little and did not share their
thoughts or feelings." As for his brother Philbert, who was two years
older and the "chromatic antithesis" of Malcolm, as dark as Malcolm
was fair, Perry writes (after interviewing Philbert) that "the rivalry
between him and Malcolm was so intense that some of their respective
friends became near-enemies."[13]

In his *Autobiography* and elsewhere, Malcolm both acknowledged
this legacy of confusion and shame and sought to cover it. He did so,
I believe, for perfectly sound reasons. His primary purpose in writing
his book was not to dwell on his misfortunes but to emphasize how he
overcame them, and thus how others could and must overcome them.
Thus political purposefulness tends to override the role and power of
accurate memory in narrative, which is to say that the text of the
Autobiography is not sacred in its details but must be studied as an
arena where effects are being created to enhance the political and
spiritual power of the book. Indeed, the very opening of the *Autobiography* is thus affected—or contaminated.

"When my mother was pregnant with me, she told me later,"
Malcolm begins, "a party of hooded Ku Klux Klan riders galloped up

to our home in Omaha, Nebraska, one night. Surrounding the house, brandishing their shotguns and rifles, they shouted for my father to come out. My mother went to the front door and opened it." Standing there, visibly pregnant with Malcolm, she stood up to the riders and told them that her husband was away. The whites "galloped around the house, shattering every window pane with their gun butts. Then they rode off into the night, their torches flaring, as suddenly as they had come" (*Autobiography*, 1). When Earl Little returns home, he is enraged. He decides to leave Omaha as soon as Malcolm is born.

This is a perfect opening for Malcolm's autobiography. It establishes, as few other opening passages could have established, his credentials as a fighter against racism, for he is depicted as, in a sense, standing up against white racism *in utero*, even before he was born. He is also standing in for his father, whose decision when he returns home, for all his customary belligerence, is to leave the city rather than face the wrath of the Klan himself. Malcolm's destiny to be a leader in the racial struggle is thus prefigured in himself, as if he is both the Messiah and John the Baptist—or, at the very least, some other militant figure associated with the Messiah's message. "I do not now, and I did not then, liken myself to Paul," Malcolm writes later, in another context. "But I do understand his experience" (*Autobiography*, 163).

Unfortunately, according to Malcolm's mother, "the incident never occurred."[14] Also speaking to Perry, her sister-in-law Rose, who at the time of the alleged incident also lived in Omaha, went on record as disputing that any such incident happened. Indeed, Rose stated that her own husband had told her that Malcolm's father had impersonated him in order to buy some clothing, then left him (Rose's husband) to deal with the bill by skipping town. The effect of these women's testimony is to strip away the mantle of heroism from much of the scene and leave in its place two tattered figures: Malcolm as possible prevaricator and Malcolm's father as petty criminal, stealing from his own trusting family.

Was Malcolm told this story by his mother, as he claimed? If not, then by whom? Did he consciously make it up? Or was it the result of a subconsciously constructed fiction on his part? Because Malcolm read the manuscript of his book more than once, one must assume that there is no likelihood of a mistake on Alex Haley's part about what Malcolm said. After all, the golden rule in their collaboration was, in Malcolm's words, that "Nothing can be in this book's manuscript that

I didn't say, and nothing can be left out that I want in it" (*Autobiography*, 387). Almost certainly, Malcolm had either been tricked by his own memory, or he had not counted on some future biographer tracking down his mother and interviewing her in the nursing home to which she had gone after spending years in a psychiatric facility.

Almost in the same breath by which this episode is revealed comes Malcolm's first portrait of his father. Malcolm first offers him as a big, brave man—"not a frightened Negro, as most then were, and many still are today. My father was a big, six-foot-four, very black man. He had only one eye" (*Autobiography*, 1–2). A Garveyite, he believes in the impossibility of blacks achieving freedom in America and advocates a return to Africa. He has seen "four of his six brothers die by violence, three of them killed by white men, including one by lynching" (*Autobiography*, 2). Malcolm looks ahead to his father's end. He was "finally himself to die by the white man's hands" (*Autobiography*, 2).

Even as Malcolm recounts it, however, what had happened to his father is by no means clear. Police came to the house to tell Mrs. Little that a terrible accident had happened and that her husband was in the hospital. But the overwhelming impression Malcolm wishes the reader to have is that there had been no accident, that his father had been murdered by whites: "My father's skull, on one side, was crushed in, I was told later. Negroes in Lansing have always whispered that he was attacked, and then laid across some tracks for a streetcar to run over him. . . . He lived two and a half hours in that condition" (*Autobiography*, 10).

Earl Little may indeed have been killed in this fashion. However, according to Perry, all the evidence suggests strongly that Malcolm's father was killed in a streetcar accident. Perry interviewed one of the policemen (all white) who had talked to Earl Little while he was still conscious. It was impossible for his head to have been crushed in, this officer told Perry, for "Mr. Little would not have been able to explain how his injury occurred." One insurance company insisted—perhaps to avoid the payment on a policy—that Earl Little had killed himself. Some people in Lansing believed that Little, apparently well known for his marital infidelities, had hurriedly tried to board the streetcar "because some irate husband was after him."[15] Records of the police and the coroner, as well as the death certificate, all listed his death as an accident.

Two other incidents in Malcolm's youth involving his father and mother are significant here. One involved a fire in the Little home, which first Earl Little in his lifetime, then Malcolm in retelling the story, attributed to hostile whites. Yet Perry's investigation suggests that the fire was set by someone in the house; and he links this fire to one that mysteriously occurred in the adult Malcolm's own home when, like his father, he was faced with what he regarded as an unfair dispossession, following his break with the Nation of Islam. Retelling the story of the fire (the police had suspected arson) in his *Autobiography*, Malcolm seems to offer a clue about its cause, even as he seems to offer only his father's version of the incident. The fire was something of a watershed in his parents' lives, he claims. After the fire, "my memories are of the friction between my father and mother. They seemed to be nearly always at odds. Sometimes my father would beat her . . ." (*Autobiography*, 4).

Malcolm is silent again on a major factor in the deterioration of his family in the long, grim aftermath of his father's death. He tells how, "about in late 1934, I would guess, something began to happen. Some kind of psychological deterioration hit our family circle and began to eat away our pride. Perhaps it was the constant tangible evidence that we were destitute. We had known other families who had gone on relief. . . . And, now, we were among them" (*Autobiography*, 14). What he does not mention is that about this time his mother gave birth to another child, born out of wedlock. Defying the welfare officials, she refused to reveal the father's name. The effect of this birth on Malcolm and his siblings, and on their effort to maintain a sense of pride, can only be imagined. But Malcolm's silence about the child in the *Autobiography* may be a token of his sense of shame.

This is by no means the only curious silence in the *Autobiography*, or the only potent revelation in Perry's *Malcolm*. Perry's revelation of homosexual involvements on Malcolm's part must be counted among the more remarkable examples of the latter. Nowhere in his own book does Malcolm appear to give a hint of such an interest or involvement. In discussing this matter, one would do well to recognize the danger of homophobia quickly muddying the issue. Homophobia undoubtedly lies behind much of the general supposition that Malcolm could not possibly have had homosexual experiences, the idea being that such experiences are at odds with his fierce teaching about manly race pride. Needless to say, homosexuality and militant race pride are not incompatible in one person. From a psychological point of view, however, the two matters, in the case of an individual with an acute moral sense who belongs to an avowedly homophobic religion, certainly can also be the source of a disruptive tension. It is Perry's belief that, in Malcolm's case, they were indeed disturbing.

In fact, Malcolm's alleged homosexual experiences, as related by Perry, are relatively few. How important these few were is another matter, but they are set by Perry mainly at a particular point in Malcolm's young manhood, and definitely before his conversion to the Nation of Islam—before, in other words, Malcolm committed himself to a transformation of virtually his entire self in order to dedicate himself to the leadership of his people. Perry believes he has proof that Malcolm indulged in homosexual behavior—the exact details of that behavior is unclear—in at least two points during his life: in his adolescence, with another youth; and in his young manhood, in his extended "hustler" period, when he may have catered to the desires of avowedly homosexual men either for money or for physical or emotional pleasure, and possibly for both.

The image of Malcolm involved with other men in this way is impossible to conceive only if we ignore the evidence of his complicated, hurtful, and quite unusual upbringing. Malcolm in his prime became synonymous with pride in black manhood, defined by many observers (perhaps by most) in terms of physical strength, physical ability, raw courage, and uncompromising pride in blackness. But Malcolm in his youth and young adulthood was nothing like this picture; in fact, one might say that he was the opposite, and that only the grating edge of poverty gave his character anything that might be interpreted as raw force and dynamism. He was, quite clearly, proud of his light skin, which he saw as a mark of superiority over other blacks. He was proud (as, apparently, his parents were) of his good relationships with whites, although he would later see that he had been their "mascot" as much as anything else. And he was, apparently, highly self-conscious, physically uncoordinated when in the public eye, highly idealistic and physically reticent about sex, and unwilling or unable to risk either physical or emotional hurt. In short, he seems to have been, as he was described by at least one of Perry's informants, something of a "sissy" as a boy even as he found favor with more discriminating observers, such as teachers or mannered girls, as boys who are called "sissies" often do.

Physically he was tall for his age and sometimes showed athletic ability, but he was terrified of violence. A boxing match ("my fighting fiasco," he himself called it in the *Autobiography* [32]) with a white youth ended in humiliation for Malcolm—not in simple defeat but in abject humiliation, as Malcolm recoiled from violence. He acquired nicknames—Harpy, "Madame Harpy," and simply "Madame"—that emphasized a tendency toward what is called effeminacy. In his own book, again, Malcolm himself spoke of a reticence about sex that was at odds with the tough conditions under which he grew up. White boys expected him to know more about sex, because he was black, than he did. He liked some of the white girls he knew, and they liked him, but "always would come up between us some kind of a wall" (*Autobiography*, 30). And with black girls there was also desire on his part but also failure, if of a possibly different kind—"with these girls, somehow, I lacked the nerve" (*Autobiography*, 30).

What caused this combination of passivity, cowardice, and reticence, of gallantry and inhibition? There is no possibility of arriving at one single, plausible cause. Certainly, concerning women, there was a complex interplay of feelings on Malcolm's part. On the one hand, this interplay prevented him in his youth (and also in much of his life, once he was done with its criminal phase) from an easy exploitation of them for the gratification of his sexual appetites. On the other, this interplay made him deeply suspicious and repressive of women and perhaps of his own sexuality. Perhaps the most striking feature of Malcolm's sexual history (as we know it) in his posthustler phase is his extraordinary self-restraint where women were concerned, which he openly discusses in his autobiography. "I had always been very careful," he declares, "to stay completely clear of any personal closeness with any of the Muslim sisters. My total commitment to Islam demanded having no other interests, especially, I felt, no women" (*Autobiography*, 225). (In her brief essay "Malcolm X as a Husband and Father," his widow, Betty Shabazz, depicted him as a cool suitor but also as a sometimes tender and solicitous husband who "taught me what every female ought to learn: to live and to love as a woman, to be true to myself and my responsibilities as a mother. And to use my spiritual, material, and intellectual capabilities to help build a better human society."[16])

Six years after his release from prison, in 1958 Malcolm married Betty X ("She was tall, brown-skinned—darker than I was" [*Autobiography*, 227]) after what must be one of the more brusque courtships in history. Only then did he seek sexual release with a woman. "From the time I entered prison until I married, about twelve years later, because of Mr. Muhammad's influence upon me, I had never touched a woman" (*Autobiography*, 294).

No one, not even the inquisitive Bruce Perry, has commented on the extent to which this reticence toward women, this Puritanism, if you will, was a factor in Malcolm's break with the Nation of Islam. Years later, the revelation of Martin Luther King's many adulteries provoked a storm of controversy. Yet, although King had been a minister and had based his career as a Civil Rights activist on moral grounds, virtually none of his colleagues and admirers took this revelation (if it was a revelation to them) as reason enough to break with him, or with his memory as an icon of morality. Even his widow has been steadfast in her loyalty to King either by ignoring or by denying the evidence of his infidelities.

Why was Malcolm different in his response to similar revelations about Elijah Muhammad? And why has he not been scrutinized on this score, as if his forbearance and his indignation were not extraordinary? He himself noted his fearsome reputation on the matter: "In my twelve years as a Muslim minister, I had always taught so strongly on the moral issues that many Muslims accused me of being 'anti-woman' " (*Autobiography*, 294). In part, the answer has to do with the prominence of strictures against infidelity in Islamic religion. But Malcolm had shown an enthusiasm beyond the expected—a zeal—in rejecting his brother Reginald on moral grounds, when Reginald was expelled from the Nation of Islam by Elijah Muhammad. Malcolm reacted explosively to news of Muhammad's infidelities. "*Adultery!*" he exclaims in his autobiography. "Why, any Muslim guilty of adultery was summarily ousted in disgrace" (*Autobiography*, 295). And previously: "For me even to consider believing anything as insane-sounding as any slightest implication of any immoral behavior of Mr. Muhammad—why, the very idea made me shake with fear. And so my mind simply refused to accept anything so grotesque as adultery mentioned in the same breath with Mr. Muhammad's name" (*Autobiography*, 295).

And yet the answer to the main question surely lies beyond the strictures of Islam and within the darkened recesses of the psychology of Malcolm himself. Perry relates how Malcolm's mother was so nauseated by the idea of filth that she remembered her children as virtually having been brought to her already toilet-trained; loathing uncleanliness, she wiped imaginary dirt from chairs before she would sit on them. How ironical it would be if Malcolm's break with Elijah and the death sentence under which he apparently was placed were both engendered primarily by an impulse deriving from hyperpuritanical notions of fidelity and chastity on Malcolm's part, with these notions themselves further tinged and tinted with elements of homoerotic desire that led both to the idealization of women and to misogyny when women failed to live up to his near-impossible ideals. And how pathetic it is when we draw back from probing such questions out of similarly misguided notions about the sanctity of Malcolm's reputation and the crystalline "purity" of his character.

"What was the color of Malcolm's eyes?" This question, posed by Perry to a would-be interviewee, so angered the man that he terminated the interview there and then. But other people responded so openly to the question that Perry was able to provide a note of about half a page on their responses (blue, green, gray, hazel, or anything but the expected brown). To the angered man, and others like him, the question was probably more than irrelevant. It was a violation of Malcolm's memory and clear evidence that Perry was about the devil's business. So, too, with the book that has resulted from these efforts.

And so, too, one suspects, with Malcolm's own autobiography. I suspect that many people, whether or not they think about this matter, probably do not accept the authenticity of much of Malcolm's narrative itself. Skeptical, even cynical, and power-starved, they may see the idea of religious conversion, of first wallowing in sin and then ascending to redemption, as quaint, or even bogus—but forgivable as a scam because the results were so spectacular, so political, so "real." They would accept Perry's subtitle, *The Life of a Man Who Changed Black America*, but would rather not answer the question why so many other men had come and gone before one was able to "change" Black America. Still, both Malcolm's *Autobiography*, for all its evasions, and a biography such as Perry's are there to remind us exactly how extraordinary—and ordinary—Malcolm was, and how curious the workings of the body and the mind can be.

NOTES

1. Bruce Perry, *Malcolm: The Life of a Man Who Changed Black America* (New York: Station Hill Press, 1991).

2. George Breitman, *Malcolm X: The Man and His Ideas* (New York: Pathfinder Press, 1969).

3. Peter Goldman, *The Death and Life of Malcolm X*, 2nd ed. (Champaign, IL: University of Illinois, 1979).

4. Hakim A. Jamal, *From the Dead Level: Malcolm X and Me* (New York: Warner Books, 1973).

5. Perry, *Malcolm*, 2.

6. Ibid., x.

7. Ibid., ix.

8. Ibid., ix–x.

9. Ibid., 3.

10. Ibid., 4.

11. Ibid., 5.

12. Ibid., 6.

13. Ibid., 7.

14. Ibid., 3.

15. Ibid., 12.

16. Betty Shabazz, "Malcolm X as a Husband and Father," in John Henrik Clarke, ed., *Malcolm X: The Man and His Times* (Trenton, NJ: Africa World Press, 1990).

Sexuality, Television, and Death: A Black Gay Dialogue on Malcolm X

RON SIMMONS AND MARLON RIGGS

RON SIMMONS: When I told some of my gay friends that we were going to discuss Malcolm X's homosexual experiences, a lot of them were apprehensive. Many of them cautioned me to be careful because they were afraid of seeing another Black icon torn down, another Black hero tarnished. How do you feel about this?

MARLON RIGGS: I'm a little bit disturbed—actually a lot disturbed— by the idea that we can't discuss the complexities of Malcolm's life, particularly in regard to his sexuality, for fear that it will be used to tarnish our hero and in turn tarnish Black America. I'm resistant to that because it says to me that this admission of Malcolm's potential— or actual—homosexuality is something that we should be ashamed of. Or that, even worse, we should simply buy into the majority culture's views about homosexuality and for that reason censor what we say, or explore, in terms of our own subjectivities as Black people. Histori- cally, there's a lot that we simply don't say about ourselves, about our sexual identities, about our actual behavior, for fear that white folks will abuse it. And that's not to say that white folks have not abused, misused, misappropriated, and distorted our character; it is to say that in the process of censoring our lives and our histories, we've failed to come to an understanding of who we really are and the complexities of Black humanity. We continue to insist that those who become Black leaders adopt these very restrictive molds, these kinds of minstrel masks. I think it's necessary for us to enter into a discussion of Malcolm's sex life not to aid in his disfigurement but aid in illuminating the realities of his life and, by extension, our own.

RS: I hear what you're saying, but at the same time I'm wondering if, as intellectuals, we are assuming too much. It's one thing for us to critically analyze Malcolm and his life, but perhaps the masses need him symbolically as an icon more than we need him as someone to critique.

MR: But this critique for me is not something that's simply intellectual. And I don't think the masses—to put it in your terms—are somehow not as critically engaged with their own lives and with notions of leadership. I don't see that division. I think that we are in effect the masses and the masses are in effect us. To censor ourselves says to me that it's better to have a lie that might mobilize people into some form of community—an artificial community—rather than to engage in real soul searching about our identities. I think if one can come through that fire, one is forged through something that's much more enduring than a fabricated myth.

RS: I would disagree with you. Many a people have been united and have grown strong on premises that were basically a lie; be it the Jews thinking that they were the chosen people, or Elijah Muhammad telling Black people that they were God at a time when they needed to hear that. One can argue that indeed both were based on lies, but look at what was accomplished.

MR: But at some point the lie becomes disabling. It becomes disempowering, and it starts to hurt various members of the community who interrogate and go deeper than the surface of the myths that we construct about ourselves. And to the degree that we hang on to these obsolete myths about Malcolm, and by extension again ourselves, then we perpetuate certain kinds of oppressions that I think are as damaging as those that have been done to us by the white majority.

RS: I think the Rodney King injustice is on my mind more than I am acknowledging. Clearly it signaled an open season on Black men, and it's probably going to be *young* Black men who are targeted. They need something—even if it's a faulty something—to believe in. They need positive symbols, positive role models. This white society has systematically stripped us of our heroes. What other icons do we really have that young people can relate to?

MR: Again, I have a problem with presenting this issue in that kind of dualistic antagonism of "white people" versus "us." It's not to say that that is not a reality, but we have to come to terms with how our refusal to look at how we hurt, and oppress, one another within the Black community is also a part of the problem. And if we don't acknowledge how Malcolm's life to some degree symbolizes that fratricidal dynamic, then we will ultimately reach an impasse and we will not be able to grow—or heal—as individuals and as community. For me, the nervousness about these revelations of Malcolm's alleged homosexuality has to be in part related to the homophobia within our communities. For many people, the idea of Black masculinity and Black leadership implicitly demands heterosexuality. It's taken for granted. And so to suggest Malcolm as a homosexual requires us really to rethink what makes for a leader. What makes for a hero in our community? I think it will only liberate us all to the degree that people come to terms with this expanded understanding of leadership and heroism. So many of us, in fact, who have been in the trenches and at the forefront of our liberation have had to do so invisibly, silently around our sexual identities.

RS: Okay, I agree with you on the need to expand the definition of Black manhood and masculinity. I believe part of the problem is that Black men have internalized a white definition of manhood rather than defined it for ourselves. And that is why today young Black men are in the streets pretending to be cowboys with Uzis.

MR: But can't you say that of Malcolm as well? Isn't it in some respect a paradox that someone who was instrumental in elevating the consciousness of Black people was in fact basing his conception of leadership and liberation on white patriarchy?

RS: You're right. One can argue that the image that Malcolm and the Nation of Islam presented—the Negro nuclear family, the conservative suit and tie, the clean-cut polite manner—comes right out of the white middle class. But at the same time wasn't that important? Didn't you, when you were a child, feel proud when you saw the Muslim brothers on the corner? I know I did. Because you so rarely saw that image of a Black man—well dressed, confident, assured, articulate—doing something for the community and himself. In the 1950s and '60s, most Black men that you saw in the so-called ghettos were blue-collar workers, if they were working at all. To see Black men starting businesses and a newspaper, and to hear Malcolm saying the kinds of things that he said, didn't it make you feel proud?

MR: Of course it gave me a sense of pride and a sense of my own possibilities to be something other than what many of our fathers and grandfathers had been forced to be. But that moment was a particular moment that required that kind of identity, and the problem is that we haven't recognized that the particularities of that moment have ceased—have changed. These new moments that we now occupy in history require something else, and instead of looking critically at what that something else might be, we simply hang on to what seemed to work—what seemed to inspire us back then. And I think that because of that desire to recapture the past, we start to engage in all kinds of subtle, as well as explicit, ways of oppression; and that for me is a problem. It's not to not acknowledge the splendor of Malcolm and the Nation at a time when many of us had an abject sense of ourselves. All of us are indebted to Malcolm for that, but we can't overlook that there were pitfalls in his strategy for our awakening. Pitfalls in how we would go about realizing and defining "nobility." Who would be noble in his utopia? That's an open-ended question, but in the way that Malcolm has been mythologized, the answers that are usually given to those kinds of questions are very constraining and at times exclusive. So that only Black men who fit that rigid image of masculinity can be "noble." Look at how we perpetuate violence against one another, psychological as well as physical. I think the models of masculinity that we have inherited from Malcolm, and the myth of Malcolm, nurture that violence.

RS: Okay, okay. I hear what you're saying. It *does* seem that the goal of many Black men, including Malcolm, is to have the power and privilege of white men—but with a Black face. Personally, I don't believe those old models of masculinity are going to free us. We don't need to out-"macho" white men in order to be liberated. Young Black males need the intellectual skills and cultural beliefs necessary to nurture, protect, and defend Black survival, but those beliefs shouldn't be homophobic and heterosexist, nor should they be exclusive and gender-specific. If Black men believe that Black masculinity requires male supremacy and heterosexism, it will only prolong conflict within the Black community.

MR: To use Audre Lorde's phrase, "The master's tools will never dismantle the master's house."

RS: However, before we go any further, I want to return to the question of Malcolm's sexuality. The biography by Bruce Perry alleges that Malcolm engaged in homosexual acts when he was "Detroit Red." After reading it, it seems to me that Malcolm may have been a man who was willing to engage in "homosex" as a way of getting over, or making money. Other than those few incidents, there is no evidence of his engaging in homosexuality once he went to prison, or once he became a Muslim. What is your feeling on this? Do you think Malcolm was a homosexual?

MR: To me, Malcolm points up the larger enigma of how we define sexuality, because within Black communities, and particularly among Black men, our sexualities have been far more fluid than the public image of our sexual identities. And whether it's one episode, or two episodes, or three episodes for me is irrelevant. What makes for sexuality is not simply the contact of genitalia but also the fantasies, the desires, and the yearnings that may many times be repressed, but still nonetheless add to the dimension of what we call sexual identity. In terms of defining Malcolm as gay, straight, homosexual, bisexual, et cetera, I think it's enigmatic because his sexuality seemed so relatively repressed, or so self-mythologized, that it's really hard to figure out who he really was in terms of his sexual behavior and what that meant to him. But again, we shouldn't fall into the pitfall of defining sexual identity simply by sex acts: That said, even with this broader definition, I wouldn't call Malcolm homosexual. I do think though that among many people who are starting to learn about the revelations of his adolescent homosexuality—or "homosex" experiences—we are seeing a refusal to deal with that, in part, because it may mean that they have to come to terms with the possibility of such feelings within themselves.

RS: I think at some level it is not only having to deal with it within themselves, but having to deal with it in the people that they call their comrades, their friends, and their brothers. If indeed Malcolm could have had those kinds of experiences and still be Malcolm, how about other Black men who are having those kinds of experiences? If Malcolm was a homosexual, it might mean that having sex with other men doesn't make that other brother less committed, or valuable, to Black enpowerment. So it could be liberating, but I don't think it often is. I think his legacy is often—in some ways—a burden for Black gay men.

MR: Yes. If you look at the myths about Malcolm in terms of defining Black masculinity, you can't help but come away with the feeling that we are, as Black gay men, burdened by this hero, this icon. And we shouldn't confine that burden simply to Black gay men, because all of us are ultimately disabled by it to the degree that we internalize these fairly rigid notions of Black masculinity. If, as Ossie Davis once said, Malcolm was Black America's "manhood," what are we defining as "man"? As "Black"? And to the degree that all of us—women, men, straight, gay, bisexual—accept a rigid icon as symbolizing Black masculinity, then it starts to burden us all in terms of demanding the repression and denial of whatever within us, and each other, doesn't fit the paradigm.

RS: Is there any way that Malcolm has been an inspiration to Black gay men?

MR: Sure, but I'd like to turn that question to you. Because you are far more explicitly Afrocentic in your perspectives.

RS: Well, when it comes to Malcolm there's a duality within me, because my admiration for Malcolm developed before I came to love myself as a gay man. Now, looking back, I can't say Malcolm was an inspiration to me as a Black gay man, unless I look at him in the sense of a man being able to change; a man who was able to reflect upon his life, set a new course, and begin moving toward it. Similar to Malcolm, gay men oftentimes find ourselves hating aspects of our identities and trying to imitate what others say we should be. But then at some point, we realize that we can set our own course.

MR: I think that's extremely critical, and for me that is really the inspiration of Malcolm. Homosexual experiences or not, he was able to do something that I think is direly needed today, particularly among Black men in America, and that is to engage in introspection without fear. To not always have to wear a mask of utter invincibility and to realize that identity, and notions of liberation, are intrinsically fluid and require a constant ongoing reflective analysis of self and of society.

RS: Now, having said that, do you think that, had Malcolm not been killed, he would have grown to the point of not being heterosexist or homophobic? Would he eventually have embraced Black gays and lesbians as allies in the Black struggle?

MR: I think there was such a potential in Malcolm because of that reflective quality in his character. Maybe not to embrace us completely as Black gay men, Black lesbians, or Black feminists, but he would have not simply closed the debate the way many of his spiritual descendants have when it comes to questions of power and identity. I think that because of the road he was journeying, given his character and his logic, he would have to have had serious conversations that admitted us into community, and therefore redefined standard notions of Black community. But I also think that because of his ability to change, Malcolm might not have retained his stature. I don't think Malcolm, had he lived, would be as important to us as he is now, dead. Malcolm constitutes the quintessential unfinished text. He is a text that we, as Black people, can finish, that we can write the ending for, that we can give closure to—or reopen—depending on our own psychic and social needs.

RS: In life, Malcolm was also a text that the white power structure used for its needs. In July 1959, a TV station in New York City aired "The Hate That Hate Produced," a news program that catapulted the Nation of Islam to the attention of white America. The program disturbed white New Yorkers so much that it was rebroadcast the following week. This was at a time when white America was deeply divided over the race issue. A year earlier Little Rock, Arkansas, had shut down its high schools rather than submit to the Supreme Court decision mandating integration. Watching a tape of that program, I couldn't help but get the impression that Mike Wallace, the host, was using the "shocking" revelations about the Nation of Islam to push for integration by showing the so-called Black hatred produced by white racism. What was your reaction?

MR: In some respects Malcolm's presence in the media illuminated how much the mainstream media was invested in a certain kind of integrationist program. I think it was partly the almost natural instincts of those media producers, and reporters, to preserve what they felt would be least threatening to their own hegemony. Integration accomplished a more gradual organic assimilation of these former disenfranchised, and disparaged, people into mainstream American life without really upsetting the basic tenets of traditionalist American ideology. What you saw in the program, and subsequent reporting, was an out-and-out attack on so-called Black extremists, militants, race haters, and Black supremacists, who wanted to undermine the existing fabric of American life and culture; who preached hatred of white supremacy and against the racism of American Christianity. In many ways, everything that was considered dear in mythic American life was now being potentially undermined by the presence of people like Malcolm X. So despite what Malcolm was saying, and despite the very cool rationality of his analysis of American racism, or his seductive presentation of the tenets of the Nation, he and the Black Muslims were constantly being contextualized in such a way as to portray them as irrational, emotionally heated, and unreasonable; thus implying that they did not have a program that was in any way reasonable or rational.

RS: I didn't get the impression that they were presenting Malcolm and the Nation of Islam as unreasonable. The way the program showed the businesses they owned, and the schools they ran; it seemed to me that the media was saying that if whites did not begin to integrate American society, they would have to contend with Blacks putting their kids in Black supremacist schools, building their own separatist communities, and destabilizing American society.

MR: I felt the show was barely above sarcasm. What I detected, for instance, in Mike Wallace's reporting was in some ways a dismissal of the Black Muslims' seriousness as a threat to the status quo. I really felt that there was something that was implicit in Wallace's voice and tone, as well as explicit in the commentary, that said this group is a threat, and it will become an increasing threat if it becomes more popular; but even so, on a certain level it can't be taken seriously because what its members are saying is really so crazy. And what must be done now is to crush the fanaticism and adopt more rational, reasonable, and less subversive ways of dealing with race in America, which meant integration.

RS: Yet as the media was using Malcolm to further its agenda, Malcolm was clearly using the media to further his. In his autobiography, he talks about how he and the Nation of Islam recognized the opportunity that that news program presented for what it was. Over time, as he began to appear on more TV and radio programs, he would rehearse his opening statement so that he could say it in one breath. He knew that the reporters, or moderators, would introduce him with a negative slant, so he would cut them off in midsentence and quickly make his statement before they could stop him. By the time he stopped to take a breath, his message was out there.

MR: Yes, Malcolm used the media to address audiences that would be empowered by his message, even when the media was trying to define his message as being a threat to social order. In interviews, Malcolm was extremely analytical and piercing, thinking critically about how to respond to questions and avoid the pitfalls that would allow him to be portrayed as simply emotional or angry. One saw a very reasoning intellect that piercingly deconstructed—to use a more modern term—how the power relationships in society subjugated Black people, and how Black cultural and political awareness was something that was necessary, and wholly reasonable and rational, for a people who had been discriminated against and disenfranchised. When he was defined and contextualized in such a way as to label him as extremist, he confounded that image by the coolness of his response to reporters' questions. And this I think was also the sexiness of Malcolm, that is, the seductive quality of his image in the media. He was compelling because even though he was being contextualized as the stereotypical "bad nigger," he was a "bad nigger" who spoke in a way that we were not accustomed to hearing. A "bad nigger" who looked like an academician, and at times spoke like an academician, but then, almost chameleonlike, could switch personalities and become an electrifying fire-breather who galvanized Black audiences to frenetic belief in ourselves and the potentials of Black power. Looking back, you realize that Malcolm's handling of the media was very sophisticated. And this for me, to some degree, demonstrated the continuing inability of the media to respond to the complexity of our identities, the complexities even of our speech.

RS: Yes, I really don't think he was addressing whites when he appeared on TV. I think he was really targeting the Black people in the audience.

MR: But what kind of Black people was he talking to?

RS: Whichever ones had a TV set.

MR: Is that so? You know, there were times Malcolm displayed explicit—and more often I think implicit—contempt for so-called house Negroes. There was contempt for the "bourgeois," those middle-class "Negroes" who supposedly so loved the white man that they could not embrace any love of self. There was contempt for the NAACP, for the philosophy that motivated nonviolent civil disobedience. And to the degree that he critiqued those Black people who hung on to traditional forms of Black leadership and nonviolent empowerment, I wonder if his message wasn't really directed at people who more closely identified with his Northern background and upbringing.

RS: But if a Southern Black sharecropper were to hear Malcolm's message, I don't think it would have thrown him. In fact, he might have been able to relate even more to the concept of the white man as a "devil" since Southern Blacks risked being brutalized almost daily, as opposed to the Blacks in the North. I think the idea of having your own separate land could really appeal to a Southern land-based people much more than a Northern urban people. And I could see the "bourgeois" and "house Negroes" admiring Malcolm for his courage to say the things they were afraid to say. Malcolm made mincemeat out of whites who debated him, and, as you said, he did it in such a controlled and refined manner that he seemed like the liberated "house Negro" who finally told the white master to go to hell. I can remember Black folks cheering as they watched him on TV. To see Malcolm in action would have thrilled any Black person, from the bourgeois to beggars.

MR: Let's pursue this a little bit further in terms of the seductiveness of Malcolm, not simply his message, but his media image. Seductiveness obviously to Black people for whom his message had special resonance, but I think seductiveness even for the media. He was an image people found useful, found in some ways powerful, whatever their particular agendas or needs were. Malcolm fulfilled the expectation of the media and all kinds of Americans—Black and white, rich and poor—that a leader should be, without question, male. He possessed the qualities typically associated with "true" masculinity: firmness, resoluteness, determination, aggressiveness, self-confidence, and control over one's emotions. Needless to say, back then, a woman displaying such qualities would have been regarded with incredulity—even as a freak—insofar as she might have attempted to command a similar public role of leadership. In actuality, and in popular mythology, commanders and generals—and messiahs—could only be men, and even today that view prevails.

RS: You're right. Malcolm's image appealed on so many levels that I think whites would have been captivated listening to him, even though they may have been appalled by what he was saying. But it's also true that things he said could not be denied. When he talked about the hell that Black folks were going through, when he talked about the contradictions in this society—be you Black or white, at some point deep down you could not deny what the man was saying. Yes, as a white person, you could deny that you were the "devil," but you could not deny the fact that whites had oppressed Black people.

MR: If his message was so well understood, and undeniable, what made it possible for people in mainstream media nonetheless to construct over and over again an image of Malcolm as wholly subversive—subversive in a way that was completely disorderly and chaotic in terms of its consequences if he, or anyone like him, was to come to power?

RS: But one could also argue that the more he presented points that could not be denied by anyone open to accepting history and the truth, the more they would have to label him as an extremist as a way of discrediting him. Throughout our history, Black leaders who refuse to "sell out" have been discredited, or assassinated. Frankly, I don't think Malcolm would get as much TV play today as he did then. I think the media would realize that to do so would be a double-edged sword. To attack him would give him more exposure, and more exposure would get him more followers because what he was saying was not crazy talk. It made a lot of sense to a lot of people.

MR: I hear you. This too is speculating, but if Malcolm could have continued his life, and if he could have assumed even greater dominance as the voice of Black America, I wonder if there wouldn't have been inevitably more and more dissent about his being presented as that preeminent Black voice. Would his message have been effectively neutralized through continually presenting him as *the* voice of Black America—as the media have historically done in elevating certain Black spokesmen—thus engendering resistance, contempt, disenchantment, or jealousy among the rest of Black leadership toward this so-called representative, whom whites select and Blacks must simply accept?

RS: I don't know, maybe the Black middle class, and the Black leadership class, would be contemptuous. Those who might aspire for high positions might say: "Why him?" But I don't think the average Black man in the street would.

MR: But wait a second, wasn't the undoing of Malcolm within the Nation in part because he was increasingly being perceived as eclipsing the authority and eminence of the Honorable Elijah Muhammad?

RS: Okay, I see your point. But, again, that's among the leadership class. I don't think that the average Muslim in the average mosque was resentful of Malcolm being on TV, saying what he was saying.

MR: That, of course, depends in part on whether the average Muslim is assumed to be male. It seems that if anyone like Malcolm or Martin or Jesse—and traditionally it has been Black men within America who are elevated thus—if anyone is deemed by the majority culture as *the* spokesperson, it inevitably breeds contempt and conflict among others—mostly men—within the Black leadership who are vying for similar preeminence and control over our communal voice. Over and over again in our history, we have had this kind of cannibalism in which our leaders become suspect of advancing a personal agenda if they receive too much media attention. Needless to say, only the individual personalities are regarded with suspicion. Few, until recently, ever bothered to question the fundamental patriarchy of our leadership.

RS: Well, I think, if anything, the lesson is how unsophisticated, or undeveloped, our leadership might be. Although one thing that strikes me about Malcolm was how naive he was about a lot of things.

MR: Naive about what things?

RS: Naive in the sense of not thinking that others would become jealous, that others in the Nation of Islam would begin to plot against him. I don't think Malcolm was seduced by the media, but I do think others were seduced by the media into resenting him.

MR: Do you think that those who are claiming the mantle of Malcolm are in some ways trying to create the aura of such power and singularity around themselves?

RS: Now, do you mean the leadership? Or do you mean the "homeboy" in the street wearing the Malcolm X T-shirt?

MR: I think perhaps both. But obviously, in terms of a media presence, those who are in the leadership, whether it's cultural leadership or political leadership; those who consider themselves cultural nationalists, Afrocentrists, or revolutionaries—to use a term that one seldom hears these days. It's as if some people are trying to claim Malcolm's spirit in order to be instilled with that almost messianic quality that others would believe in and follow. This is problematic not only because of the narrow political motivation behind their claiming of Malcolm, but also because of their petty psychological and egotistical drives to become the new media "darlings," whether in entertainment or in news. And often, as with groups like Public Enemy, it straddles both arenas: the desire to be *the* diva for all disciplines.

RS: That's an interesting point. Rap artists like Public Enemy are basically entertainers, but they view themselves—and many of the youth see them—as political philosophers, and leaders. But instead of critical analysis and community discussion, they offer catchy phrases and choreographed dance routines.

MR: There's another fallout from Malcolm's legacy: a political maliciousness that centered on the use of name-calling to discredit one's adversaries, or opponents, whether it's the "white devils," the "house Negroes," or the "bourgeois." And I think, unfortunately, that legacy continues today. It's not something that Malcolm originated, but it is something he really did catapult into public discourse in a way that no other Black leader before him had. And what we see today, whether it's in the rhetoric of someone like Baraka or in the rap artists who "dis" various members of the Black community and use language in which one is reduced to "faggot" or "punk" or "ho" or "bitch," is the silencing of the rebellious or threatening "other" in Black communities. Such name-calling is a way of justifying that silencing because the "others" are seen as destructively deviant from what should be the norm, and what should be—

RS: The answer?

MR: Yes, the answer for a progressive liberated community. Malcolm definitely used such language. I mean, he didn't use "faggot" or "punk," but he did use other kinds of terms that in many ways short-circuited any need for real critical analysis and grossly oversimplified the relationships of power and disenfranchisement in our society. That too is a part of the media legacy of Malcolm X that I think still resides with us.

RS: Ironically, the contemporary analysis of Malcolm is being short-circuited and oversimplified by the commodification of his image, what I call "Malcolm as wallpaper." He's been dead for so long, but now he's reappearing larger than life, bought and sold as merchandise in department stores and on street corners. The X has become a contemporary crucifix mourning someone who was crucified to save us. On the surface, it seems progressive the way today's youth adorn themselves with images of a hero they never knew, a hero we remember so fondly. But I think the price we pay for Malcolm as a commodity is far more than we realize.

MR: As a commodity, the complexity of Malcolm has simply been flattened. He's like a statue in a museum, which if you turn this way you see one side of him, and if you turn that way you see another side;

and each side that you see reflects something that you want to have affirmed in yourself. That which does not please you, or provokes anxiety or discomfort in you, you turn away from, you ignore. I think that what we are seeing in the flattened images of Malcolm on T-shirts, or even reduced more to simply the X, is the ridding of Malcolm's complexity, of his humanity, so that we can make use of him to affirm what we need in ourselves. But the danger—the great danger—in that is that what we see over and over again is Malcolm as the defiant warrior, the angry Black man, Malcolm as the quintessential icon of Black rage.

RS: Yes, and it's usually his single face you see, sometimes with a pointed finger, or a gun. You very rarely see any commercial images of Malcolm in the context of community, or even family. You don't see images of him and Betty Shabazz. You don't see him with his children. Sometimes you may see him with another Black leader, but that's about it.

MR: That is an amazing witness. Because even as we're trying to achieve solidarity with Malcolm on a symbolic level—by wearing his image—that solidarity extends only to him, not to the larger Black community. What we're in touch with, more so than anything, is Malcolm's alienation not only from white America but from his own Black community. And I don't believe people think about this on a conscious level. I wonder—particularly for young Black men who are wearing Malcolm with a kind of ritualistic obsession—whether the identification is not simply with Malcolm as besieged angry Black man, but also Malcolm as this individual loner who is alienated from any of the structures of society and is simply trying to assert and fight his way to some form of redemption.

RS: I disagree. True, we don't see images of Malcolm in the context of community, but the subtext of his image symbolizes community. There is a shared community response to the icon of Malcolm. Members of the Black community are using his image to signify that indeed there is a community, and the individuals who wear the icon are saying they belong. Malcolm symbolizes the "elder" who provides a base, a history for others to gather around. In that sense, he is a symbolic father figure for young Black men who have none.

MR: Or are they trying to capture a sense of a self that they hold inside, that they want to be? I mean, it's both the father and the self. Many of the men—gay men as well as straight men—who have adopted the Malcolm style have adopted that "gaze," that sense of "don't fuck with me," that sense of "I will take nothing from anyone," that sense of "I will be who I damn well want to be, in defiance of all of your expectations, and on my own terms."

RS: And, if you look at the publicity photos of some of the rap artists, they give that "gaze"—arms folded, nonsmiling, a rigid sort of militaristic look—similar to the way Malcolm is portrayed in the icons.

MR: Black masculinity has become conflated with militarism.

RS: But I still believe that they are basically imitating a white masculinity that has been depicted as militarism and conquering the world.

MR: I don't think you can just reduce it to that. It's not just simply imitating "the master." I think that because young Black men are in many respects an endangered species, under attack, they identify naturally with the warrior. The warrior worn on one's chest, or on one's head, or as a medallion, signifies a certain level of fortitude in the face of worsening adversity.

RS: But I don't think that nullifies the idea of it being a white imitation. It's still the lone cowboy, but it's a Black urban cowboy with few, if any, allies; and unlike the white cowboys who rallied to conquer a people of color, today's Black cowboys are most often slaughtered by their own. The death that haunts them is a Black death, a "Black-on-Black" death.

MR: Exactly. I think there's a very acute realization of the precarious nature of a young Black male's existence today, and because of that, Malcolm—who died young and who died at the hands of his brothers—symbolizes this condition. And I think through the identification with him, as this revolutionary warrior, one's anticipated premature death is transformed, alchemized, into something important, something meaningful.

RS: You mean to be killed becomes a glorious act?

MR: Yes, because you become a martyr. To be killed means you'll be remembered as a warrior, as a hero. And maybe your level of heroism is less than someone who has achieved national preeminence, but within the block, within the "hood," you're remembered nonetheless as a hero, as a martyr, as one who sacrificed his life for something.

RS: But that's the loophole, because you haven't. If you get shot over a drug deal, I doubt the neighborhood would say you died sacrificing your life for the greater good.

MR: But you *are* asserting your manhood. You're dying because you're protecting your turf. You're dying because you're trying to live a level of existence in which you're not wholly dependent upon somebody else.

RS: You're dying as a man.

MR: Yes, you're dying as a man. I mean, isn't that the great affliction in our psychologies as Black men, that we all face? That we all suffer from? We have this extremely obsolete notion of manhood for which we are willing to give up our lives. And Malcolm on a certain almost metaphysical level symbolizes someone who sacrificed his life for the same reasons, and the way in which we treasure his memory has justified that sacrifice.

RS: I hear you. But at the same time, we don't want to go too far and say that indeed the struggle for the liberation of Black people is not something worth dying for.

MR: No, I don't think we're saying that, but I am saying that the preservation of an antiquated, patriarchal, heterosexist belief about manhood is definitely not worth dying for.

RS: You know, premature death seems to be a relentless stalker of Black men, straight and gay. Death by man. Death by privation. Death by disease. The decimation of Black gay men through AIDS results in our having symbolic needs, similar to our straight brothers. We too have a precarious existence, and thus we have a similar need for a hero like Malcolm.

MR: Yes, Malcolm's death connects to our own personal death, as well as to that of our communities and our brothers who are killing each other and are being killed by outside forces. In some ways, it's hard to break through to what Malcolm's death means for us because what we may end up with is an extremely nihilistic view of Black life in contemporary society. No matter what we do—whether we're sexually repressed or sexually promiscuous, whether we assert our identities or police them—the end result is always death. And death not in some natural sense of having lived a life full of contradictions . . .

RS: No, it's premature death.

MR: Yes, death that cuts one off before one is even able fully to recognize the contradictions. That's the scary part, and at the same time the extremely resonant part, of Malcolm's life for the present generation. Even when it's not consciously perceived, we identify with him as the defiant warrior, and unfortunately most warriors get killed.

RS: So we identify with him because we are defiantly facing our own possible death. Identifying with the slain Malcolm gives our own early death symbolic meaning. We seek salvation, and understanding, through his sacrifice.

MR: I even wonder if the identification is therefore in some ways a death wish because of feeling trapped in society, trapped either by our sexuality, or because of our racial, or masculinist, identities. In a society that demands our assimilation and erasure, death seems like an apt metaphor for the condition of our lives. No matter where we turn, or what we do, no matter what strategies we adopt in order to survive, in the end we're obliterated.

RS: I can see how our condition may foster a sense of nihilism, but again I think you're going a bit too far. I don't think that the way the

Black population is identifying with the Malcolm X icon, and the X symbol, is a death wish. I think if anything it is more of a . . . I don't want to say an affirmation of life, but perhaps a fortification of life—meaning the will to fight. And I don't think it's fighting with the idea of wanting to die. Maybe it's accepting death as the inevitable price one pays to be free.

MR: I wonder if it's welcoming death.

RS: Welcoming death?

MR: Yes, death redeems the warrior. Death is what Christ, King, Malcolm—the warrior—has to pay ultimately in the effort of waging the good fight. I wonder if in accepting the kinds of battles that we're engaged in now for our survival, we also to some degree welcome death, partly because it will relieve us of the struggle, but also because it will insure that we're looked at in a way that's worth remembering. Whether it is to protect our turf as drug lords, or whether it is to demand acknowledgment of our sexual identities or to call America on its entrenched and enduring racism; whatever the battleground, to die in the act of fighting remains heroic. Malcolm symbolizes this for all kinds of Black men in America today. On a certain level, he is so seductive for so many of us because he makes death meaningful.

RS: But doesn't the commodification of his life take away from the real tragedy of his death? Malcolm's death was not heroic, it was a senseless murder committed by other Black men.

MR: Well, one can be both tragic and heroic simultaneously. Malcolm's life in many ways was a tragedy, and I think partly through our mythology we try to metamorphosize his life into a heroic triumph. And for me that too is the seduction of Malcolm's life—and the inseparable myth of Malcolm. His life, even after death, can remain heroic because its spirit of survival, of defiance, of self-assertion and self-determination, still lives. Malcolm remains symbolic of a struggle that continues to this day, particularly for a class of young Black men within our inner cities, but also for many of us who are struggling with our identities in a nation that demands the adoption of mythic cardboard constructs of self in order to fit in. And rather than continue to internalize the oppressive beliefs about whom they should be, people start to fight back. They begin to assert identities that challenge the dominant society, and that may mean within our own home and tribe. Like Malcolm, they begin to ask critical questions that inevitably move them along an autonomous, deeply reflective, and ultimately deeply transforming self-evolution.

The Riddle of the Zoot:
Malcolm Little and Black
Cultural Politics During
World War II*

ROBIN D. G. KELLEY

> *But there is rhythm here. Its own special substance:*
> *I hear Billie sing, no good man, and dig Prez, wearing*
> *the Zoot*
> *suit of life, the pork-pie hat tilted at the correct angle,*
> *through the Harlem smoke of beer and whiskey, I*
> *understand the*
> *mystery of the signifying monkey,*
> *in a blue haze of inspiration, I reach to the totality*
> *of Being.*
> *I am at the center of a swirl of events. War and death.*
> *Rhythm. Hot women. I think life a commodity*
> *bargained for*
> *across the bar in Small's.*
> *I perceive the echoes of Bird and there is a gnawing in*
> *the maw*
> *of my emotions. . . .*
> *—Larry Neal, "Malcolm X—An Autobiography"*

*The author is indebted to Diedra Harris-Kelley, Akinyele Umoja, Joe Wood, George Lipsitz, Peter Linebaugh, Tom Holt, and participants in the seminar on Race and Racism at the University of Chicago, for their comments, criticisms, and conversation.

*Much in Negro life remains a mystery; perhaps the zoot suit conceals
profound political meaning; perhaps the symmetrical frenzy of the
Lindy Hop conceals clues to great potential power—if only Negro
leaders would solve this riddle . . .*
—*Ralph Ellison*

Like hundreds of thousands of country-bred Negroes who had come
to the Northern black ghetto before me, and had come since,"
Malcolm X recalled in his autobiography, "I'd also acquired all the
other fashionable ghetto adornments—the zoot suits and conk that I
have described, the liquor, cigarettes, the reefers—all to erase my
embarrassing background" (*Autobiography*, 56). His narrative is familiar: the story of a rural migrant in the big city who eventually finds
social acceptance by shedding his country ways and adopting the
corrupt life-styles of urban America. The big city stripped him of his
naïveté, ultimately paving the way for his downward descent from
hipster, to hustler, to criminal. As Malcolm tells the story, this period
in his life was, if anything, a fascinating but destructive detour on the
road to self-consciousness and political enlightenment.

But Malcolm's narrative of his teenage years should also be read
as a literary construction, a cliché that obscures more than it reveals.[1]
The story is tragically dehistoricized, torn from the sociopolitical context that rendered the zoot suit, the conk, the lindy hop, and the
language of the "hep cat" signifiers of a culture of opposition among
black, mostly male, youth. According to Malcolm's reconstructed
memory, these signifiers were merely "ghetto adornments," no different from the endless array of commodities black migrants were introduced to at any given time. Of course, Malcolm tells his story from
the vantage point of the Civil Rights movement and a resurgent Pan-
Africanism, the early 1960s when the conk had been abandoned for
closely cropped hairstyles, where the zoot had been replaced with the
respectable jacket and tie of middle-class America (dashikis and Afros
from our reinvented Mother Country were not yet born), and where the
sons and daughters of middle-class African Americans, many of whom
were themselves college students taking a detour on the road to respectability to fight for integration and equality, were at the forefront of
struggle. Like the movement itself, Malcolm had reached a period of

his life when opposition could be conceived only as uncompromising and unambiguous.

The didactic and rhetorical character of Malcolm's *Autobiography*—shaped by presentist political concerns of the early 1960s and told through the cultural prism of Islam—obscures the oppositional meanings embedded in wartime black youth culture. And none of Malcolm's biographers since have sought to understand the history and political character of the subculture to which he belonged.[2] The purpose of this brief chapter, then, is not merely to "correct" Malcolm's or his biographers' narratives but to recontextualize his teenage years by reexamining the discursive practices and styles of the hipster subculture and their relation to wartime social, political, economic, and ideological transformations. World War II was a critical turning point not only for Malcolm but for many young African Americans and Latinos in the United States. Indeed, it was precisely the cultural world into which Malcolm stepped that prompted future novelist Ralph Ellison to reflect on the political significance of the dance styles and attire of black youth. Ironically, one would think that Malcolm, himself a product of wartime black youth culture and one of the world's most influential organic intellectuals, was uniquely situated to solve the riddle posed by Ellison in 1943. Nevertheless, whether or not Malcolm acknowledged the political importance of that era on his own thinking, it is my contention that his participation in the underground subculture of black working-class youth during the war was not a detour on the road to political consciousness but rather an essential element of his radicalization.

"I AM AT THE CENTER OF A SWIRL OF EVENTS"

The gangly, red-haired young man from Lansing looked a lot older than fifteen when he moved in with his half sister Ella, who owned a modest home in the Roxbury section of Boston. Little did he know how much the world around him was about to change. The bombing of Pearl Harbor was still several months away, but the country's economy was already geared up for war. By the time U.S. troops were finally dispatched to Europe, Asia, and North Africa, many in the black community restrained their enthusiasm, for they shared a collective memory of the unfulfilled promises of democracy generated by the First World War. Hence, the Double-V campaign, embodied in A. Philip Randolph's threatened march on Washington to protest racial discrimination in employment and the military, partly articulated the sense of hope and pessimism, support and detachment, that dominated a good deal of daily conversation. This time around, a victory abroad without annihilating racism at home was unacceptable. As journalist Roi Ottley observed during the early years of the war, one could not walk the streets of Harlem and not notice a profound change. "Listen to the way Negroes are talking these days! . . . Black men have become noisy, aggressive, and sometimes defiant."[3]

The defiant ones included newly arrived migrants from the South who had flooded America's northeastern and midwestern metropolises. Hoping to take advantage of opportunities created by the nascent wartime economy, most found only frustration and disappointment, because a comparatively small proportion of African Americans gained access to industrial jobs and training programs. By March of 1942, black workers constituted only 2.5 to 3 percent of all war production workers, most of whom had been relegated to low-skill, low-wage positions. The employment situation improved more rapidly after 1942: By April of 1944, blacks made up 8 percent of the nation's war production workers. But members of the African American community did not all benefit equally. For example, the United Negro College Fund was established in 1943 to assist African Americans attending historically black colleges, but during the school year 1945–46, undergraduate enrollment in those institutions amounted to fewer than 44,000. On the other hand, the number of organized black workers increased from 150,000 in 1935 to 1.25 million by the war's end. The Congress of Industrial Organization's (CIO) organizing drives ultimately had the effect of raising wages and improving working conditions for these black workers, though nonunion workers, who made up roughly 80 percent of the black working class, could not take advantage of the gains. And the upgrading of unionized black workers did not take place without a struggle; throughout the war white workers waged "hate strikes" to protest the promotion of blacks, and black workers frequently retaliated with their own wildcat strikes to resist racism.[4]

In short, wartime integration of black workers into the industrial economy proceeded unevenly; by the war's end most African Americans still held unskilled, menial jobs. As cities burgeoned with working people, often living in close quarters or doubling up as a result of housing shortages, the chasm between middle-class and skilled working-class blacks, on the one hand, and the unemployed and working poor, on the other, began to widen. Intraracial class divisions were exacerbated by cultural conflicts between established urban residents and the newly arrived rural folk. In other words, demographic and economic transformations caused by the war not only intensified racial conflict but led to heightened class tensions within urban black communities.[5] For Malcolm, the zoot suit, the lindy hop, and the distinctive lingo of the "hep cat" simultaneously embodied these class, racial, and cultural tensions. This unique subculture enabled him to negotiate an identity that resisted the hegemonic culture and its attendant racism and patriotism, the rural folkways (for many, the "parent culture") that still survived in most black urban households, and the class-conscious, integrationist attitudes of middle-class blacks.

"THE ZOOT SUIT OF LIFE"

Almost as soon as Malcolm settled into Boston, he found he had little tolerance for the class pretensions of his neighbors, particularly his peers. Besides, his own limited wardrobe and visible "country" background rendered him an outsider. He began hanging out at a local pool hall in the poorer section of Roxbury. Here, in this dank, smoky room, surrounded by the cracking sounds of cue balls and the stench of alcohol, Malcolm discovered the black subculture that would ultimately form a crucial component of his identity. An employee of the pool room, whom Malcolm called "Shorty" (most likely a composite figure based on several acquaintances, including his close friend Malcolm Jarvis), became his running partner and initiated him into the cool world of the "hep cat."[6]

In addition to teaching young Malcolm the pleasures, practices, and possibilities of hipster culture, Shorty had to make sure his homeboy wore the right uniform in this emerging Bebop army. When Malcolm put on his very first zoot suit, he realized immediately that the wild sky-blue outfit, the baggy punjab pants tapered to the ankles, the matching hat, gold watch chain, and monogrammed belt was more than a suit of clothes. As he left the department store he could not contain his enthusiasm for his new identity. "I took three of those twenty-five-cent sepia-toned, while-you-wait pictures of myself, posed the way 'hipsters' wearing their zoots would 'cool it'—hat dangled, knees drawn close together, feet wide apart, both index fingers jabbed toward the floor" (*Autobiography*, 52). The combination of his suit and body language encoded a culture that celebrated a specific racial, class, spatial, gender, and generational identity. East Coast zoot suiters during the war were primarily young black (and Latino) working-class males whose living spaces and social world were confined to northeastern ghettos, and the suit reflected a struggle to negotiate these multiple identities in opposition to the dominant culture. Of course, the style itself did not represent a complete break with the dominant fashion trends; zoot suiters appropriated, even mocked, existing styles and reinscribed them with new meanings drawn from shared memory and experiences.[7]

While the suit itself was not meant as a direct political statement, the social context in which it was created and worn rendered it so. The language and culture of zoot suiters represented a subversive refusal to be subservient. Young black males created a fast-paced, improvisational language that sharply contrasted with the passive stereotype of the stuttering, tongue-tied sambo, and in a world where whites commonly addressed them as "boy," zoot suiters made a fetish of calling each other "man." Moreover, within months of Malcolm's first zoot, the political and social context of war had added an explicit dimension to the implicit oppositional meaning of the suit, making it a plainly un-American style. By March 1942, because fabric rationing regulations instituted by the War Productions Board forbade the sale and manufacturing of zoot suits, wearing the suit (which had to be purchased through informal networks) was seen by white servicemen as a pernicious act of anti-Americanism—a view compounded by the fact that most zoot suiters were able-bodied men who refused to enlist or found ways to dodge the draft. Thus when Malcolm donned his "killer-diller coat with a drape-shape, reat-pleats and shoulders padded like a lunatic's cell," his lean body became a dual signifier of opposition—a rejection of both black petit-bourgeois respectability and American patriotism.[8]

The urban youth culture was also born of heightened interracial violence and everyday acts of police brutality. Both Detroit and Harlem, two cities in which Malcolm spent considerable time, erupted in massive violence during the summer of 1943. And in both cases riots were sparked by incidents of racial injustice.[9] The zoot suiters, many of whom participated in the looting and acts of random violence, were also victims of, or witnesses to, acts of outright police brutality. In a description of the Harlem Riot, an anonymous zoot suiter (who sounds more like he stepped out of an NWA or Ice Cube track) expresses both disdain for and defiance toward police practices:

> A cop was runnin' along whippin' the hell outa [sic] colored man like they do in [the] slaughter pen. Throwin' him into the police car, or struggle-buggy, marchin' him off to the jail. That's that! Strange as it may seem, ass-whippin' is not to be played with. So as I close my little letter of introduction, I leave this thought with thee:
>> Yea, so it be
>> I leave this thought with thee
>> Do not attempt to fuck with me. . . .[10]

For Malcolm reflecting backward through the prism of the Nation of Islam and Pan-Africanism, the conk was the most degrading aspect of the hipster subculture. In his words, it was little more than an effort to make his hair "as straight as any white man's." "This was my first really big step toward self-degradation: when I endured all of that pain, literally burning my flesh to have it look like a white man's hair. I had joined that multitude of Negro men and women in America who are brainwashed into believing that the black people are 'inferior'— and white people 'superior'—that they will even violate and mutilate their God-created bodies to try to look 'pretty' by white standards" (*Autobiography*, 54).

Malcolm's interpretation of the conk, however, conveniently separates the hairstyle from the subculture of which it was a part and the social context in which such cultural forms were created. The conk was, as cultural theorist Dick Hebdige might put it, a "refusal" to look like either the dominant, stereotyped image of the Southern migrant or the black bourgeoisie, whose "conks" were closer to mimicking white styles than those of the zoot suiters. Besides, to claim that black working-class males who conked their hair were merely parroting whites ignores the fact that specific stylizations created by black youth emphasized difference—the ducktail down the back of the neck; the smooth, even stiff look created by Murray's Pomade; the neat side parts angling toward the center of the back of the head. More important, once we contextualize the conk and consider the social practices of young hep cats, the totality of ethnic signifiers from the reat pleats to the coded language, their opposition to war, and emphasis on pleasure over waged labor, we cannot help but view the conk as part of a larger process by which black youth appropriated, transformed, and reinscribed coded oppositional meanings onto styles derived from the dominant culture. For as Kobena Mercer recently observed, "the conk was conceived in a subaltern culture, dominated and hedged in by a capitalist master culture, yet operating in an 'underground' manner to subvert given elements by creolizing stylization. Style encoded political 'messages' to those in the know which were otherwise unintelligible to white society by virtue of their ambiguous accentuation and intonation."[11]

"BUT THERE IS RHYTHM HERE"

Once properly attired ("togged to the bricks," as his contemporaries would have said), sixteen-year-old Malcolm discovered the lindy hop, and in the process expanded both his social circle and his politics. The Roseland Ballroom, and in some respects the Savoy in Harlem, constituted social spaces of pleasure free of the bourgeois pretensions of "better class Negroes." His day job as a soda fountain clerk in the elite section of black Roxbury became increasingly annoying as he endured listening to the sons and daughters of the "Hill Negroes," "penny-ante squares who came in there putting on their millionaires' airs" (*Autobiography*, 59). Home (his sister Ella's household) and spaces of leisure (Roseland's Ballroom) suddenly took on new significance, for they represented the negation of black bourgeois culture and a reaffirmation of a subaltern culture that emphasized pleasure, rejected work, and celebrated a working-class racial identity. "I couldn't wait for eight o'clock to get home to eat out of those soul-food pots of Ella's, then get dressed in my zoot and head for some of my friends' places in town, to lindy-hop and get high, or something, for relief from those Hill clowns" (*Autobiography*, 59–60).

For Malcolm and his peers, Boston's Roseland Ballroom and, later, Harlem's Savoy afforded the opportunity to become something other than workers. In a world where clothes constituted signifiers of identity and status, "dressing up" was a way of shedding the degradation of work and collapsing status distinctions between themselves and their oppressors. In Malcolm's narrative, he always seemed to be shedding his work clothes for his zoot suit, whether it was the apron of a soda jerk or the uniform of a railroad sandwich peddler. At the end of his first run to New York on the *Yankee Clipper*, he admitted to having donned his "zoot suit before the first passenger got off" (*Autobiography*, 72). Seeing oneself and others "dressed up" was enormously important in terms of constructing a collective identity based on something other than wage work, presenting a public challenge to the dominant stereotypes of the black body, and reinforcing a sense of dignity that was perpetually being assaulted. Malcolm's images of the Roseland were quite vivid in this respect: "They'd jampack that ballroom, the black girls in wayout silk and satin dresses and shoes, their hair done in all kinds of styles, the men sharp in their zoot suits and crazy conks, and everybody grinning and greased and gassed" (*Autobiography*, 49).

For many working-class men and women who daily endured back-breaking wage work, low income, long hours, and pervasive racism, these urban dance halls were places to recuperate, to take back their bodies. Despite opposition from black religious leaders and segments of the petit bourgeoisie, as well as some employers, black working people of both sexes shook and twisted their already overworked bodies, drank, talked, engaged in sexual play, and—in spite of occasional fights—reinforced their sense of community. The sight of hundreds moving in unison on a hardwood dance floor unmistakably reinforced a sense of collectivity as well as individuality, as dancers improvised on the standard lindy hop moves in friendly competition, like the "cutting sessions" of jazz musicians or the verbal duels known as the dozens. Practically every Friday and Saturday night, young Malcolm experienced the dual sense of community and individuality, improvisation and collective call and response. "The band, the spectators and the dancers, would be making the Roseland Ballroom feel like a big rocking ship. The spotlight would be turning, pink, yellow, green, and blue, picking up the couples lindy-hopping as if they had gone mad.

'*Wail, man, wail!*' people would be shouting at the band; and it *would* be wailing, until first one and then another couple just ran out of strength and stumbled off toward the crowd, exhausted and soaked with sweat" (*Autobiography*, 51).[12]

It should be noted that the music itself was undergoing a revolution during the war. Growing partly out of black musicians' rebellion against white-dominated swing bands and partly out of the heightened militancy of black urban youth—expressed by their improvisational language and dress styles, as well as by the violence and looting we now call the Harlem Riot of 1943—the music that came to be known as "bebop" was born amid dramatic political and social transformations. Minton's Playhouse and Monroe's Uptown constituted the social spaces where a number of styles converged; the most discerning recognized the wonderful collision and reconstitution of Kansas City big band blues, East Coast swing music, and the secular as well as religious sounds of the black South. The horns, fingers, ideas, and memories of *young* black folk such as Charlie Parker, Thelonius Monk, Dizzy Gillespie, Mary Lou Williams, Kenny Clarke, Oscar Pettiford, Tadd Dameron, Bud Powell, and a baby-faced Miles Davis, to name only a few, gave birth to what would be called "bebop." Coinciding with the emergence of Modernism, bebop was characterized by complex and implied rhythms frequently played at blinding tempos, dissonant chord structures, and a preelectronic form of musical "sampling" in which the chord changes for popular Tin Pan Alley songs were appropriated, altered, and used in conjunction with new melodies. Although the music was not intended as dance music, folks found a way to lindy hop to some remarkably fast tempos and in the process invented new dances such as the "apple jack." Although the real explosion in bebop occurred after Malcolm began his stay at Charleston State Penitentiary, no hip Harlemite during the war could have ignored the dramatic changes in the music or the musicians. Even the fairly conservative band leader Lionel Hampton, a close friend of Malcolm's during this period, linked bebop with oppositional black politics. Speaking of his own music in 1946, he told an interviewer, "Whenever I see any injustice or any unfair action against my own race or any other minority groups 'Hey Pa Pa Rebop' stimulates the desire to destroy such prejudice and discrimination."[13]

Finally, although neither the lindy hop nor the apple jack carried intrinsic political meanings, the social act of dancing was nonetheless resistive—at least with respect to the work ethic. Cultural critic Paul

Gilroy insists that black working people who spent time and their precious little money at dance halls and house parties regarded "waged work as itself a form of servitude. At best, it is viewed as a necessary evil and is sharply counterposed to the more authentic freedoms that can only be enjoyed in nonwork time. The black body is here celebrated as an instrument of pleasure rather than an instrument of labor. The nighttime becomes the right time, and the space allocated for recovery and recuperation is assertively and provocatively occupied by the pursuit of leisure and pleasure."[14]

"WAR AND DEATH"

From the standpoint of most hep cats, the Selective Service was an ever-present obstacle to "the pursuit of leisure and pleasure." As soon as war broke out, Malcolm's homeboys did everything possible to evade the draft. (Malcolm was only sixteen when Pearl Harbor was attacked, so he hadn't yet reached draft age.) His partner Shorty, a budding musician hoping to make a name for himself, was "worried sick" about the draft. Like literally dozens of young black musicians (most of whom were drawn to the dissonant, rapid-fire, underground styles of bebop), Shorty succeeded in obtaining 4F status by ingesting something that made "your heart sound defective to the draft board's doctors" (*Autobiography*, 71)—most likely a mixture of benzedrine nasal spray and cocaine.[15] When Malcolm received notice from the draft board in October of 1943, he employed a variety of tactics in order to attain a 4F classification. "I started noising around that I was frantic to join . . . the Japanese Army. When I sensed that I had the ears of the spies, I would talk and act high and crazy. . . . The day I went down there, I costumed like an actor. With my wild zoot suit I wore the yellow knob-toed shoes, and I frizzled my hair up into a reddish bush conk" (*Autobiography*, 105). His interview with the army psychiatrist was the icing on the cake. In a low, conspiratorial tone, he admitted to the doctor, "Daddy-o, now you and me, we're from up North here, so don't you tell nobody. . . . I want to get sent down South. Organize them nigger soldiers, you dig? Steal us some guns and kill up crackers [*sic*]!" (*Autobiography*, 106). Malcolm's tactic was hardly unique, however. Trumpeter John "Dizzy" Gillespie, a pioneer of bebop, secured 4F status and practically paralyzed his army recruitment officer with the following story: "Well, look, at this time, at this stage in my life here in the United States whose foot has been in my ass? The white man's foot has been in my ass hole buried up to his knee in my ass hole! . . . Now you're speaking of the enemy. You're telling me the German is the enemy. At this point, I can never even remember having met a German. So if you put me out there with a gun in my hand and tell me to shoot at the enemy, I'm liable to create a case of 'mistaken identity,' of who I might shoot."[16]

Although these kinds of "confessions" were intended to shake up military officials, both Malcolm and Dizzy were articulating the feelings of a great majority of men who shared their inner cultural circle—feelings that a surprisingly large number of African Americans identified with. The hundreds, perhaps thousands, of zoot suiters and musicians who dodged the draft were not merely evading responsibility. They opposed the war altogether, insisting that African Americans could not afford to invest their blood in another "white man's war." "Whitey owns everything," Shorty explained to Malcolm. "He wants us to go and bleed? Let him fight" (*Autobiography*, 71). Likewise, a Harlem zoot suiter interviewed by black social psychologist Kenneth Clark made the following declaration to the scholarly audience for whom the research was intended: "By [the] time you read this I will be fighting for Uncle Sam, the bitches, and I do not like it worth a dam [*sic*]. I'm not a spy or a saboteur, but I don't like goin' over there fightin' for the white man—so be it."[17] We can never know how many black men used subterfuge to obtain a 4F status, or how many men— like Kenneth Clark's informant—complied with draft orders but did so reluctantly. Nevertheless, what evidence we do possess suggests that black resistance to the draft was more pervasive than we might have imagined. By late 1943 African Americans comprised 35 percent of the nation's delinquent registrants, and between 1941 and 1946, over two thousand black men were imprisoned for not complying with the provisions of the Selective Service Act.[18]

While some might argue that draft dodging by black hipsters hardly qualifies as protest politics, the press, police, and white servicemen thought otherwise. The white press, and to a lesser degree the black press, cast practically all young men sporting the drape shape as unpatriotic "dandies."[19] And the hep cats who could not escape the draft and refused to either submerge their distaste for the war or discard their slang faced a living nightmare in the armed forces. Labeled "Jody" by other servicemen, zoot suiters and jazz musicians were frequently the subject of ridicule, severe punishment, and even beatings. Civilian hipsters fared no better. That black and Latino youth exhibited a cool, measured indifference to the war, as well as an increasingly defiant posture toward whites in general, annoyed white servicemen to no end. Tensions between zoot suiters and servicemen consequently erupted in violence; in June 1943, Los Angeles became the site of racist attacks on black and Chicano youth, during which white soldiers engaged in what amounted to a ritualized stripping of the zoot. Such tensions were also evident in Malcolm's relations with white servicemen. During a rather short stint as a sandwich peddler on the *Yankee Clipper* train, Malcolm was frequently embroiled in arguments with white soldiers and on occasion came close to exchanging blows.[20]

"I THINK LIFE A COMMODITY BARGAINED FOR"

Part of what annoyed white servicemen was the hipster's laissez-faire attitude toward work and his privileging of the "pursuit of leisure and pleasure." Holding to the view that one should work to live rather than live to work, Malcolm decided to turn the pursuit of leisure and pleasure into a career. Thus after "studying" under the tutelage of some of Harlem's better-known pimps, gangsters, and crooks who patronized Small's Paradise, Malcolm eventually graduated to full-fledged hustler.

Bruce Perry and other biographers who assert that, because Malcolm engaged in the illicit economy while good jobs were allegedly "a dime a dozen," we should therefore look to psychological explanations for his criminality, betray a profound ignorance of the wartime political economy and black working-class consciousness.[21] First, in most northeastern cities during the war, African Americans were still faced with job discrimination, and employment opportunities for blacks tended to be low-wage, menial positions. In New York, for example, the proportion of blacks receiving home relief *increased* from 22 percent in 1936 to 26 percent in 1942, and when the Works Progress Administration (WPA) shut down in 1943, the percentage of African Americans employed by the New York WPA was higher than it had been during the entire depression.[22] Second, it was hard for black working people not to juxtapose the wartime rhetoric of equal opportunity and the apparent availability of well-paying jobs for whites with the reality of racist discrimination in the labor market. Of the many jobs Malcolm held during the war, none can be said to have been well-paying and/or fulfilling. Third, any attempt to understand the relationship between certain forms of crime and resistance must begin by interrogating the dominant view of criminal behavior as social deviance. We should not presume, for instance, that wage employment is natural and/or desirable, for to do so would be to naturalize the mythic "Protestant work ethic," private property, and capitalist relations in general. As a number of criminologists and urban anthropologists have suggested, "hustling" or similar kinds of informal/illicit economic strategies should be regarded as efforts to escape dependency on low-wage, alienating labor.[23]

The zoot suiters' collective hostility to wage labor became evident to young Malcolm during his first conversation with Shorty, who promptly introduced the word "slave" into his nascent hipster vocabulary. A popular slang expression for a job, "slave" not only encapsulated their understanding of wage work as exploitative, alienating, and unfulfilling, but also implied a refusal to allow *work* to become the primary signifier of identity. (This is not to say that "hustlers" adamantly refused wage labor; on the contrary, certain places of employment were frequently central loci for operations.) Implied, too, is a rejection of a work ethic, a privileging of leisure, and an emphasis on "fast money" with little or no physical labor. Even Shorty chastised Malcolm for saving money to purchase his first zoot suit rather than taking advantage of credit (*Autobiography*, 44, 51).[24]

Malcolm's apprenticeship in Boston's shoeshine trade introduced him to the illicit economy, the margins of capitalism where commodity relations tended to be raw, demystified, and sometimes quite brutal. Success here required that one adopt the sorts of monopolist strategies usually associated with America's most celebrated entrepreneurs. Yet, unlike mainstream entrepreneurs, most of the hustlers with whom Malcolm was associated held on to an antiwork, anti-accumulation ethic. Possessing "capital" was not the ultimate goal; rather, money was primarily a means by which hustlers could avoid wage work and negotiate status through the purchase of prestigious commodities. Moreover, it seems that many hustlers of the 1940s shared a very limited culture of mutuality that militated against accumulation. On more than one occasion, Malcolm gave away or loaned money to friends when he himself was short of cash, and in at least one case "he pawned his suit for a friend who had pawned a watch for him when he had needed a loan."[25]

Nevertheless, acts of mutuality hardly translated into a radical collective identity; hustling by nature was a predatory act that did not discriminate by color. Moreover, their culture of mutuality was a male-identified culture limited to the men of their inner circle, for, as Malcolm put it, the hustler cannot afford to "trust anybody." Women were merely objects through which hustling men sought leisure and pleasure, prey for financial and sexual exploitation. "I believed that a man should do anything that he was slick enough, or bad and bold enough, to do and that a woman was nothing but another commodity" (*Autobiography*, 134). Even women's sexuality was a commodity to be bought and sold, though for Malcolm and his homeboys selling made more sense than buying. (In fact, Bruce Perry suggests that Malcolm pimped gay men and occasionally sold his own body to homosexuals.)[26]

At least two recent biographies suggest that the detached, sometimes brutal manner with which Malcolm treated women during his hipster days can be traced to his relationship to his mother.[27] While such an argument might carry some validity, it essentially ignores the gendered ideologies, power relationships, and popular culture that bound black hipsters together into a distinct, identifiable community. Resistance to wage labor for the "hep cat" frequently meant increased oppression and exploitation of women, particularly black women. The hipsters of Malcolm's generation and after took pride in their ability to establish parasitical relationships with women wage earners or sex workers. And jazz musicians of the 1940s spoke quite often of living off women, which in many cases translated into outright pimping.[28] Indeed, consider Tiny Grimes's popular 1944 recording featuring Charlie Parker on alto:

> Romance without finance is a nuisance,
> Mama, mama, please give up that gold.
> Romance without finance just don't make sense,

Baby, please give up that gold.

You're so great and you're so fine,
You ain't got no money, you can't be mine,
It ain't no joke to be stone broke,
Honey you know I ain't lyin'. . . .[29]

Furthermore, the hustler ethic demanded a public front of emotional detachment. Remaining "cool" toward women was crucial to one's public reputation and essential in a "business" that depended on the control and brutal exploitation of female bodies. In the words of black America's most noted pimp scribe, Iceberg Slim, "The best pimps keep a steel lid on their emotions."[30]

These gendered identities, social practices, and the discursive arena in which pimping and hustling took place were complicated by race. As in the rest of society, black and white women did not occupy the same position; white women, especially those with money, ranked higher. Once Malcolm began going out with Sophia, his status among the local hipsters and hustlers rose enormously: "Up to then I had been just another among all the conked and zooted youngsters. But now, with the best-looking white woman who ever walked in those bars and clubs, and with her giving me the money I spent, too, even the big important black hustlers and 'smart boys' . . . were clapping me on the back, setting us up to drinks at special tables, and calling me 'Red' " (*Autobiography*, 68). As far as Malcolm and his admirers were concerned, "Detroit Red" conquered and seized what he was not supposed to have—a white woman. Although some scholars and ordinary folk might view Malcolm's dangerous liaison as an early case of self-hatred, the race/gender politics of the hustling community and the equally cool, detached manner with which they treated white women suggests other dynamics were operating as well. White women, like virtually all women (save one's mama), were merely property to be possessed, sported, used, and tossed out. But unlike black women, they belonged to "Charlie," the "Man," "whitey," and were theoretically off limits. Thus, in a world where most relationships were commodified, white women, in the eyes of hustlers at least, were regarded as stolen property, booty seized from the ultimate hustle.

Hustling not only permitted Malcolm to resist wage labor, pursue leisure, and demystify the work ethic myth, but in a strange way the kinds of games he pulled compelled him to "study" the psychology of white racism. Despite the fact that members of this subaltern culture constructed a collective identity in defiance of dominant racist images of African Americans, the work of hustling "white folks" often required that those same dominant images be resurrected and employed as discursive strategies. As a shoeshine boy, for example, Malcolm learned that extra money could be made if one chose to "Uncle Tom a little," smiling, grinning, and making snapping gestures with a polishing rag to give the impression of hard work. Although it was nothing more than a "jive noise," he quickly learned that "Cats tip better, they figure you're knocking yourself out" (*Autobiography*, 48). The potential power blacks possessed to manipulate white racial ideologies for their own advantage was made even clearer during his brief stint as a sandwich salesman on the *Yankee Clipper*: "It didn't take me a week to learn that all you had to do was give white people a show and they'd buy anything you offered them. . . . We were in that world of Negroes who are both servants and psychologists, aware that white people are so obsessed with their own importance that they will pay liberally, even dearly, for the impression of being catered to and entertained" (*Autobiography*, 75). Nevertheless, while Malcolm's performance enabled him to squeeze nickels and dimes from white men who longed for a mythic plantation past where darkeys lived to serve, he also played the part of the model Negro in the watchful eye of white authority, a law-abiding citizen satisfied with his "shoeshine boy" status. It was the perfect cover for selling illegal drugs, acting as a go-between for prostitutes and "Johns," and a variety of other petty crimes and misdemeanors.[31]

In some respects, his initial introduction to the hustling society illumined the power of the trickster figure or the signifying monkey, whose success depended not only on cunning and wiles, but on knowing what and how the powerful thought. Yet the very subculture that drew Malcolm to the hustling world in the first place created enormous tension, as he tried to navigate between Sambo and militant, image and reality. After all, one of the central attractions of the zoot suiters was their collective refusal to be subservient. As Malcolm grew increasingly wary of deferential, obsequious behavior as a hustling strategy, he became, in his words, an "uncouth, wild young Negro. Profanity had become my language" (*Autobiography*, 77). He cursed customers, took drugs with greater frequency, went to work high, and copped an attitude that even his co-workers found unbecoming. By the war's end, burglary became an avenue through which he could escape the masking of petty hustling, the grinning and Tomming so necessary to cover certain kinds of illicit activities. Although burglary was no less difficult and far more dangerous than pulling on-the-job hustles, he chose the time, place, and frequency of his capers, had no bosses or foremen to contend with, and did not have to submit to time clocks and industrial discipline. Furthermore, theft implied a refusal to recognize the sanctity of private property.

Malcolm's increasingly active opposition to wage labor and dependence on the illicit economy enabled him partially to penetrate or demystify capitalist relations, but at the same time it led to a physically deleterious lifestyle, reinforced his brutal exploitation of women, and ensured his downward descent and subsequent prison sentence. Nevertheless, Malcolm's engagement with the illicit economy offered important lessons for future analysis. Unlike nearly all of his contemporaries during the 1960s, he was fond of comparing capitalism with organized crime and refused to characterize looting by black working people as criminal acts—lessons he clearly did not learn in the Nation of Islam. Just five days before his assassination, he railed the mainstream press's coverage of the 1964 Harlem riot for depicting "the rioters as hoodlums, criminals, thieves, because they were abducting some property." Indeed, Malcolm insisted that dominant notions of criminality and private property only obscure the real nature of social relations: "instead of the sociologists analyzing it as it actually is . . . again they cover up the real issue, and they use the press to make it appear that these people are thieves, hoodlums. No! They are the victims of organized thievery."[32]

"IN A BLUE HAZE OF INSPIRATION, I REACH THE TOTALITY OF MY BEING"

Recalling his appearance as a teenager in the 1940s, Malcolm dismissively observed, "I was really a clown, but my ignorance made me think I was 'sharp' " (*Autobiography*, 78). Forgetting for the moment the integrationist dilemmas of the black bourgeoisie, Malcolm could reflect: "I don't know which kind of self-defacing conk is the greater shame—the one you'll see on the heads of the black so-called 'middle-class' and 'upper class,' who ought to know better, or the one you'll see on the heads of the poorest, most downtrodden, ignorant black men. I mean the legal-minimum-wage ghetto-dwelling kind of Negro, as I was when I got my first one" (*Autobiography*, 55). Despite Malcolm's sincere efforts to grapple with the meaning(s) of "ghetto" subculture, to comprehend the logic behind the conk, the reat pleat, and the lindy hop, he ultimately failed to solve Ralph Ellison's riddle. In some ways this is surprising, for who is better suited to solve the riddle than a former zoot suiter and brilliant organic intellectual who rose to become one of America's most insightful social critics of the century?

When it came to thinking about the significance of *his own* life, the astute critic tended to reduce a panoply of discursive practices and cultural forms to dichotomous categories—militancy versus self-degradation, consciousness versus unconsciousness. The sort of narrow, rigid criteria Malcolm used to judge the political meaning of his life left him ill-equipped to capture the significance of his youthful struggles to carve out more time for leisure and pleasure, free himself from alienating wage labor, survive and transcend the racial and economic boundaries he confronted in everyday life. Instead, "Detroit Red" in Malcolm's narrative is a lost soul devoid of an identity, numbed to the beauty and complexity of lived experience, unable to see beyond the dominant culture he mimics.

This is not at all to suggest that Malcolm's narrative is purposely misleading. On the contrary, precisely because his life as a pimp, prostitute, exploiter, addict, pusher, and all-purpose crook loomed so large in his memory of the 1940s, the thought of recuperating the oppositional meanings embedded in the expressive black youth cultures of his era probably never crossed his mind. Indeed, as a devout Muslim recalling an illicit, sinful past, he was probably more concerned with erasing his hustling years than reconstructing them. As bell hooks surmises, Malcolm's decision to remain celibate for twelve years probably stems from a desire to "suppress and deny those earlier years of hedonistic sexual practice, the memory of which clearly evoked shame and guilt. Celibacy alongside rigid standards for sexual behavior may have been Malcolm's way of erasing all trace of that sexual past."[33]

In the end, however, Malcolm did not need to understand what the zoot suit, bebop, the lindy, or even hustling signified for black working-class politics during the war. His hipster past continued to follow him, even as he ridiculed his knob-toed shoes and conked hair.

His simple but colorful speaking style relied on an arsenal of words, gestures, and metaphors drawn in part from his street-corner days. And when he lampooned the black bourgeoisie before black working-class audiences, he might as well have donned an imaginary zoot suit, for his position had not changed dramatically since he first grew wary of the "Hill Negroes" and began hanging out in Roxbury's ghetto in search of "Negroes who were being their natural selves and not putting on airs" (*Autobiography*, 43). There, among the folks today's child gangstas might have called "real niggaz," fifteen-year-old Malcolm Little found the uniform, the language, the culture that enabled him to express a specific constellation of class, racial, generational, and gendered identities.

What Malcolm's narrative shows us (unintentionally, at least) is the power of cultural politics, particularly for African-American urban working-class youth, to both contest dominant meanings ascribed to their experiences and seize spaces for leisure, pleasure, and recuperation. Intellectuals and political leaders who continue to see empowerment solely in terms of "black" control over political and economic institutions, belittle or ignore class distinctions within black communities, and insist on trying to find ways to quantify oppression need to confront Ellison's riddle of the zoot suit. Once we situate Malcolm Little's teenage years squarely within the context of wartime cultural politics, it is hard to ignore the sense of empowerment and even freedom thousands of black youth discovered when they stepped onto the dance floor at the Savoy or Roseland ballrooms, or the pleasure young working-class black men experienced when they were "togged to the bricks" in their wild zoot suits, strolling down the avenue "doin' the streets up brown."

Whatever academicians and self-styled nationalist intellectuals might think about Malcolm Little's teenage years, the youth today, particularly the hip-hop community, are reluctant to separate the hipster from the minister. Consider, for example, W.C. and the Maad Circle's sampling of Malcolm's voice to open their lyrical recasting of the political economy of crime "If You Don't Work, You Don't Eat," in which Los Angeles rapper Coolio asserts, "A hustle is a hustle, and a meal is a meal/that's why I'm real, and I ain't afraid to steal." Or consider Gangstarr's video, "Manifest," in which the Boston-bred rapper shifts easily between playing Malcolm—suit, rimmed glasses and all—rapping behind a podium before a mosque full of followers, to rollin' with his homeboys, physically occupying an abandoned, deteriorating building that could have easily been a decaying Roseland Ballroom. Not coincidentally, beneath his understated tenor voice switching back and forth between sexual boasting and racial politics, one hears the bass line from Dizzy Gillespie's bebop classic, "A Night in Tunisia." Through an uncanny selection of music, an eclectic mix of lyrics, and a visual juxtaposing of young black men "hanging out" against Malcolm the minister, Gangstarr and D.J. Premier were able to invoke two Malcolms, both operating in different social spaces but sharing the same time—or, rather, timelessness. While some might find this collapsing of Malcolm's life politically and intellectually disingenuous, it does offer a vehicle for black (male) youth to further negotiate between culture as politics and culture as pleasure.

But "collapsing" the divisions Malcolm erected to separate his enlightened years from his preprison "ignorance" also compels us to see him as the product of a *totality of lived experiences*. As I have tried to suggest, aspects of Malcolm's politics must be sought in the riddle of the zoot suit, in the style politics of the 1940s that he himself later dismissed as stupidity and self-degradation. This realization is crucial for our own understanding of the current crisis of black working-class youth in urban America. For if we look deep into the interstices of the postindustrial city, we are bound to find millions of Malcolm Littles, male and female, whose social locations have allowed them to demystify aspects of the hegemonic ideology while reinforcing their ties to it. But to understand the elusive cultural politics of contemporary black urban America requires that we return to Ellison's riddle posed a half century ago and search for meaning in the language, dress, music, and dance styles rising out of today's ghettoes, as well as the social and economic context in which styles are created, contested, and reaccented. Once we abandon decontextualized labels such as "nihilism" or "outlaw culture," we might discover a lot more *Malcolm Xes*—indeed, more El-Hajj Malik El-Shabazzes—hiding beneath hoods and baggy pants, Dolphin earrings and heavy lipstick, Raider's caps and biker shorts, than we might have ever imagined.

NOTES

1. A number of scholars, from a variety of different disciplines and standpoints, have illustrated the extent to which the *Autobiography* depended on various rhetorical strategies and literary devices (that is, conversion narrative). See especially Thomas Benson, "Rhetoric and Autobiography: The Case of Malcolm X," *Quarterly Journal of Speech* 60 (February 1974): 1–13; Werner Berthoff, "Witness and Testament: Two Contemporary Classics," *New Literary History* 2 (Winter, 1971); Nancy Clasby, "Autobiography of Malcolm X: A Mythic Paradigm," *Journal of Black Studies* 5, no. 1 (September 1974): 18–34; David Demarest, "*The Autobiography of Malcolm X*: Beyond Didacticism," *CLA Journal* 16, no. 2 (December, 1972): 179–187; Carol Ohmann, "The Autobiography of Malcolm X: A Revolutionary Use of the Franklin Tradition," *American Quarterly* 22, no. 2 (1970): 131–149; John Hodges, "The Quest for Selfhood in the Autobiographies of W.E.B. DuBois, Richard Wright, and Malcolm X," Ph.D. diss., University of Chicago, 1980; Stephen Whitfield, "Three Masters of Impression Management: Benjamin Franklin, Booker T. Washington, and Malcolm X as Autobiographers," *South Atlantic Quarterly* 77 (Autumn, 1978).

2. Part of the reason for this, I believe, has something to do with the unusual proclivity of most Malcolm biographers to adopt a psychobiographical approach in place of an analysis that places the subject within specific historical and cultural contexts. Examples include Bruce Perry, *Malcolm: The Life of a Man Who Changed Black America* (New York: Station Hill Press, 1991), and Perry's three articles, "Malcolm X in Brief: A Psychological Perspective," *Journal of Psychohistory* 11, no. 4 (Spring, 1984): 491–500; "Malcolm X and the Politics of Masculinity," *Psychohistory Review* 13, nos. 2 and 3 (Winter, 1985): 18–25; "Escape from Freedom, Criminal Style: The Hidden Advantages of Being in Jail," *Journal of Psychiatry and Law* 12, no. 2 (Summer, 1984): 215–230; Lawrence B. Goodheart, "The Odyssey of Malcolm X: An Eriksonian Interpretation," *The Historian* 53 (Autumn 1990): 47–62; Frederick Harper, "Maslow's Concept of Self-Actualization Compared with Personality Characteristics of Selected Black American Protestors: Martin Luther King, Jr., Malcolm X, and Frederick Douglass," Ph.D. diss., Florida State University, 1970; Cedric J. Robinson, "Malcolm Little as a Charismatic Leader," *Afro-American Studies* 3 (1972): 81–96; Eugene Victor Wolfenstein, *The Victims of Democracy: Malcolm X and the Black Revolution* (London: 1989; orig. 1981). The worst example thus far is clearly Bruce Perry's massive psychobiography. Ignoring African-American urban culture in general, and black politics during World War II in particular, enables Perry to treat Malcolm's decisions and practices as manifestations of a difficult childhood, thus isolating him from the broader social, cultural, and political transformations taking place around him. Throughout the book Perry betrays an incredible ignorance of black culture and cultural politics, and the

fact that standard works are omitted from the notes and bibliography further underscore this point. On the other hand, Wolfenstein makes some reference to black politics during the war, but his very thin discussion focuses almost exclusively on organized, relatively mainstream black politics, such as A. Philip Randolph's March on Washington Movement. The cultural politics of black zoot suiters, for all its contradictions and apparent detachment from social struggle, is ignored. See also George Breitman, *The Last Year of Malcolm X: The Evolution of a Revolutionary* (New York: Pathfinder Press, 1967); Breitman, *Malcolm X: The Man and His Ideas* (New York: Pathfinder Press, 1965); John Henrik Clarke, ed., *Malcolm X: The Man and His Times* (New York: Macmillan, 1969); James Cone, *Martin and Malcolm and America: A Dream or Nightmare* (Maryknoll, NY: Orbis Books, 1991); Peter Goldman, *The Death and Life of Malcolm X* (New York: Harper & Row, 1973); William Moore, "On Identity and Consciousness of El Hajj Malik El Shabazz (Malcolm X)," Ph.D. diss., University of California, Santa Cruz, 1974.

3. Roi Ottley, *New World A-Coming: Inside Black America* (New York and Boston: Houghton and Mifflin, 1943), 306. On black politics during the war, see Richard Dalfiume, *Fighting on Two Fronts: Desegregation of the Armed Forces, 1939–1953* (Columbia, MO: University of Missouri Press, 1969) and "The 'Forgotten Years' of the Negro Revolution," *Journal of American History* 55 (June 1968): 90–106; Herbert Garfinkel, *When Negroes March: The March on Washington Movement in the Organizational Policies for FEPC* (Glencoe, IL: Free Press, 1959); Lee Finkle, "The Conservative Aims of Militant Rhetoric: Black Protest During World War II," *Journal of American History* 60 (December 1973): 692–713; Peter J. Kellogg, "Civil Rights Consciousness in the 1940's," *The Historian* 42 (November 1979): 18–41; Neil A. Wynn, *The Afro-American and the Second World War* (New York: Holmes and Meier Publishers, 1975); John Modell, Marc Goulden, and Magnusson Sigurdur, "World War II in the Lives of Black Americans: Some Findings and an Interpretation," *Journal of American History* 76 (December 1989): 838–848; Harvard Sitkoff, *A New Deal for Blacks: The Emergence of Civil Rights as a National Issue* (Oxford and New York: Oxford University Press, 1978), 298–325, and "Racial Militancy and Interracial Violence in the Second World War," *Journal of American History* 58 (December 1971): 661–681; Robert Korstad and Nelson Lichtenstein, "Opportunities Found and Lost: Labor, Radicals, and the Early Civil Rights Movement," *Journal of American History* 75 (December 1988): 786–811; Herbert Shapiro, *White Violence and Black Response: From Reconstruction to Montgomery* (Amherst, MA: University of Massachusetts Press, 1988), 301–348.

4. Manning Marable, *Race, Reform, and Rebellion: The Second Reconstruction in Black America, 1945–1990* (Jackson and London: University Press of Mississippi, 1991, 2nd ed.), 14–17; Philip Foner, *Organized Labor and the Black Worker, 1619–1981* (New York: International Publishers, 1981), 239, 243; Daniel R. Fusfield and Timothy Bates, *The Political Economy of the Urban Ghetto* (Carbondale, IL: Southern Illinois University Press, 1984), 48; William H. Harris, *The Harder We Run: Black Workers Since the Civil War*

(New York and Oxford: Oxford University Press, 1982), 113–122; George Lipsitz, *Class and Culture in Cold War America: "A Rainbow at Midnight"* (New York: Praeger, 1981), 14–28; Nelson Lichtenstein, *Labor's War at Home: The CIO in World War II* (New York and Cambridge: Cambridge University Press, 1982), 124–126.

5. Wolfenstein (*Victims of Democracy*, 175–176) makes a similar observation about the intensification of intraracial class divisions, although we disagree significantly as to the meaning of these divisions for the emergence of black working-class opposition. Besides, I am insisting on the simultaneity of heightened intraracial class struggle and racist oppression.

6. Perry, *Malcolm*, 48–49; Malcolm X, *Autobiography*, 38–41; Wolfenstein, *Victims of Democracy*, 154–157.

7. I am making a distinction here between African-American zoot suiters and the Chicano zoot suiters in the Southwest. In predominantly Mexican-American urban communities, especially Los Angeles, the zoot suit emerged about the same time, but it also has its roots in the pachuco youth culture, an equally oppositional-style politics emerging out of poverty, racism, and alienation. The youth reappropriated aspects of their parents' and grandparents' Mexican past in order to negotiate a new identity, adopting their own hip version of Spanish laced with English words and derived from a very old creolized dialect known as Calo. For more on Chicano zoot suiters and pachuco culture, see Stuart Cosgrove, "The Zoot-Suit and Style Warfare," *History Workshop Journal* 18 (Autumn 1984): 78–81; Mauricio Mazon, *The Zoot-Suit Riots: The Psychology of Symbolic Annihilation* (Austin, TX: University of Texas Press, 1984); Marcos Sanchez-Tranquilino and John Tagg, "The Pachuco's Flayed Hide: Mobility, Identity, and *Buenas Garras*," in Lawrence Grossberg, Cary Nelson, and Paula Treichler, eds., *Cultural Studies* (London: Routledge, 1992), 566–570; Marcos Sanchez-Tranquilino, "Mano a mano: An Essay on the Representation of the Zoot Suit and Its Misrepresentation by Octavio Paz," *Journal of the Los Angeles Institute of Contemporary Art* (Winter 1987): 34–42; Ralph H. Turner and Samuel J. Surace, "Zoot Suiters and Mexicans: Symbols in Crowd Behavior," *American Journal of Sociology* 62 (1956): 14–20; Octavio Paz, *The Labyrinth of Solitude: Life and Thought in Mexico* (New York: Grove Press, 1962): 5–8; Arturo Madrid-Barela, "In Search of the Authentic Pachuco: An Interpretive Essay," *Aztlan* 4, no. 1 (Spring, 1973). The best general discussions of the zoot in African-American culture are Cosgrove, "The Zoot-Suit," 77–91; Bruce M. Tyler, "Black Jive and White Repression," *Journal of Ethnic Studies* 16, no. 4 (1989): 32–38; Steve Chibnall, "Whistle and Zoot: The Changing Meaning of a Suit of Clothes," *History Workshop*, 20 (Autumn 1985): 56–81. Malcolm's own description of his zoot suits can be found in *Autobiography*, 52, 58.

8. Cosgrove, "The Zoot Suit," 78, 80; LeRoi Jones, *Blues People* (New York: William Morrow, 1963), 202; Eric Lott, "Double V, Double-Time: Bebop's Politics of Style," *Callaloo* 11, no. 3 (1988): 598, 600; Ben Sidran, *Black Talk* (New York: Holt, Rinehart and Winston, 1971), 110–111; Tyler, "Black Jive and White Repression," 31–66.

9. Dominic J. Capeci, Jr., *Race Relations in Wartime Detroit* (Philadelphia:

Temple University Press, 1984), and *The Harlem Riot of 1943* (Philadelphia: Temple University Press, 1977); Harvard Sitkoff, "The Detroit Race Riot of 1943," *Michigan History* 53 (Fall 1969): 183–206; Shapiro, *White Violence*, 310–337.

10. Clark and Barker, "The Zoot Effect," 146; for a broader discussion of police brutality in Harlem during the late 1930s and 1940s, see Cheryl Greenberg, *Or Does It Explode: Black Harlem in the Great Depression* (New York and Oxford: Oxford University Press, 1991), 193–194, 211.

11. Kobena Mercer, "Black Hair/Style Politics," *New Formations* 3 (Winter 1987): 49; also see Lawrence Levine, *Black Culture and Black Consciousness: Afro-American Folk Thought from Slavery to Freedom* (New York and Oxford: Oxford University Press, 1977), 291–292. For a general discussion of the ways oppositional meaning can be reinscribed in styles that are essentially a recasting of aspects of dominant culture, see Dick Hebdige, *Subcultures: The Meaning of Style* (London: Methuen, 1979), 17–19. Although Wolfenstein does not completely accept Malcolm's description of the conk as an act of self-degradation, he reduces his transformation to hipster entirely to a negation of waged work, ignoring the creative construction of an ethnic identity that celebrates difference as well as challenges the hegemonic image of the black male body. In Wolfenstein's schema, oppositional identity becomes merely caricature. Thus he writes, "he was trying to *be* white, but in a black man's way" (*Victims of Democracy*, 157).

12. For a description of the Savoy in Harlem, see Jervis Anderson, *This Was Harlem: A Cultural Portrait, 1900–1950* (New York: Farrar, Straus and Giroux, 1981), 307–314.

13. Quoted in Lott, "Double V, Double Time," 603. Lott's essay is by far the best discussion of the politics of bebop. See also Ira Gitler, *Swing to Bop: An Oral History of the Transition in Jazz in the 1940's* (New York and Oxford: Oxford University Press, 1985); Jack Chambers, *Milestones 1: The Music and Times of Miles Davis to 1960* (Toronto and Buffalo: University of Toronto Press, 1983); Ira Gitler, *Jazz Masters of the 1940's* (New York: Collier Books, 1984, orig. 1966); Jones, *Blues People*, 175–207; Frank Kofsky, *Black Nationalism and the Revolution in Music* (New York: Pathfinder Press, 1970), chapter 1; Robert Reisner, *Bird: The Legend of Charlie Parker* (New York: Citadel Press, 1962); Sidran, *Black Talk*, 78–115; John Wilson, *Jazz: The Transition Years, 1940–1960* (New York: Appleton-Century-Crofts, 1966). Malcolm's claim to having been friends with Lionel Hampton was recently challenged by Bruce Perry. Gladys Hampton, whom Perry interviewed, insists that Malcolm was not a close friend. See Perry, *Malcolm*.

14. Paul Gilroy, "One Nation Under a Groove: The Cultural Politics of 'Race' and Racism in Britain," in David Theo Goldberg, ed., *Anatomy of Racism* (Minneapolis: University of Minnesota Press, 1990), 274; see also discussions of the social meaning of dance halls black life in Tera Hunter, "Household Workers in the Making: Afro-American Women in Atlanta and the New South, 1861–1920," Ph.D. diss., Yale University, 1990, 92–93; and Katrina Hazzard-Gordon, *Jookin': The Rise of Social Dance Formations in African-American Culture* (Philadelphia: Temple University Press, 1990).

15. Gerald R. Gill, "Dissent, Discontent and Disinterest: Afro-American Opposition to the United States Wars of the Twentieth Century" (ms. 1988), 166–167; Gitler, *Swing to Bop*, 115–116; Tyler, "Black Jive," 34–35. It is interesting to note that in Germany, a subculture emerged in opposition to "Nazi regimentation" that resembled African-American hipsters. They wore zoot suits, listened to jazz, grew their hair long, and spent as much time as possible in the clubs and bars before they were closed down. The "swing boys," as they were called, faced enormous repression; jailings and beatings were common for merely possessing jazz records. Earl R. Beck, "The Anti-Nazi 'Swing Youth,' 1942–1945," *Journal of Popular Culture* 19 (Winter 1985): 45–53; "Hans Massaquoi," in Studs Terkel, ed., *The Good War: An Oral History of World War Two* (New York: Pantheon Books, 1984), 500–01; Michael H. Kater, "Forbidden Fruit?: Jazz in the Third Reich," *American Historical Review* 94 (February 1989): 11–43.

16. Dizzy Gillespie with Al Fraser, *To Be or Not . . . to Bop: Memoirs* (Garden City, NY: Doubleday, 1979), 119–120. Malcolm's later speeches returned to this very theme. The military was initially reluctant to draft African Americans, Malcolm explained to his audiences, because "they feared that if they put us in the army and trained us in how to use rifles and other things, we might shoot at some targets that they hadn't picked out. And we would have." George Breitman, ed., *Malcolm X Speaks: Selected Speeches and Statements* (New York: Pathfinder Press, 1965), 140; "Not Just an American Problem, but a World Problem," in Bruce Perry, ed., *Malcolm X: The Last Speeches* (New York: Pathfinder Press, 1989), 176.

17. Kenneth B. Clark and James Barker, "The Zoot Effect in Personality: A Race Riot Participant," *Journal of Abnormal and Social Psychology* 40, no. 2 (April 1945): 145.

18. Gill, "Dissent, Discontent, and Disinterest," 164–168; George Q. Flynn, "Selective Service and American Blacks During World War II," *Journal of Negro History* 69 (Winter 1984): 14–25. Ironically, one of the most widely publicized groups of black conscientious objectors happened to be members of the Nation of Islam. About one hundred of its members were arrested for resisting the draft, even its spiritual leader Elijah Muhammad. Yet, despite the fact that a number of jazz musicians had converted to Islam and even adopted Arabic names (e.g., Sahib Shihab, Idris Sulieman, and Sadik Hakim) during the war, Malcolm claims complete ignorance of the Nation prior to his prison stint. On the Nation of Islam during the war, see Gill, *Dissent, Discontent, and Disinterest*, 156–157; E. U. Essien-Udom, *Black Nationalism: A Search for Identity* (Chicago: University of Chicago Press, 1962), 80–81; Sidran, *Black Talk*, 82.

19. See especially Tyler, "Black Jive," 34–39 passim.

20. Tyler, "Black Jive," 38; Mazon, *Zoot Suit Riots*, 54–77; Cosgrove, "The Zoot-Suit," 80–88; C.L.R. James, George Breitman, Edgar Keemer, et al., *Fighting Racism in World War II* (New York: Pathfinder Press, 1980), 254–255; Malcolm X, *Autobiography*, 77.

21. Bruce Perry, for example (who characterizes Malcolm's entire family as a bunch of criminals), not only suggests that theft is merely a manifestation of deviant behavior rooted in unfulfilled personal relationships, but he naturalizes the "Protestant work ethic" by asserting that Malcolm's resistance to "steady employment" reflected a reluctance to "assume responsibility" (*Malcolm*, 57–61 passim).

22. Greenberg, *"Or Does It Explode?"* 198–202; Busfield and Bates, *Political Economy*, 45–46.

23. Carol B. Stack, *All Our Kin: Strategies for Survival in a Black Community* (New York: Harper & Row, 1974); Betty Lou Valentine, *Hustling and Other Hard Work: Life Styles in the Ghetto* (New York: Free Press, 1978); for comparative contemporary and historical examples from Britain, see the brilliant book by Peter Linebaugh, *The London Hanged: Crime and Civil Society in the Eighteenth Century* (London: Allen Lane, The Penguin Press, 1991); Steven Box, *Recession, Crime, and Punishment* (Totowa, NJ: Barnes and Noble Books, 1987); J. Ditton, *Part-Time Crime* (London: Macmillan, 1977); R.C. Hollinger and J.P. Clark, *Theft by Employees* (Lexington, MA: Lexington Books, 1983); and for a general discussion of the informal economy and working-class opposition, see Cyril Robinson, "Exploring the Informal Economy," *Crime and Social Justice* 15, nos. 3 and 4 (1988): 3–16.

24. Wolfenstein, *Victims of Democracy*, 157. For a discussion of the "hustler's ethic" as a rejection of the "Protestant work ethic," see Julius Hudson, "The Hustling Ethic," in Thomas Kochman, ed., *Rappin' and Stylin' Out: Communication in Urban Black America* (Urbana, IL: University of Illinois Press, 1972), 414–416.

25. Wolfenstein, *Victims of Democracy*, 155; Perry, *Malcolm*, 72. Horace Cayton and St. Clair Drake found numerous examples of poor black residents in Chicago's Southside mutually supporting one another while simultaneously engaged in the illicit economy. *Black Metropolis: A Study of Negro Life in a Northern City* (New York: Harper & Row, 1962, 2nd ed.), vol. 2, pp. 570–611 passim.

26. Perry, *Malcolm*, 77–78, 82–83. The evidence Perry provides to make this assertion (which includes simplistic Freudian interpretations of later speeches!) is slim, to say the least. But even if the hearsay Perry's informant passed on is true, it would not contradict my argument. For the manner in which Malcolm allegedly exploited gay men positioned them as Other, and in the cases Perry cites obtaining money was far more important than sexual pleasure. He apparently did not identify with an underground gay community; rather, it was merely another "stunt" in the life of a hustler.

27. Perry, *Malcolm*, 51–52; Wolfenstein, *Victims of Democracy*, 162–163.

28. See, for example, Miles Davis with Quincy Troupe, *Miles: The Autobiography* (New York: Simon and Schuster, 1989), 87–189 passim; Charles Mingus, *Beneath the Underdog* (Harmondsworth: Penguin, 1969); and for some postwar examples beyond the jazz world, see Elliot Liebow, *Tally's Corner: A Study of Negro Streetcorner Men* (Boston and Toronto: Little, Brown & Co.,

1967), 137–144; Christina Milner and Richard Milner, *Black Players: The Secret World of Black Pimps* (Boston and Toronto: Little, Brown & Co., 1973); Susan Hall and Bob Adelman, *Gentleman of Leisure: A Year in the Life of a Pimp* (New York: NAL, 1972).

29. "Romance Without Finance," *Bird/The Savoy Recordings [Master Takes]* (Savoy, 2201).

30. Iceberg Slim, *Pimp: The Story of My Life* (Los Angeles: Holloway House, 1969), vi.

31. A number of scholars have suggested that pimps and hustlers, at least in black folklore, were more like modern-day tricksters than "bad men." See, for example, Levine, *Black Culture and Black Consciousness*, 381–382; Milner and Milner, *Black Players*, 242.

32. "Not Just an American Problem, but a World Problem," in Perry, ed., *Malcolm X: The Last Speeches*, 161.

33. bell hooks, "Sitting at the Feet of the Messenger: Remembering Malcolm X," in *Yearning: Race, Gender and Cultural Politics* (Boston: South End Press, 1990), 84.

"Can This Be the End for Cyclops and Professor X?"

GREG TATE

'm not a race man. I'm an X-man," says Bullrose to Dravidiana, the she-ra with the high-8 video camera.

"As in Malcolm, of course?" she cracks, whopping them blond dreads out of her face with ye olde roundhouse swing of the dome.

"No, as in Ice Man, Angel, Cyclops, and The Beast. My **slave name** used to be Scott Summers, dig?" The list does not leave Dravidiana perplexed, just provoked to jump deeper into Bullrose's bushwah.

"Whoa, Troop! What happened to X-Girl? You just erasin' her from the pages of Marvel history?"

The gender interrogation feels like déjà vu to Bullrose. It takes him back. Back before Dravidiana turned that lesbonic corner, back when she was his woman and he was her man, back when she routinely took him to task for the masculinist infractions.

"I remember back in the day when being up on Marvel Comics' lore was strictly a brother-thang. Can't nothing be strictly a brother-thang anymore? I know how them all-white country clubs feel. Can't get away from these niggas nowhere."

"And woman is the nigga of the world," proclaimed the she-ra. "But let's stick to the point. The original question was . . ."

". . . how many peckers did Peter Piper prick?"

"The original question was, why are so many young brothers sweatin' Malcom X's dick so hard these days? Is it 'cause of Spike Lee, Chuck D, BDP? Why you got the sleaze-ass likes of Big Daddy Kane saying he aspires to be a combination of Malcolm X and Marvin

Gaye, a great black leader and a sexy entertainer? And a virtual humanist like Vernon Reid coming out the box like he wants to be X and Hendrix rolled into one? How cum? Huh? Huh?"

"Well, all the brothers you mentioned led the way far as the resurrection goes, but X wouldn't be making this kind of comeback if he wasn't a bona fide superstar. I mean, the brother had style. He never took a bad photograph in his life. His records still sound dope. And no matter what kinda nigga you are, if you read his book you can see yourself in him. Like Chaka Khan said she was everywoman, X was every black man. I mean, the brother had a multiple-identity crisis going on. Count 'em off: preacher, poet, pimp, prostitute, prophet, player, political activist, warrior-king, husband, father, martyr.

"X occupies so many housin'-units in the black male psyche, a brother can't erase X without erasing himself. I don't think he shot hoop, and he wasn't a jazz musician, but he was a great jazz dancer, which is close enough to confer jazzman/jock cache on his godhead too."

"But what do these brothers really know about brother Malcolm? All they seem to know is what other niggas say about what a bad nigga he was. Jockin' on the T-shirts, buttons, and shit. What do they know about his politics, particularly his gender politics, which were like totally fucked up?"

"What else does a young brother got to know? X was a smooth operator from the streets with a dope rap who stood up for black folks and got shot down for doing it. That's the stuff black heroes are made of. Staying black and dying for it. It's a mytho-pop-poeic world out there. Brothers been brought up on it same as everybody else. Malcolm was like JFK or Elvis. He was made for the TV age, the information age and the hip-hop age. Brother man was videogenic and gave great soundbites. The hip-hop nation got to dig him because he could rap, he had street knowledge, mother wit, and supreme verbal flow. You know how we value verbal prowess in the black community. The brother or sister who can make stone rhetoric swing like a pickax to the brain. All of that is why the young brothers are on Malcolm's jock so hard."

"Do you think they'd be following him if he was alive today?"

"If he was alive today they wouldn't need to be following him. I mean, do you realize how different America would be today if King and X had been around to provide moral leadership and militant thrust

to the Panthers and the Yippies and all them muhfuhkuhs instead of
them being left out there to freelance and fuck it up for themselves?
But, you know, it's cool, because Malcolm left the brothers their first
revolutionary pop ikon. Nat Turner don't count. Who even knows what
he looked like? Coulda been a nerd. And when you dealing with
American superstars, baby, all you need to know is he lived fast and
died young, a martyr who went out in a blaze of glory. Dying under
suspicious and mysterious circumstances helps too. That way you can
really hype the conspiratorial element. Live heroes are a problem.
They be getting all soft and wet and problematic on you. If you're
lucky enough to die young you can be remembered for being a hard
muhfuhkuh forever. We celebrate the death of Malcolm X for what it
is—the birth of a new black god. X is dead, long live X. He's like
the Elvis of black pop politics—a real piece of Afro-Americana. That's
why Spike's X logo is branded with an American flag. Malcolm couldn't
have happened anywhere else."

"Do you think Malcolm's spirituality makes a difference to the
youth at all?"

"Sure it does because that's all part of the package, the construct
we know as X the martyr. But spirituality is like anything else in
America, you got to package it right. Malcolm had the right package.
If being Muslim is how you get to be a righteous black man like
Malcolm, then you become Muslim. When you're young, dumb, and
full of cum and, lord knows, you gonna get you some, you like to think
you got juice to pass judgment on the world, that youth makes right.
Self-righteousness comes with the territory: You think however you
living is justifiable because you a sexy young thing, maybe good with
your hands or in some sport. But maybe not, because it really ain't as
important as being proficient in Black Male Posturing. BMP is a bitch.
Carry you farther than you will ever imagine in this world because the
whole world gives it so much power. Except for the butch breed like
yourself who on the whole are probably less impressed than anybody.
And cocky because of it. Yeah, I be checking how arrogantly y'all will
ignore a fine brother just because you know it fucks up his whole
program. Y'all eat that shit up."

"You mean like you, boy-Romeo?"

"Being a loveman is a tough job but somebody has to do it, right?
Anything else you want to ask me?"

"When did you first hear about Malcolm?"

"In my house, growing up. I'm an old muhfuhkuh so we talking

'65, '66 when I was around eight or nine. He was a regular on the turntable, 'longside Otis, Coltrane, and Nina Simone. We lived in a big three-story house. The stereo was a big old piece of furniture. So when my people played Malcolm on a Sunday it would fill up the house, every nook and cranny, you could almost smell Malcolm's voice smoking up the joint. Seems like on Sunday my people kept Malcolm going like we keep candles and incense going today. Except for Nina Simone and Otis Redding and John Coltrane, the only records I can remember my people playing was X. Now all my mother listens to besides jazz-lite radio and weight-loss tapes is Public Enemy. There's some kinda continuity there, I guess. I don't know what happened to all those X records she had. Probably got stolen, or borrowed and never returned. They're collector's items really. Probaly fetch a fine price on the open market."

"What do you remember from the X oeuvre?"

"Certain phrases will stick with me forever. 'I'm the man you think you are.' 'I'd do the same as you, only more of it.' 'You can't get a chicken from a duck egg.' I always liked that image. It always made me see a baby chick flopping around in an eggshell three sizes too big. 'You can't have a revolution without bloodshed.' 'Doesn't matter if you're a Baptist or a Methodist, you'll still catch hell.' That conjured an image in my mind too: churches burning down. That one where he talks about how if you were a citizen you wouldn't need no Civil Rights bill. What's funny is that even as a child—and I'm talking seven, eight years old—X made perfect sense to me. Maybe because he was talking about right and wrong in such binary terms, like in fairy tales. You know he painted the world as black equals good and white equals evil. Black could be stupid, punk ass, and illogical but not evil. And white couldn't be nothing but evil. Do I still believe that? Not expressly. On the other hand I'm not impressed by much of anything white people do except for some painters and photographers, a couple stand-up comics and the theoretical physicist types."

"Not to digress but you can be hard on our black visual artists. Why is that?"

"The evidence speaks for itself. It's not even about where's the Coltrane, the Baraka, the Lady Day, the Fannie Lou Hamer of painting, sculpture, and photography. It's about where is the Jr. Walker, the Iceberg Slim, the Gloria Lynne, the Shirley Chisholm. There's very little black visual work that personifies blackness. You got people that do good work but rarely does it not lack for the wit, pathos, and absurdity of black existential reality. We got people that have rolled up close up on it. But it can get even blacker than that. I think so, anyway."

"How can you quantify the blackness of visual practice and phenomena?"

"Only by the way it does things white boys can't even contemplate. Like being a Malcolm X, Bob Marley, Miles Davis. If you a white boy you know there's no way in hell you could be one of them because you could never step inside of history in their skin. Race doesn't prescribe experience or predict emotional depth, but there are historical experiences that only being black in space, time, and mind will make possible. You get my drift?"

"Sounds kinda essentialist to me. What's really the difference between what you're saying and calling white folks grafted devils?"

"Are we gonna have that old debate again? Look, there is a special kind of alienation you possess as a black person in this society that is all mashed up with your feelings of love and loathing and loyalty to black folks as a whole. Unless you were raised among black people you never develop certain sensitivities or neuroses about race and culture and identity that I believe are a fundamental inspiration for black creative genius. Du Bois talked about black folks and double consciousness. I think if you're a black intellectual you got quadruple, sextuple, octagonal consciousnesses beaming around your brain. You're always trying to square things that have no liners and hard edges. Like where Africa ends and Europe begins. How to develop yourself without alienating those who aren't interested in development on whose behalf you are developing yourself. You know if Malcolm hadn't had the Nation of Islam's save-a-sinner program behind him to smooth all that kinda shit out he woulda been another alienated Black intellectual in deep crisis. Trying to figure out how to relate to the masses and redeem 'em without romanticizing or patronizing or, worst of all, pandering to them. It's easy to challenge black folks on self-destructive behavior. Harder to challenge us on reactionary practices like misogyny, homophobia, and thinking that intellectual development is a white thang. But what is Malcolm to you, Dravi? What are you looking for from these interviews and whatnot?"

"Well, like, I was never raised to have heroes. I was raised to listen to what people said and look for how it contradicted what they did. I learned that the person who did a constructive thing for the community today could be about tearing it down tomorrow. I was taught how fragile and selfish most human beings are—except for black mothers—and that holding power over people makes them even more fragile, vain and lonely and dangerous. Dangerous to others because their charisma makes folks want to let them do their thinking for them. Dangerous to themselves because they have to give up their humanity on the way to the hall of glory.

"I think history shows us that the revolutionaries and prophets that the state killed got a better deal than the ones who became living symbols. Because there's nothing at the end of that road but bitterness, regret, and tyranny. How can you respect the common humanity of people who hold your ideas, your utterances as more valid than their own lives? That's why I got no use for heroes. I can respect heroic acts but I can't respect anybody who'd want idolatry for breakfast, lunch, and dinner."

"You don't think that's what Malcolm wanted, do you?"

"I don't know that any real revolutionary starts out wanting that. It's what people want for you. And the only way you can defeat that kind of imposed demogogic status is by rejecting the people and the power they invest in you. Malcolm was one of the lucky ones. History swallowed him before he swallowed it."

"Ahh, the humanist response. Deep. Far as it goes. But if you want to know the real deal, I think X was swallowed by the world of the assassins."

"The what?"

"The world of the assassins. The world he renounced after his trip to Mecca and after he renounced the Nation of Islam. Anywhere you have a politicized secret society you're going to draw the secret order of the assassins. They're a guild that's been around since about the eleventh century. For more on this than I got time for here I suggest you check out Ishmael Reed, Thomas Pynchon, and Robert Anton Wilson. I think X became a target when he threatened to come out of the cultish darkness of Islamic separatism and into the light of pantheistic humanism. The assassins thrive wherever humans dispute over difference, borders, territories, or identity—anywhere difference becomes politicized, the assassins have got a stake and probably a hand in it. They killed JFK and RFK when they threatened to bridge differences between nations. And they did it to Martin when he threatened the Vietnam project as well as their program of American economic apartheid. They could have killed Castro but they realized his presence provided the 'logic' that kept state terror and the assassins' order alive and well in Latin America.

"The assassins uphold no ideology, no. The assassins live only for chaos, disunion, and the perfectability of the art of the political murder. To perpetuate themselves they have to practice their craft. Anyone with political power who renounces them in pursuit of dissolving human difference is dangerous. The assassins want to keep us in that Tower of Babel state. That's why they had to take out Coltrane, Redding, Hendrix, Marley, and X, and neutralize Clinton and Sly. That's why you see cats likes Chuck D and KRS-One only flirt with humanism but not really embrace it. They know that the assassins are on the nether side of bringing folk together, with a vengeance. When you can convince folks they don't need ignorance, hatred, and fear or the ism-schisms to survive, you've effectively cut the heads off the assassins and tossed their mangy torsos into the streets to be mulled over and masticated by the dogs in the clear light of day. Malcolm was on the way to taking them out of the darkness and into the light like every other progressive prophet who ever came down the pike, and that's why 'history' swallowed him. Dig?"

"Dig? Niggapleeze. If you don't get out my face with that warmed-over Illuminati Tragedy-Mumbo-Jumbo Rainbow Coalition bushwah— I still say we don't need another hero."

"And I say you still don't get it. It's not about us. It's about an ancient conflict over how the soul of the world should turn."

"No, it's about the souls of men and how easily they turn to violence when they can't control the earth, nature, or women. If any of these prophets you speak of were truly progressive, they'd realize the only way your assassins could be assassinated will be when the planet is ruled by the cult of woman, which is the cult of the earth. But men are too into keeping up the body count because all they can bring into existence on the planet without bowing down to the feminine principle is murder."

"I ain't even steppin' up into that nonsense. Baby, I'm 5000."

"5000? Not even that high. More like 33 and a third."

Clarence X, Man of
the People

PATRICIA J. WILLIAMS

As a child of the Civil Rights movement, I find it amazing to wake up and find that a black neoconservative Supreme Court justice named Clarence Thomas has suddenly become the symbolic guardian of racial justice in America. And as if that weren't amazement enough, it turns out that Clarence Thomas's erstwhile hero is, was, or has been none other than Malcolm X.

It took me a long time to sort out what on earth was going on when the newspapers reported that Malcolm X was one of Clarence Thomas's role models. I just didn't get it: Malcolm, man of the people, outspoken firebrand of his day, religious fundamentalist, and radical black nationalist? And Clarence?! Lonely disdainer of the group-no-matter-what-group, not outspoken about much of anything he wasn't later willing to disclaim, confused theologian in the church of an undefined, mushy breed of so-called natural law.

A friend of mine tried to reconcile it all for me by saying "Oh, it's not about politics—it's a male thing. You wouldn't understand." (Maybe. But the sentiment was at least one I could place. When asked to explain why he delivered the eulogy at Malcolm X's funeral, for example, actor Ossie Davis told a reporter: ". . . you always left his presence with the sneaky suspicion that maybe, after all, you were a man! . . . However much I disagreed with him, I never doubted that Malcolm X, even when he was wrong, was always that rarest thing in the world among us Negroes: a true man" (*Autobiography*, 458–459).

Then another friend said, "Malcolm represented manhood. It's as simple as that." (This, of course, is literally how Ossie Davis characterized Malcolm X in the eulogy itself: "Malcolm was our manhood, our living black manhood! This was his meaning to his people. And, in honoring him, we honor the best in ourselves" (*Autobiography*, 454).

And then, just to make sure things stayed complicated, yet a third friend observed, "Malcolm wasn't just a role model; he's become the ultimate pornographic object." Against the backdrop of rumored affidavits that Clarence Thomas had a penchant for the pornographic, I found this last particularly provocative; so I went to the library and started reading and thinking about pornography in this larger sense, in the beyond-role-model sense, as part of a scheme of thought that has no necessary connection to sex.

I started to think about pornography as the habit of thinking that it is a relation of dominance and submission. A habit of thinking that permits the imagination of the voyeur to indulge in autosensation that obliterates the subjectivity of the observed. A habit of thinking that allows that self-generated sensation to substitute for interaction with a whole other human being, to substitute for listening or conversing or caring. In which the object becomes passified, a malleable object upon which to project. In which the object becomes interchangeable with the will of the voyeur, in which the insatiable lust of Wanda the Wench is representational of the insatiable lust of all women. In which Wanda the Wench may profess deepest delight in the unspeakable pain of having unspeakable acts of violence enacted upon her, because she "delights" "in being a real woman" and real women are defined as the sum of their body parts, bared, open, and eternally available for use and abuse. In which Wanda says she would never want to be a feminist because they don't believe in having fun and they emasculate men and besides women should be free to experience the joys of a little bondage.

And from this thinking I began to extrapolate, hypothesize, do a little imagining of my own: Here we have Clarence Thomas, man of the moment, whose biggest appeal is that he will stand in and speak for all black people while speaking exclusively about himself. Not that he will represent their interests, but that he will represent their image. He will be a role model, but more in the sense of a runway model than of a modeler of actions, or a propounder of ideas; as a Supreme Court justice, he would be seen but not heard. Clarence Thomas says he loves the good old days when a little oppression was good for the soul and brought black people together and taught them the true meaning of community; Clarence Thomas hangs a Confederate flag in his office and says it makes him think of home. Affirmative action just emasculates him, and besides blacks should be free to experience the self-help joys of a little bondage.

I can't help wondering what Wanda and Malcolm would have to say about all this, if she weren't bleeding and he weren't dead.

Recently I have begun to appreciate why there is so much controversy about Spike Lee's film of Malcolm X's life. As Alex Haley recounts, "After signing the contract for [the autobiography], Malcolm X looked at me hard. 'A writer is what I want, not an interpreter.' I tried to be a dispassionate chronicler. But he was the most electric personality I have ever met, and I still can't quite conceive him dead. It still feels to me as if he has just gone into some next chapter, to be written by historians" (*Autobiography*, 456). So perhaps it doesn't really matter who would do such a movie: The effrontery is the transition from literary imagination to the filmic, the iconographic.

And with that shift of perception, I begin to see the extent to which a whole generation of us have grown up pretenders to the Malcolm legacy; I see it in the faces of my friends; I hear it in the inflections of our voices. I see it in myself: iconette-in-the-making, dedicatedly pursuing the path of liberatory potential. Who knows if Malcolm would have approved. But that's the beauty of it all, the achingly postmodern transformativity of the singular imagination, floating somewhere in the misty blue angst of annibus domini 1980 to 2001. Who knows, who cares. And if the complexity that was Malcolm X survives this moment as only a T-shirt or a trademark, then it is no wonder that Clarence Thomas has emerged as the perfect co-optive successor—an heir-transparent, a product with real producers; the new improved apparition of Malcolm, the cleaned-up version of what he could have been with a good strong grandfather figure to set him right. Clarence X gone good.

Clarence Thomas is to Malcolm X what "Unforgettable. The perfume. By Revlon" is to Nat King Cole. A sea change of intriguing dimension, like when Eldridge Cleaver came back from Algeria preaching the good news of free enterprise and started marketing trousers with codpieces and barbecue sauce. Or when Ray Charles proclaimed that, while he sang "America the Beautiful" at the 1988

Republican National Convention, he would have done it for the Democrats "if they had paid me some money. I'm just telling the truth."[1]

Symbolic complication was a feature of Clarence Thomas's entire
nomination process, right down to the "symbolic" swearing-in cere-
mony on the White House lawn, which turned out to be an entirely
different event from the "real" swearing in—so that even the oath-
taking to uphold the Constitution broadcast to Us the People was a
reenactment for prime-time consumption. Many blacks supported him
because his success was a symbol of those heights to which a black man
could aspire. His strong-but-simple, rags-to-riches stories symbolized
triumph over adversity, knowledge over darkness, industry over idle-
ness. His powerful mythology, helpfully concocted by some of the very
same public relations people who designed Ronald Reagan's, George
Bush's, and Jesse Helms's campaigns, presented Thomas as the product of a land where dreams come true, where odds are always overcome, where workers whistle (even at the risk of a few sour *feminists*
misunderstanding the bright innocence of it all), and where the rainbow
is enuf. Clarence Thomas looked like Horatio Alger, Miss Jane Pitt-
man, and Colin Powell all wrapped into one.

If, as some assert, in sexual pornography men act and women
appear, and if, in racial pornography white people act and black
people appear, a classic moment in the political pornography of the
Malcolmized moment is exemplified by when President Bush invited
the Black Caucus, who represent many millions of black and white
voters, on up to the White House to sit and chat about their concerns for
a while. As it turned out, of course, the whole event was a magnificently
choreographed photo opportunity, the entire point of which were the
images—stills of Bush *looking* as if he were listening, disseminated
to the media all over America. Similarly, the entire arrangement of
witnesses in the confirmation process—four witnesses for, four witnesses against—replicated a kind of "he said–she said" setup if there
ever was one, belied the extent to which the witnesses represented
complex and vastly differing constituencies, and disguised completely
the extent to which the witness who represented the NAACP also
represented a membership of thousands upon thousands yet was made
the imagistic equivalent of the witness who represented the relatively
minuscule membership of the black bailiff's association of Southern
California.

There has been a lot written about role models and the black
community. Some of it undoubtedly is a good thing. I am a firm

believer that there is great power in seeing ourselves in others, likable, respectable, and socially desirable, in the world. But models are not enough, and I am increasingly concerned that *all* we are left with is "players" in "roles" rather than substantive, interactive beings—people as labels rather than complexly situated bundles of fluid allegiances.

During the Gulf War, a black friend of mine expressed her unswerving pride and support of General Colin Powell: "Black people can sleep better knowing that a black man has his finger on the button." (Actually I've been losing a lot of sleep lately. In my dreams, I am toiling endlessly in a world where hard labor is supposed to be eternally ennobling rather than ever degrading or even just exhausting, where ignorance is glorified, where creativity is vilified as mental disobedience and cruelty rationalized as preemptive necessity. In *my* dreams, there's just a big button, with this disembodied finger on it.)

I worry about this tendency to indulge in figureheading our ideals. I think that the habit of imbuing humans with ideal or essential traits is a formula for either dashed ideals or corruption of them. It is a formula as well for cynicism on the one hand or intolerance on the other. It prevents us from engagement with the shortcomings of idols; it requires that our public figures be monolithic—saints or sinners. It is no wonder we end up with a lot of liars in public office. Malcolm was both saint and sinner and, in his insistence to just *be*, paid dearly. No one knew better than he how complicated is heroism; how much the product of good acts and bad, of bravery, craft, dumb luck, and brilliant insight—all mixed up in serendipitous proportion. If Malcolm had conformed himself to the politically pornographic imagination of his generation's fixed ideals—even just a little—he would no doubt be alive today, hosting a talk show, lunching with Clarence. But Malcolm never was one for mannered acquiescence.

The substitution of role models for complete understanding of the political implications of certain philosophical doctrines results in the privatization of the political and shifts focus from the implications of philosophy to the personalities of its proponents. It also makes those proponents *very* authoritative. It cedes to them enormous and total power over the consequences of "their" theories, as if theory had no life beyond birth, no interpretive generative property as taken up and reiterated by others. As if the life of the mind were physical, rigid, bounded as the body—as if you could pick an idea up and lay it down, this concrete, static, three-dimensional club of an idea spat forth like law upon the earth. As if the idea might die like the man.

Given all that, it is simultaneously true that the ideals embodied in the role modeling, like laws themselves, are frequently a way of presenting, and are premised on, certain kinds of statistical probabilities. Thus, when Clarence Thomas's image as a black man was advanced as a reason why he should be on the Supreme Court, black people frequently used it to mean that the experience of being black increases the likelihood of being sympathetic to the advancement of particularly situated collective agendas. So it was that many people asked with disarming credulousness of the Thomas situation: How could a once-poor black man turn on his people? (One heard the same sorts of veiled statistical wistfulness at the other end of the political spectrum: Tom Metzger, founder of the White Aryan Resistance, said of his support of David Duke, "I think David Duke will make a great politician, because politicians make themselves acceptable to a majority of people."[2])

What has not sufficiently captured the public imagination about all this, however, is the degree to which we live in a moment in which political ad agencies have perfected the art of exploiting symbolic properties while severing them from the statistical likelihoods that gave rise to them. Thus Clarence Thomas could simultaneously exploit his roots as a poor black man, while denying that the poverty and material degradation in which millions of other poor blacks live is anything more than a state of mind. And thus, Virginia Lamp Thomas, of all people, could, in the pages of *People* magazine, of all places, exploit the status of rape victim by dressing herself in the language of "survivor"—as a way of denying another woman's allegations of sexual harassment.[3] (This entire article in *People* is a fascinating study in the metaphors of embattlement, and weirdly evocative of Malcolm X's stories. Compare, for example:

Malcolm X:

. . . It was Allah's intent for me to help Cassius prove Islam's superiority before the world—through proving that mind can win over brawn. I don't have to remind you how people everywhere scoffed at Cassius Clay's chances of beating Liston.

This time, I brought from New York with me some photographs of Floyd Patterson and Sonny Liston in their fight camps, with white priests as their "spiritual advisors." Cassius Clay, being a Muslim, didn't need to be told how white Christianity had dealt with the American black man. "This fight is the *truth*," I told Cassius. "It's the Cross and the Crescent fighting in a prize ring—for the first time. It's a modern Crusades—a Christian and a Muslim facing each other with television to beam it off Telstar for the whole world to see what happens!" I told Cassius, "Do you think Allah has brought about all this intending for you to leave the ring as anything but the champion?" (*Autobiography*, 306–307)

. . . and Virginia Lamp Thomas:

Clarence knew the next round of hearings to begin that day was not the normal political battle. It was spiritual warfare. Good versus evil. We were fighting something we didn't understand, and we needed prayerful people in our lives. We needed God.

So the next morning, Wednesday, we started having these two couples in our home to pray for two or three hours every day. They brought over prayer tapes, and we would read parts of the Bible. We held hands and prayed. What got us through the next six days was God. We shut the kitchen blinds and turned on Christian praise music to survive the worst days. . . .

Later, after two hours sleep, we walked into the hearing room, and people were lining the hallways, urging him on. "Who are these people?" Clarence asked me, and I said, "I think they are angels."[4]

These calculated disjunctures, rhetorical rearrangements, and surgical revisionism have resulted in such strange symbolic cyborgs that I sometimes think the President could appoint a practicing Nazi to the Supreme Court, as long as he could find the right packaging—a black Hispanic lesbian one, say, in a wheelchair. (This is, of course, exactly what the voters of Louisiana too nearly did, in their rush to endorse the boyish good looks and the political plastic surgery of the "new" David Duke's new words. "When David Duke entered a hotel ballroom here today, JoAnn Jernigan, a retired nurse and lifelong Democrat, jumped to her feet and applauded. . . . 'I've got to see my candidate,' she said of Mr. Duke, the Republican candidate for governor and former grand wizard of the Ku Klux Klan. 'He's so cute. How can someone who looks like that be bad?' "[5] And it is what David Duke himself did when, "under the pseudonym 'Mohammed X,' he wrote 'African Atto,' a martial arts manual for black militants. He later said it was a way to develop a mailing list to keep track of potential black agitators. Under the pseudonym 'Dorothy Vanderbilt,' he wrote 'Finderskeepers,' a dating-and-sex manual for women."[6] This is, after all, pornography's great power: to disguise, to dehistoricize, to decontextualize, to isolate.

Against this backdrop, it seems weirdly fitting that one of the most distinguishing features of Clarence Thomas's judicial philosophy is his wholesale rejection of statistics and other social science data, and with it the dismissal of a range of affirmative action remedies that have been central to blacks' social and economic progress over the last thirty years or so. For all of his quite moving anecdotalizing about his own history, Thomas by this gesture effectively supplants a larger common history with individualized hypotheses about free choice, in which each self chooses her destiny even if it is destitution. Clarence Thomas has not clearly committed himself to taking into account past and present social constraints as realistic infringements on the ability to exercise choice. He ignores that history which gives at least as much weight to the possibility that certain minority groups have not had many chances to be in charge of things as to the possibility that they just don't want to, or that they just can't.

While self-help and strong personal values are marvelous virtues, they are no stand-in for the zealous protection of civil and human rights—that protection being the paramount task of the judiciary in any democracy, and of the Supreme Court in greatest particular. The problem with Clarence Thomas's espousal of these self-help values is that he positions them in direct "either/or" tension with any other value; self-help is presented as bitterly competitive rather than in complete concert with those social measures that would help ever more rather than ever fewer people. Thus while some commentators have observed that Clarence Thomas and Malcolm X share a common thread of black nationalism, Clarence Thomas has added a peculiarly stultifying, nullifying twist—that of simultaneously individualizing nationalism and nationalizing individualism.

Thomas's insistence on a hyperindividualistic case-by-case analytic in race and gender cases, for example, is itself nothing more than another way of insisting on a very high statistical probability, by narrowing the range of reference and narrowing the number of parties at issue. The difficulty with that, of course, is that the evidence is narrowed from probabilities in the population at large to the credibility of sometimes a single witness. It does not deal with the unconscious or unexpressed probabalistic presumptions that judges as well as juries bring to the calculation of credibility itself. Blacks are "more likely" to be criminals, for example: Hispanics "probably" steal cars; and women are "undoubtedly hysterics."

Evidence of disparate impact in a larger population is one very effective way of countering such free-floating presumptions or prejudices.[7] Imagine, for example, how powerful it would have been if (*hypothetically*) there had been evidence that 99 percent of the female Yale Law School graduates who worked at the EEOC during Thomas's tenure never advanced beyond the lowest G-level ranking, while (still hypothetically) John Doggett and 99 percent of the rest of the male Yalies sailed to the top within two years. Yet this disparate impact evidence is precisely the sort of stuff that Thomas's judicial philosophy *excludes*—thus, in a very real and ironic way, making sure that the vast majority of race- and gender-discrimination complaints rarely get past the "he said-she said" stage, unless there is a posse of independent, ironclad, preferably hostile, Alan Simpson–like witnesses on hand. It amounts to the kind of credibility test it took finally to wake the country up to the mere possibility of racially motivated police-citizen violence: the amateur videotape of the brutal beating of Rodney King in Los Angeles. It is an insistence that amounts to having been there, video being a kind of mechanical or substitute eye, the insistent voyeur that must be satisfied before racial disbelief is overcome.

(And not even then. The eye for an eye, video for a video media analyses of the Reginald Denny beating as counterpart to the beating of Rodney King became a wierd echo of the "he said–she said" configuration that so successfully dead-ended the Clarence Thomas–Anita Hill confrontation.)

Against this, consider the utter disarray of any data about Clarence Thomas's judicial philosophy—the complete, calculated lack of a basis upon which to form an opinion or fashion a likelihood about what Thomas would do on the Supreme Court. (And contrary to the many careless aspersions about how "politicized" the hearings became, it must be kept in mind that the Constitution expressly makes the senatorial process of inquiry a political one. The Constitution specifies that no nominee shall be confirmed without the "advice and consent" of the Senate.) If the Senate is confronted with a tabula rasa—or even a tabula-not-so clara, a "mystery," as some of the senators openly acknowledged—then there is little basis for either knowledgeable advice or informed consent. And this is a severe threat to the functioning of our tripartite system of government, to the balance of political input that the involvement of the several branches of government must provide before someone is placed into that most sensitive position of discretionary insularity, that shielded office of highest trust that is the Supreme Court.

Nevertheless, in the face of this senatorial duty to inform itself about a judicial candidate's philosophy, there was a deeply disconcerting pattern of Judge Thomas either revising or disclaiming much of the most troubling aspects of his record over the past decade. If one believed this epiphanous recanting, we were left with the disturbing phenomenon of a Supreme Court nominee who didn't read his own citations, who misunderstood the legal import of his own obstructionist administrative actions, and who didn't really mean most of what he said—a disdain for accountability made even more alarming in its implications by the degree to which it was being echoed in the CIA director's hearings just down the hall: "In explanation of his flagging memory, Robert Gates recently told the Senate confirmation committee, 'I have to admit to you that when I left the C.I.A. in 1989 . . . I did a major data dump.' "[8]

And if one is not inclined to believe that Clarence Thomas's keen intelligence could leave him in quite so disingenuous a state of disarray, then we the people must come to terms with the fact that we were confronted with an outright, practiced refusal to answer questions. This, again, is a tremendously serious violation of the Senate's right to answers about any nominee's views and disposition to uphold precedent as well as judge facts and interpret new law. The Senate has a constitutional *duty* to ensure that the Court remains a place where voices of dissent and unpopular causes may be heard. Ambiguity is not the standard. A senatorial leap of faith, as the Philadelphia *Enquirer* urged in an editorial, should not have been good enough. Much of the vocabulary that even some senators have employed during the course of the hearings—"impression," "faith," "instinct," "hope," and "trust"—simply did not amount to a reasoned "choice" to support Clarence Thomas.

(But the truth was, I suppose, that through all the masquerade, there really was lots of evidence about what Clarence Thomas was likely to do on the Supreme Court, just none that anyone ever talked about straightforwardly or sustainedly. We were left instead with the ghostly, enigmatic trace of Senator Thurmond's smile.)

* * *

"There but for the grace of God, go I," said Clarence Thomas of the prisoners he saw being shuttled back and forth from the District Courthouse in Washington, D.C. These words were uttered during his confirmation hearings, an attempt to reassure senators of his compassion, which was in question. Barely four months later, from his post on the Supreme Court, Thomas wrote, in a dissenting opinion, that a prisoner who was beaten, bloodied, and had had his teeth loosened by prison guards should have no constitutional claim under the Eighth Amendment proscription against cruel and unusual punishment, even where the violence was undue, wanton and excessive.[9] It's not a constitutional issue, in the world according to Clarence, until they *have* to go to the hospital.[10]

Malcolm X once said: "It didn't take me a week to learn that all you had to do was give white people a show and they'd buy anything you offered them. It was like popping your shoeshine rag. The dining car waiters and Pullman porters knew it too, and they faked their Uncle Tomming to get bigger tips. We were in that world of Negroes who are both servants and psychologists" (*Autobiography*, 75).

(I wonder from the sidelines: If, again, in sexual pornography men act and women appear, and if in racial pornography white people act and black people appear, then what happens in the intersectional politics of race and gender, when a black woman suffers sexual abuse at the hand of a black man, against the gladiatorial backdrop of a white theater? In order to win, will he have to act as an aggressive racial observer [or "play the race card"]? Will he have to appear the sexual victim, malleable and open and available [or "lynched," castrated, skewered]? In order for her to win, will she, paradoxically, have had to appear sexually assertive? And act racially passive? Or vice versa? Would any matrix of asserted attributes work in her case, or would she always just disappear? Is the double-binded double burden of the intersectionality of her race and her gender simply too great a confluence of appearances for her to ever successfully transgress into the role of actor? [As opposed to that sly counterfeit, the "mere actress."] What arrangement of ingredients from the archetypal stewpot would allow her interpretive apotheosis into the cult of true womanhood?)

* * *

In today's world, discrimination and the deprivation of cherished civil liberties have taken new forms, unforms, and wordlessness that our labor and civil rights laws are hard-pressed if not outright refusing to recognize. One reason, of course, is a sociopolitical climate in which both formal and informal burdens of proof make it harder and harder to have anything recognized as discrimination. Another is a kind of calculated confusion and rhetorical gaming, of which the spectacle of Clarence Thomas's hearing was exemplary, that clouds all discussion of the rights of minorities and women in the U.S., and of Thomas himself. A friend of mine writes, "Thomas invokes a mythical image of Malcolm X to serve his own needs. . . . Thomas's use of X is the theft of a religious icon from a people whose religious and spiritual [ties come not from triptychs or cathedrals, but] memories. . . . In short, Thomas is a thief in the temple."[11] And in that move, Malcolm X has become a signifier of the female, a space for subjugation, a debased emptiness, a loss for which there is no voice.

In today's world, this repeated emptying of all of our cultural coffers, of all of our sources of both self and unity, has left us much the poorer. It has left us with an atmosphere in which public relations firms, like mean-spirited astrologers, dictate presidential politics, and TV call-in polls divine the course of governance. In which David Duke's plastic surgery is a metaphor for the cosmetizing of Nazi policies made mainstream. In which if calling a black person nigger is bad, then calling a white person racist must be Exactly the Same Thing Only Twice As Bad. In which sexual harassment is shrugged off as a hopeless morass of impossible children playing that annoying little game of "he said–she said," so better for the parents to just never get involved. In which parties in relationships of political trust are replaced by game-show contestants for verisimilitude. In which reality is a stranger category than fantasy. In which reality is just a high-priced form of fantasy. In which marketing trends are the new-age demonstration of democracy-in-action. In which there is justice for sale and media moments for all.

NOTES

1. Interview on *The Today Show*, November 7, 1991.

2. Peter Applebome, "Duke: The Ex-Nazi Who Would Be Governor," *New York Times*, November 10, 1991, A17.

3. Virginia Lamp Thomas, "Breaking Silence," *People*, November 11, 1991, 111.

4. Ibid., 111, 112. Excerpt is reprinted by permission of *People*.

5. Don Terry, "In Louisiana, Duke Divides Old Loyalties," *New York Times*, October 31, 1991, 1.

6. Applebome, "Duke," A17.

7. The phrase "disparate impact" implies a legal presumption, perhaps most famously confronted in the 1971 case of *Griggs v. Duke Power Company*. There, the Court held statistical disparities between the numbers of black applicants available and the numbers of blacks hired to be admissible evidence of the necessity for affirmative action.

8. "Speeches," *The New Yorker*, November 4, 1991, 35.

9. *Hudson v. McMillian*, 112 S. Ct. 995, L. Ed. 2d 156, 60 U.S.L.W. 4151.

10. In a majority opinion joined in or concurred with by everyone else on the court but Scalia, Sandra Day O'Connor chided Thomas's use of this "substantial injury" test, pointing out that if the cutoff for constitutional claims is whether someone requires medical attention, this literally sanctions forms of torture that stop just short of leaving marks on the body.

11. Margaret Fernandez, letter to the author, February 25, 1992.

The Allure of Malcolm X
and the Changing Character
of Black Politics

≡

ADOLPH REED, JR.

t is difficult to recall precisely when I first became aware of Malcolm X, but I was fourteen or fifteen, which would make it either 1961 or 1962. I was in the midst of negotiating adolescence in the lifeworld of a black New Orleans bounded by the regime of racial segregation, a boundary no doubt made all the more palpable by increasing contestation. Jim Crow had been eliminated on public transportation only a year or so before I started high school, so I had fresh memories of learning the ritual of making certain to sit behind—or to place on top of the seat in front of me—a movable "For Colored Patrons Only" sign. By adolescence, when I would have had to depend on my mastery of the ritual, the signs were gone. Holes for the signs remained on the seat tops, as did the unofficially enforced residues of segregation's racial etiquette, to remind of what had changed and what had not.

My freshman year in high school began shortly after the highly publicized lynching of Mack Charles Parker in nearby Mississippi, where only four years earlier Emmett Till's murder had received even more attention. Adults made sure we knew of those horrible crimes and thus, among other things, of the dangers surrounding being in the presence of white women. The Greensboro sit-in occurred in February of that school year, and SNCC was founded soon thereafter. At the same time, our civics teacher declaimed throughout the year on the splendor and superiority of the American way of life. Then, preparing us for a field trip, she reminded us of the imperative to use only Jim Crow facilities. (She could not imagine us overtly challenging the racial order; she feared only that some of our number might "pass.") She saw—or would admit—no contradiction. We were generally cognizant of these events, but only in the muted and diffuse way that adolescents experience the world outside teenage concerns. Mrs. Avery's admonition alone brought the segregated order to our shared consciousness, and provoked an inarticulate discomfiture.

Public school desegregation, however, began in my sophomore year, and the sociopolitical forces that channeled and constrained our adolescent pursuits erupted into everyday consciousness. (One of the selected elementary schools—named after Judah P. Benjamin, the Jewish Confederate official—was around the corner from my house, so I had to walk past barricades, police and their dogs to get to my bus every morning. I also watched my neighborhood turn in a few months from evenly mixed by New Orleans standards—alternate blocks or half blocks, different sides of the same street—to very nearly all black.) Whites rioted endlessly and spewed venom all over the city. Our principal kept us in school an hour late to protect us and to keep us from fighting the marauding bands of white boys who roamed Canal Street—the center of the city—attacking black people. I recall the anger and frustration my friends and I felt at being kept in. We wanted, if only in the abstract, to go fight back.

The school crisis waxed and waned as an intrusion into our mundane lives. Toward the end of the year it was joined first by the Bay of Pigs invasion, which stood out because of the city's economic and cultural inflection toward the Caribbean Basin, and then the Freedom Rides. New Orleans was the Freedom Riders' ultimate destination, and their bloody journey received enough news coverage to penetrate the parochial universe of youth.

By my junior year the direct action phase of the Civil Rights movement was in full swing. SNCC organizers were in the city, and the local NAACP youth group was recruiting pickets to demonstrate in front of stores on Canal Street, near my transfer point for the bus home. Both live and on television we regularly saw people—among them slightly older, more precocious members of our social world—being attacked and dragged roughly off to jail, singing and passively resisting all the while. We were awed by the demonstrators. As urban, adolescent males, all engaged in swaggering vaguely toward adulthood, we thought them crazy to take what they did, admired them, and were quietly enraged and humiliated by the treatment they received. Meek acceptance of being beaten and limply carted off carried, in our view, a taint of cowardice, no matter how modified. And the gleeful taunts and physical abuse from white bystanders seemed to reinforce that opinion, even while stoking our empathy with the demonstrators and hatred for their victimizers. (I do not remember any particular surge of animus toward the police in this regard. I suspect the reason is that their behavior was consistent with our normal experience of them. The police existed in our lives only as the embodiment of an absolute, hostile, and arbitrary authority, and they cultivated that role. The hypocrisy emblazoned on the Parish court house—"The Impartial Administration of Justice Is the Foundation of Liberty"—was transparent even to distracted teens.)

This was the context in which I learned of Malcolm X, some time between the Bay of Pigs invasion and the Cuban Missile Crisis, when many of us fretted that nuclear war was imminent. I think the first reference was on television news, in a story raising the specter of dangerous "Black Muslims" and "black separatists." I recall my father remarking favorably, albeit with reservations, about Malcolm's criticisms of the Civil Rights establishment, the Kennedy administration, imperialism, and the pervasiveness of white supremacist ideology. I saw and heard more of Malcolm later, especially during the period between John Kennedy's assassination and his own. By 1968, like so many others in my cohort, I had been swept up into the movement and was looking for an organizational affiliation. The Socialist Workers Party attracted me, a few months prior to the King assassination, in part because the SWP actively sought to identify itself with Malcolm, promising to bridge Marxism and the Black Power sensibility that seemed to be his legacy.

My purpose in taking this excursus into personal reflection is not to embrace the vogue of establishing authorial "positionality," which, I confess, most often strikes me as self-indulgent posturing. Rather, I draw on my own experience as part of a concern to situate Malcolm— and particularly the iconic appeal of the image of Malcolm—in historical context.

I realize that my circumstances were in meaningful ways idiosyncratic. Some of the events I have noted were, largely for familial reasons, more prominent in my consciousness than they probably were for many others in my age-set, even in the same social circle. Also, familial environment and networks predisposed me to range toward the most politically attentive end of my high school cohort. The narrative I have presented, however, centers on phenomena that my peers generally noted in some degree—the large happenings that we discussed in current events classes and, occasionally at least, in informal conversations among ourselves, that we confronted conspicuously in our daily life—and our most broadly consensual reactions to them. I believe that it is fair to assume, therefore, that these occurrences and reactions typically formed part of the experiential backdrop of black, particularly male, urban youth in the early to middle 1960s. Outside the South, I suspect, the specific campaigns and symbols of the Civil Rights movement were likely to blend into a more remote, homogenized blur of things going on "down there," and some of them certainly were uniquely resonant in New Orleans. Nevertheless, they all are representative of the stream of events and dispositions in which young black (again, particularly male and urban) people at that time found the raw material for fashioning political consciousness, and thus for assigning significance to Malcolm X.

The clock, moreover, hardly stopped in 1962. Malcolm became much more visible beyond the ranks of the political cognoscenti later, after the 1963 March on Washington, the Birmingham church bombing, and the Kennedy assassination. In fact, he was most visible after he broke with Elijah Muhammad and the Nation of Islam. That was a period marked by the Harlem Uprising, Freedom Summer, and the murder of Schwerner, Goodman, and Chaney, the sellout of the Mississippi Freedom Democratic Party at the Democratic National Convention, passage of the 1964 Civil Rights law that finally outlawed segregation in public accommodations, and proclamation of the War on Poverty. Malcolm himself was killed just before the crest of the brutal struggle in Selma, Alabama, that resulted in passage of the 1965 Voting Rights Act.

Rehearsing this background helps to recall that both Malcolm and the construction of his image exist within specific circumstances in concrete history. That perspective is important for making sense of the recent "rediscovery" (though insofar as it is a generational matter, "discovery" is probably nearer the mark) that a colleague has dubbed Malcolmania. It is first of all a reminder that the time in which Malcolm lived and the issues and problems that defined him as a public figure differ sharply from those confronting black Americans today. Keeping that distinction in mind, moreover, suggests that getting at the sources of Malcolm's current popularity requires examination of the ways in which politics among black Americans has altered since his death. Only then can we form an idea of what young people are responding to and doing now in identifying with him.

The main difference separating the two generations' attraction to Malcolm is that the Malcolm to whom my generation was drawn was alive. That difference is so obvious that its significance can easily be overlooked. However, the Malcolm X who engaged us was moving inside the history that we were living. He responded to it, tried to understand and describe it, to shape its course. He was, as an image, a hologram produced by the same forces that made our immediate reality. In fact, Malcolm's appeal grew largely from the way that he counterpunched in very concrete terms against the changing elements of that reality—for example, in his responses to the Birmingham church bombing, the sanctimony surrounding the Kennedys, the Civil Rights movement's strategic reliance on the stereotype of the patient-suffering-slow-to-anger Negro. Malcolm emboldened us, or those of us whom he did, because he was an interlocutor with current orthodoxy, expressing forbidden black silences of our time; he energized us by playing the dozens on the official narratives of race and power under which we strained.

Only a dead Malcolm X is available to young people today. He was killed five years before the birth of the typical member of the 1992 college graduating class. More important, though, is another sense in which their Malcolm is dead. He has no dynamic connection to the lived reality of the youth who invoke him. He is grafted onto their world of experience as a frozen icon to be revered, a reification of other people's memories. This Malcolm X does not encourage by providing a running critique of the prevalent narrative of oppression as it evolves. His voice is like that of a biblical figure or a computerized toy: a set of prepackaged utterances that can be accessed arbitrarily and that seem more or less pertinent depending on listeners' interpretive will. To that extent today's Malcolm is marked for and by objectification.

That is the deeper truth beneath complaints about the penumbra of commodification surrounding Malcolm's new popularity. Malcolm's reduction to a logo on a baseball cap only reflects his prior reduction to a soothing object of contemplation, a talismanic image. Yes, it is ironic that Malcolm—whose appeal in life was linked in so many ways to being militantly *un*fashionable—has become a fashion statement. Those with older recollections of him understandably bristle at seeing

Malcolm lined up alongside Black Bart Simpson in the urban trinketry outposts of the mass consumer market. That phenomenon, however, is less the real problem than it is a symptom. Malcolm's incorporation into the logic of merchandising was enabled by his already having been turned into a transcendent symbol, which is, at bottom, a decontextualized, hollow *thing*. Purists' old codgerlike laments about bowdlerization of Malcolm thus not only miss the point; they are betrayed by their own self-righteousness. What is being bowdlerized is an already romanticized image, a hero larger than—and therefore outside of—life, an *object* of reverence.

Malcolm X is attractive to young people today in part because he was attractive to young people when he was alive. Those who are now drawn to Malcolm are therefore especially likely to take their elders' constructions of him and his significance as foundation for their own. What they have been given is a Malcolm X fabricated within an abstracted discourse of black "greatness," a discourse that lines up public figures like trading cards. (In this respect the Malcolm v. Martin cliché brings to mind debates in the late 1960s over whether it was Hank Aaron or Willie Mays who was the best baseball player of all time, or the one in the 1950s pitting Mays against the White Hope, Mickey Mantle.) This notion of greatness even undermines the injunction to "learn from" Malcolm, which is a commonly proposed alternative to purely commercialized identification with him. Nothing can be learned from a decontextualized icon except timeless wisdom. And timeless wisdom is worse than useless for making sense of social life inside real history. It inevitably boils down either to tag phrases and slogans or to allegorically driven platitudes. The former function only as rhetorical parsley, an authenticating garnish ("As Malcolm said," etc.) in the patter of those who parrot them; the latter—for example, "when Malcolm (was in prison, went to Mecca, broke with Elijah Muhammad) he learned that" et cetera—in addition replace thought and analysis with truisms and empty pieties. Both are ideally suited for inscription on buttons and T-shirts.

The current Malcolmania is not simply the product of clever marketing and merchandising. For many people, of course, the fad is just that, and the object could as easily be Black Bart or Michael Jordan. At the other end of the continuum are those who experience their embrace of the Malcolm imagery self-consciously as political behavior. Most probably fall some place in between, in the big region where existential statement, political statement, and fashion statement swirl together into a more or less emphatic, but generally inchoate, attitude. Especially in these dispiriting times, though, the temptation is to read more coherence, strategy, and critique into the phenomenon than are warranted. Among those of us desperate for signs of political mobilization, it is all too easy to believe that Malcolm's apparent popularity either reflects or may crystallize a rising tide of activism. This temptation persists despite the existence of clear precedent to the contrary.

In the late 1960s and early 1970s the proliferation of Black Power *chatchke* washed out the boundary between ideology and fad and exposed the inherent limitations of inferring outlook from either choices made among the artifacts of mass consumption culture or the vagaries of tonsorial and sartorial style. Anyone could cultivate an afro, listen to the Last Poets, wear a dashiki or red, black, and green button, and doing so was in no way a reliable indication of any concrete views concerning political, social, or economic life. Individuals who consumed Black Power paraphernalia typically may have understood themselves to be endorsing or asserting a pro-Black attitude through their choices. However, the symbols expressing that attitude—refracted as they were through the mass market's least common denominator—were so amorphous as to accommodate any sort of substantive belief or practice. As a popular recruiting slogan of the time put it, "You can be black and Navy too."

Black Power consumerism (as distinguished from Black Power ideology), however, developed in an environment defined by political activism; it was parasitic, therefore, on a rhetoric of black assertiveness that presumed the centrality of ideological programs and strategic agendas. To that extent, the consumerist construction of radical black identity was regularly criticized as superficial, an inadequate proxy for concerted political thought and action. Of course, the ideologies and strategies on whose behalf critics disparaged the equation of commodities and consciousness were usually themselves neither free from mystification nor pragmatically acute as radical politics. Nevertheless, the critics nearly all insisted that claims to serious commitment or sophisticated analysis be judged in relation to an objective of changing social conditions affecting black people. And that view entailed an orientation to strategic thinking that paid at least instrumental attention to the institutions and processes of public authority. That inflection was encouraged, of course, by material inducements generated through War on Poverty and Great Society programs (for example, Community Action or Model Cities funding) as well as the energy created around the rise of black public officialdom. The key fact remains, though, that radical black consciousness in the 1960s and 1970s was largely a discourse about and intersecting with public power—from protests against police behavior and displacement for urban renewal to demands for community control, welfare rights, and tenants' rights. Even Pan-Africanists and cultural nationalists, whose ideologies supported quietistic withdrawal from American politics, consistently sought to align themselves with black public officials (with the 1972 Gary Convention, the National Black Assembly, and 1970 Congress of African Peoples as the most prominent examples) and to mobilize around contesting the exercise of public authority in the black community.

My point is not to romanticize that period as a Golden Age of black radicalism. On the contrary, the forces critical of Black Power consumerism, despite their genuflections to the need for practical action and concrete program, tended less toward coherent critique than to the kind of self-righteous denunciations of impiety or impurity we now hear from codgers (and wannabe codgers) concerned to protect the sanctity of Malcolm's image. Nor were those forces ever dominant in Afro-American political or ideological life. Although the previous decade had been a time of fairly open-ended struggle for the hearts and minds of black America, by the middle of the 1970s radicalism had been generally marginalized. Primacy in articulating the discourse of black consciousness had been won by mainstream politicians, the centrist Civil Rights establishment, and the purveyors of sitcoms and blaxploitation films. (Watching children act out a perception of their authentic blackness derived from Jimmy "J.J." Walker on *Good Times*—"DY-NO-MIIITE!"—chastened at least some of us grappling with the slippery problem of crafting a critical politics tied to notions of cultural authenticity.)

Radicalism's defeat, moreover, resulted in part from internal tendencies. Because Black Power activism's sole critical category was race, radicals were generally unprepared to respond when the new, mainstream black political elite gained momentum in the late 1960s and began to consolidate a new kind of racially assertive but still accommodationist politics. The rising stratum of black officeholders and public managers advanced a model of racial empowerment defining incremental adjustment of the routine operations of institutions in their charge—for example, increasing minority personnel ratios, opening access to minority competitors for public contracting, fine-tuning mechanisms to reduce potential conflict arising in human service delivery, appointment of more black officials—and other forms of insider action as the only legitimate political goals. This definition drastically narrowed the horizon of political activity by denying the efficacy of all strategies geared to challenging entrenched policy priorities. The model also directly endorsed demobilization of the black citizenry by limiting the scope of legitimate participation to ratifying agendas set by elites; in this view voting on command becomes the standard of active participation, and simple acquiescence replaces engagement. A radical discourse that presumed uncomplicated uniformity of purpose in an organic "black community" was short-circuited by this outcome of the demand for community control; Black Power sensibility could neither anticipate nor effectively criticize the appearance of a cohort of (more or less decent and humane, more or less venal and reactionary—but all militantly race conscious) Bantustan administrators as a stratum-for-itself. This problem was only compounded by the main Civil Rights organizations' incorporation into public management processes. The Urban League, NAACP, Operation PUSH, and SCLC all found their way into public budgets and the inner circles of policy implementation and thereby legitimized accommodationist, insider politics as the proper legacy of protest activism. The new elite gained ground rapidly, aided by the greater access to material and ideological resources that insider status confers and the related capacity to promise, and deliver, immediate benefits. As that occurred, radicalism increasingly took refuge in ideological purification.

In this context, the turn to ideology over the decade after the 1966 proclamation of Black Power aimed not so much to make sense of what was going on politically as to avoid confronting it by constructing alternative narratives in which mundane politics was ephemeral. Those narratives—chiefly Kawaida nationalism, Pan-Africanism, and increasingly esoteric brands of axiomatic Marxism-Leninism—also were intended to define a black political agenda different from and more authentic than mainstream black accommodationism. They sought fundamentally, however, to preempt rather than to challenge the new political elite's vision. To that extent, the turn to ideology was an evasive maneuver, as even its form suggests.

The search for a guiding ideology usually began with disattending from the really existing situation to work out, in the abstract, an internally consistent cosmology, propagation of which then became the basis for attracting adherents. Ideology's relation to current practice was thus inevitably arcane and rested on a logic of imaginative rationalization that was vulnerable to the worst extremes of opportunism. After all, any specific action might be linked to one of the Seven Principles of the Nguzo Saba, might contribute to the millennial emancipation of Africa, might be historically correct for the appropriate stage of a class struggle that had no empirical referents. This notion of ideology was formulaic and, even in its allegedly Marxist variants, shared as much with religion as with politics. More significantly, in positing the "real" concerns—inculcation of a "black value system," liberation and unification of Africa, a resuscitated Comintern version of socialist revolution—to lie on a different plane from the agendas projected by elite politicians, radicals in effect conceded the latter's dominance by refusing to engage it head-on.

By the 1980s the mainstream elite was hegemonic in Afro-American politics and political discourse. Popular mobilization had dissipated; radical activism was a memory, and the ideological affiliations of the late 1960s and early '70s existed mainly as relics. Not even the growing threat of the Reagan/Bush assault on black Americans could rekindle an assertive, popular political movement. The earlier failure to formulate a critical response to the postsegregation era's mainstream accommodationism had culminated in an inability to develop an effective language or practice of political opposition. Indeed, as the hegemonic national political discourse has moved ever more in a conservative, victim-blaming direction, the black elite has moved along with it. We have seen the steady expansion of a rhetoric of special black middle-class responsibility for impoverished Afro-Americans, calls for moral rearmament, and complaints about pathology, social disorganization, and self-defeating behavior—all tied together by a quasi-nationalist insistence on "self-help." As in the society at large, this rhetoric is not merely the province of avowed conservatives. Black liberals, even leftists, and of course nationalists of all stripes have embraced this line even as it becomes the era's common sense.

Beginning in the 1980s also, the invention of a youth-centered hip-hop culture, whose iconic markers allegedly constitute an immanent form of social criticism, once again has blurred the lines between ideology and style, political action and consumer preference. This time the tendency to read critical consciousness into fashion and fad is even less restrained than a generation earlier. Certain features of the Reagan/Bush/hip-hop era combine particularly to obscure the faultiness of conflating political outlook and identification with a consumer taste community. On the one hand, the relatively low level of political mobilization among black Americans (and its corollary, absence of a dynamic political movement) has removed a pragmatic constraint on the ways people think and talk about alternative politics—at the same time that the official narratives have come to seem suffocatingly inadequate. On the other hand, the influence of a "cultural politics" discourse—an outgrowth of the structuralist and post-structuralist trends in radical social theorizing—denies the possibility of a problem in this regard by defining identification with a "taste community" as intrinsically political behavior, on an equal status with purposive contests over state action.

This is the context in which the rediscovery of Malcolm X has occurred. To be sure, much of the ubiquity of X trinkets can be attributed to the snowball effects of Spike Lee's marketing campaign. Lee's concerted efforts and talent as a hypester—fueled by and fueling his own iconic presence—no doubt explain much of the greater visibility this phenomenon has enjoyed in relation to the era's previous inner-city youth fads, for example, Africa medallions in the late eighties and coonskin or Confederate battle caps (so much for immanently revolutionary consciousness) a few years earlier. It is also probably easier to produce Malcolmania knockoffs; all that it takes is sticking X appliqués onto existing merchandise. Even when those factors are taken into account, though, a residuum of autonomous attraction to Malcolm's image almost certainly remains. And, in any case, the marketing blitz clearly has stimulated interest, which in turn has taken on a life of its own. So, the main questions persist: Why does the Malcolm image have so much resonance now? What can its popularity tell us about our situation? Is there any way to look to Malcolm X for practical commentary on the present?

Those questions stand out especially when we consider that all of the most significant tendencies in postsegregation era black politics matured after his death. Malcolm was killed nearly six months before the Watts uprising, nearly a year and a half before Willie Ricks and Stokely Carmichael introduced the Black Power slogan on the Meredith march in 1966, two years before Ron Karenga invented kwanzaa. Malcolm was dead more than two years before the election of the first black big-city mayor, more than a year before establishment of the

HUD Model Cities program that became a principal training ground for black urban managers. (And died months before the first major escalation of the war in Vietnam, almost three years before the Tet offensive.)

By the time Black Power consumerism took hold, Malcolm had been dead for long enough to have been turned into a beatific symbol invoked as an emblem of righteousness rather than as a guide to action. "Niggers loved to hear Malcolm rap, but they didn't love Malcolm," declaimed the ever-didactic Last Poets in "Niggers Are Scared of Revolution." In fact, during the 1970s Malcolm was already being rediscovered in fabulous terms, as the *Autobiography* became a frequently assigned text—characteristically as a *Bildungsroman*—in college and high school black studies courses.

In the early 1980s, things changed. A story making black academic rounds during that period had a perplexed student asking a professor earnestly, "Who was this Malcolm the Tenth?" The story reflected recognition of a generational passage; it was the signal of the first cohort to approach maturity with no clear memories of '60s activism or the specific injustices it fought. The average college freshperson in 1980 had been at most three years old when Malcolm was murdered and barely into school when the movement began to decompose. Also, the national ideological climate shifted toward out-of-hand dismissal of that activism as a benighted, outmoded style like long hair. Young black people were no less inclined than others to distinguish themselves from their elders in the terms provided by mass culture, and they had also grown up with perceptions of the 1960s acquired through *Laugh-In* and B-movies. (A little-remarked feature of the blaxploitation genre was its standard depiction of "militants" as incompetent, naive, and "out-of-touch" with "real," apolitical blackness.) Even those who had read *The Autobiography of Malcolm X* as the disconnected story of a great, perhaps tragic, personality were no more knowledgeable than others in this respect.

As the popularity of the tale of the perplexed undergraduate attests, many in the older generation were alarmed by young people's dismissive ignorance. I confess to having been stopped in my tracks in a New Haven laundry upon seeing my first black teen in a Confederate battle cap, complete with stars and bars on top. (My query confirmed the obvious; he had not a clue about the Civil War or the Confederacy, much less either's relation to his choice in haberdashery.) Stories like these gained velocity, so that by the middle of the decade they combined to support an almost ritualistic lament that "Our young people don't know anything about (our, their own) history." Embedded in this lament was a call for remedial action.

Unfortunately, the easiest, most immediately available alternative was one familiar from a decade of Black History Month ads and public service announcements, the compendium of Black Contributions and Accomplishments and/or Great Black Historical Figures. This approach, sort of a hybrid Homeric narrative and Afrocentric version of *Jeopardy!*, bears traces of a pattern—reaching back through the turn of the century—of subordinating historical analysis to the project of vindicating the race's image. It is itself profoundly ahistorical and was one of the reasons that young people were so poorly informed in the first place. Television crews' trips to inner-city schools around Martin Luther King, Jr.'s birthday annually exposed its limitations. In response to variants of the question "What do you know about Martin Luther King?" students—K through 12—invariably returned answers with the same structure: A long time ago Black people didn't have any freedom, and then Martin Luther King came, and they got their freedom. (As a product of Catholic education under the regime of Pius XII, this is a form of call-and-response I knew only too well; the *Baltimore Catechism* is not a good model for understanding anything, least of all history.)

Those who had formed their political consciousness in the 1960s were somewhere between settled adulthood and middle age when they encountered this shift in the youth population. Therefore, the latter's apparent passivity and lack of appreciation for an epic past rang an especially discordant note against an older generation's slide toward nostalgic reflection on its own youth, a mood illustrated in (and encouraged by) the oldies' music boom during those years. Such nostalgia naturally feeds on invidious comparisons with "today's" youth, whose folkways thus appear increasingly opaque and irrational. The concern with historical amnesia and political inertness in this way flowed into stereotypical anxieties about the younger generation's deficiencies, which in turn commingled with the burgeoning "underclass" ideology that traded on images of widespread "cultural pathology" among inner-city black and Hispanic youth. The trope of black pathology also has blended with nationalist psychobabble about the need to repair supposedly damaged self-respect by teaching black people about "themselves." So a parade of racial self-esteem experts, who themselves had grown up with—depending on their ages—pink suits, konks, and the Cadets ("Stranded in the Jungle"), twelve-inch afros, bell-bottom pants and Archie Bell and the Drells; or pimp hats, new-style konks, platform shoes, and Bootsy's Rubber Band, came forward to pronounce on side-turned baseball caps, Gumby haircuts, and rap music as evidence of a rampant nihilism threatening to destroy the black social fabric. (Oh, I know, "but this is different because . . .")

In these circumstances it is not difficult to imagine how the desire to improve young people's civic education was—with notable exceptions, such as the *Eyes on the Prize* series—absorbed by an increasingly prominent fixation on finding "role models," a black manifestation of the decade's trickle-down ideology. But a focus on role models distorts history toward the search for heroes. Similarly, linking examination of the past to a therapeutic project destroys a sense of history as process and reduces it to a field of static, decontextualized parables. Both traits suffuse the prevailing constructions of Malcolm X, and, as I have noted, they yield an objectified image primed for commercial exploitation.

This generational dynamic was overlapped by the instability arising from Reaganism's matter-of-fact break with the established model of race relations management. Not only was the Reagan agenda forthrightly hostile to black interests, it also explicitly rejected and set out to discredit the conventional practice of insider negotiation with black political elites. Prominent black elected officials and Civil Rights technicians complained repeatedly during Reagan's first term that the administration had not made overtures toward the black leadership establishment and was in fact refusing access. The administration and its allies responded by challenging the mainstream political elite's legitimacy as representatives of racial interests and pursued an overt strategy of creating an alternative "voice" of pro-Reaganite blacks.

These developments exacerbated tensions at the core of the post-segregation era's style of political accommodationism, and the Reaganite strategy exposed and manipulated the points at which the new black political elite is most vulnerable. The pattern of race relations engineering that had congealed over the 1970s pivots, in its logical essence, on a quid pro quo: black retreat from a politics based on popular mobilization and potentially disruptive protest activism in exchange for a regime that guarantees regular, if only incremental or symbolic, payoffs. Central to this arrangement is a very delicate balancing act by the new Bantustan administrators. On the one hand, they must secure black acquiescence to the regime and its terms of governance. Realizing this objective has meant, in practice, channeling black political participation into support for the regime—in part by defining any other course as illegitimate and in part by successfully representing the payoffs generated as both significant and optimal. Because incremental or symbolic payoffs are hardly adequate to overcome systemic disadvantage and inequality, though, they must be buttressed by a justifying rhetoric of steady, even if very gradual, progress. On the other hand, the black political elite's capacities for generating payoffs rest ultimately on the specter of disruptive, popular mobilization, to which the regime of incrementalist race relations engineering is presented as a preferable alternative. Well into the 1970s, for example, arguments for meliorative initiatives regularly evoked the fear of a "long, hot summer" that might ensue from failure to pursue the desired course.

Over time, the new regime's success has made the prospect of disruptive mobilization ever more remote. Incumbent leadership is incumbent leadership regardless of race or electoral status, and incumbents generally prefer to minimize the size of the attentive public in order to maximize their loyal supporters' relative strength. Black elected officials, like others, are not particularly interested in increasing voter registration or turnout once they have carved out electoral bases that will dependably reelect them. Infusions of new voters both increase the cost and effort of campaigning and introduce a potentially volatile element into the electorate. Similarly, Civil Rights organizations operate most comfortably with a strategy of insider advocacy. This strategy is incompatible with popular mobilization because its principal audience is policy-making elites, and it is embedded in a technicistic discourse that requires insider knowledge. The insider advocacy strategy reorients these organizations as professional agencies of race relations administration. As a result, they function both as an independent brokerage elite and as auxiliary branches of public management. Both functions are averse to popular mobilization, and for similar reasons. Commitment to a professionalistic ideology that mystifies expertise reinforces class prejudice and defense of privilege. Also, the incremental and symbolic nature of the payoffs in this arrangement exerts a further pressure toward demobilization. It is just as well for those who do not benefit from the payoffs to be alienated or inattentive; otherwise, they might become actively dissatisfied and uncontrollably disruptive politically.

Successful institutionalization of postsegregation era elite-brokerage politics, therefore, has undercut the principal leverage (besides the ability to deliver a large bloc of Democratic voters) that the new black political elite has in negotiating payoffs. The Reaganite right exploited this contradiction. In staking out a position expressly antagonistic to blacks and in challenging the black establishment's legitimacy, the Reagan administration in effect called the tacit bluff and dared the political elite to mobilize popular opposition. In the parlance of bid whist, the Reaganites called for trumps and caught black leadership with a void.

Recognition that Reaganism was a qualitative departure from politics as usual settled in only slowly. Even Nixon, after all, had not completely broken with the elite-brokerage model; despite its willingness to court white *ressentiment* rhetorically, the Nixon administration did not stonewall the black political establishment in the way that Reagan did. Indeed, the transition from agitation to technical administration as the substance of Civil Rights advocacy occurred mainly under Nixon. I suspect that the Nixon/Ford precedent may have led to discounting the manifest hostility of Reagan's rhetoric. Some probably treated even his inflammatory policy agenda as a grandstand play, imagining that he would, like Nixon, slouch toward the center.

In any event, the dawning truth of the Reagan agenda precipitated anxious groping for a proper response. But lack of commitment to a larger vision of social, political, and economic organization, a related entrapment within an incrementalist discourse suddenly without pragmatic basis, and a flickering hope that the apparent was not real combined to undermine those efforts, rendering them contradictory and strangely anticlimactic. Statements whose structure and context implied the indictment and militant demand characteristic of protest politics were tepid in their actual complaints, tentative and indirect in their accusations, and likely to dribble off into bland calls for improved communication. The 1983 March on Washington for Jobs and Freedom exemplifies the extent of the problem. The march was packaged by its organizers largely as a nostalgic event—a gathering to commemorate the famous Civil Rights march on the same site twenty years earlier. This focus muted the counterattack on Reagan by mixing it with a celebration of past glories. Moreover, in attempting opportunistically to draw energy from nostalgia, it in effect acknowledged the inadequacy of the black political elite's purchase on the current situation. Insofar as the turn to nostalgia was not opportunistic, it reflected the persistence of the evasive tendency in postsegregation era black politics. Constructing a supposedly simpler, clearer time in the past and then projecting it as a model for the present is, when all is said and done, a move that yearns for a different reality in lieu of engaging the one that actually confronts us.

Totemic nostalgia for Civil Rights activism converged with the ongoing reconstruction of Martin Luther King as singular embodiment of the movement. Intensification of a campaign to declare King's birthday a national holiday both reflected and drove this convergence. The attempt to define the holiday issue as the central racial concern also indicates how desperate and pathetically inadequate the black leadership stratum was in the face of the Reagan juggernaut. Anxiety about Reaganism grew among black Americans generally, as could be seen in a surge in voting that sharply narrowed the racial gap in voter turnout in 1982. And a backdrop blended of King idolatry and yearning for the Civil Rights movement's apparent clarity gave rise to a view that the black political elite's palpable failure stemmed from the absence of a comparable leader in the present. (Never mind that compression of Civil Rights activism into King's persona was a myth that became orthodoxy only in the 1980s.) Then, riding on the wave of pertinent symbolism condensed by the 1983 march, Jesse Jackson stepped forward to present himself as heir to King's fictitious legacy.

Jackson had been campaigning since the early 1970s to be appointed National Black Leader, a job description for which historically there had never been appreciable demand from putative constituents. Significantly, the one period during which there had been anyone approximating a singular race spokesperson was during what remains the worst time in Afro-American history since Emancipation. Booker T. Washington asserted greater influence over initiatives regarding black Americans than any individual before or since, and his preeminence corresponded almost identically with the years during which the gains of Reconstruction were largely overturned and black people were driven to the margins of American life. The relation, moreover, was not coincidental. Washington, whose agenda was by no means consensually accepted by Afro-Americans, was denominated National Black Leader by the dominant white political, economic, and philanthropic interests precisely because he preached accommodation to their program of black marginalization. To be sure, because Afro-Americans have had no referendum or other forum for legitimizing claims to be a national leader, the support of white opinion-makers has been key for all aspirants to such *Rassenführer* status. From Marcus Garvey to Elijah

Muhammad to Louis Farrakkan to Jackson—all have reproduced the
ironic strategy of seeking to become the Black Leader by means of
white acclamation.

Jackson's quest has shown another ironic characteristic of the
National Black Leader status today. Race leaders work best if they
are already dead when appointed. Through two campaigns for the
Democratic presidential nomination Jackson produced few benefits
besides his own aggrandizement—no shift in public policy, no institu-
tionalized movement, not even a concrete agenda (except, again, Jackson's aggrandizement) around which to mobilize. At the same time, the
rightist program has become increasingly hegemonic and has tightened
steadily around the lives and aspirations of the most vulnerable strata
in the black population. Under these circumstances, a doggerel rhetoric of hope, calls for self-esteem, platitudes about caring for the
unfortunate, and promises of oceanic identification with the Leader's
prowess could be expected to lose appeal after eight years.

Jackson exploited nostalgic yearning during the summer and fall
of 1983 by staging a Potemkin grass-roots movement, a speaking tour
through the South, centered in churches and the occasional campus
and ostensibly connected to a voter registration drive. Mass-mediated
projections of the tour evoked images of Civil Rights activism's heroic
phase and enshrined Jackson's claim to be an activist-outsider with a
mobilized popular base. (Public acceptance of his self-representation
as an outsider is in a way an equal-opportunity spur of a line of political
gullibility running from Jimmy Carter in 1976 to Jerry Brown and H.
Ross Perot in 1992—the consummate insider as outsider, Pericles
dressed up as Cincinnatus. Jackson had been incorporated into the
inner circles of elite race relations management by the early 1970s.
His presidential endorsement had been sought since 1972, when he
flirted with Richard Nixon, and, as head of Operation PUSH, he had
for about as long been negotiating covenants with major corporations
and administering substantial public grants and contracts.) He par-
layed the persona thus created and the stirrings of germinal black
impatience with incumbent leadership, along with calls to racial patriotism, to generate heavy black voting for himself in the 1984 Democratic primaries.

Local activists and fringe politicos sought to use the visibility
surrounding Jackson's bid to advance their own objectives. The campaign's newsworthiness promised to enhance individual and organizational name recognition, and the motion around the candidacy opened

possibilities for greater leverage vis-à-vis entrenched elites. Black elected officials in particular had come around to supporting Jackson only slowly. Some already were committed to Mondale. Some questioned or opposed the idea of a black candidacy on pragmatic grounds. Some were open to a candidacy in principle but resented Jackson's presumptuousness in putting himself forward. However motivated, their reluctance to join what soon became a bandwagon appeared to make them vulnerable to insurgents. But marginalized activists' and aspiring politicians' enthusiastic embrace of Jackson was not merely strategic; the Jackson phenomenon's cathartic aspect appealed to them as well as to others. All these factors underwrote a wishful scenario in which Jesse Jackson, reborn as noble outsider and self-proclaimed "moral force" in American politics, would embody and authorize a redemptive movement—and maybe even become President, or at least nominee.

Between 1984 and 1988, however, Jackson moved his image back inside. Rather than a lightning rod for black insurgents, he operated more as symbolic first among equals and authenticating touchstone for the black establishment. The most regular of black regular Democrats—for instance, David Dinkins—jumped to the forefront of Jackson motion at the local level. Jackson assured national Democratic leadership that he most of all wanted to be a member of the inner circles of the party; he could be trusted, therefore, not to support activity that would actually violate the going regime of race relations management. Simple familiarity also made Jackson's new persona part of normal politics. As his status thus became normalized, the potential costs of identification with him receded toward zero for mainstream black politicians. The stage was set for them to position themselves as principal manipulators (and beneficiaries) of the symbolism that many activists had hoped would galvanize an insurgent opposition. Moreover, when establishment and activist factions squared off for control of local organizations, as in New Jersey, Jackson gave the nod of legitimacy to the former. (This disposition reflected both the practical advantage of supporting the claimants who have greater resources and Jackson's fundamental commitment to the stratum of black insiders, a commitment that later led him even to defend Marion Barry.) As had happened with Black Power, mainstream elites co-opted the putative symbols of insurgency. In this case, moreover, the co-optation occurred more smoothly. It was facilitated by Jackson's presence as exclusive arbiter of the main symbol—himself—and by the relative absence of contestation of elite hegemony over the terms of black political debate.

Jackson's 1988 campaign presumed that he had proven his status as the National Black Leader in 1984, and he did seem to have united insiders and outsiders consensually under the umbrella of his candidacy. So uncontested was his claim to be the Black Leader that the campaign focused most concertedly on demonstrating his broader appeal as spokesman for the generically "locked out." When the dust settled, though, Jackson had been able to draw only about 10 percent of the white vote. And he had won no concessions from the party or the nominee except use of an airplane for his efforts on behalf of Dukakis in the race against Bush.

The official script of hope, excitement, enthusiasm, and so on, attendant to Jackson's 1988 effort obscured at least two of its dangerous characteristics. Jackson's success in forging consensual black identification with his candidacy effected the most radical narrowing of the focus of Afro-American political action to date. He managed more thoroughly than in 1984 to squeeze the totality of recognized black concern with presidential politics into his demand for personal "respect" from the Democratic party leadership and, eventually, its standard-bearer. That the payoff was so skimpy only adds insult to injury.

Similarly, Jackson's custodianship of black voting power allowed the other Democratic candidates to avoid directly courting black voters during the primary season. Instead, it was entirely reasonable for them to concede the black primary vote to Jackson. The eventual nominee then would be free to cut a separate deal with the Black Leader and would thus be able to benefit from black electoral support without being stigmatized as blacks' candidate. Jackson's candidacy, therefore, probably made it easier for the white candidates to act out the belief—formalized in the party by the Democratic Leadership Council, formed in 1985 after Mondale's defeat—that the party had fallen onto hard times in presidential politics because of its too-close identification with minorities, labor, and other "special interests."

This perspective puts new light on the lovefeast shared in 1988 by Jackson and Bert Lance, who had always been associated with the party's conservative, Southern white wing. Jackson's visibility aided the DLC's agenda both by keeping the specter of racial polarization in the limelight and by giving the other candidates space to refine a pattern of debate that excluded explicit concern with issues bearing on specifically Afro-American interests. When Jackson succeeded in becoming the symbolic embodiment of black interests in the campaign, he also helped those forces seeking to marginalize blacks among the agenda-setting constituencies in the Democratic party.

After two emotional campaigns and incessant maneuvering and posturing between them, Jackson apparently had no further moves to make. Despite his contention that his candidacy was necessary to stop white Democrats from taking black voters for granted, he had contributed to producing just the opposite effect. In positioning himself as National Black Leader, he also has claimed the status of singular broker of a black population whose interests and concerns are isomorphic with his own. In the process he has helped to diminish black Americans' autonomous significance in the party by insisting that their preferences be channeled through him. Insofar as satisfying him can be construed as satisfying black Americans, Jackson has seriously reduced the level of black demand on the party and the political system. At the turn of the century, making a private railroad car available so that Booker T. Washington could avoid the indignities of Jim Crow was less costly than protecting black people's civil rights; in the same way, giving Jesse Jackson an airplane for campaigning and recognition in inner circles (in his phrase, "a seat at the table") is more convenient than trying to craft a political agenda that actually safeguards and advances social justice and racial equality.

So, on the verge of becoming a black Harold Stassen, Jackson decided not to run in 1992. The damage, though, had already been done. Political and economic conditions have continued steadily to deteriorate within the Afro-American population, and demoralization seems ever more pronounced. Even activists who had steered by their own lights for decades before Jackson's rise to prominence find themselves hamstrung conceptually and programmatically, trapped by a narrative that requires Jackson as Black Leader to provide a basis and direction for action. Politics seems not to offer avenues for response, ironically, in part because the National Black Leader myth, particularly as realized in the Jackson phenomenon, has cut political action loose from its moorings in practical activity and reconfigured it as existential drama. This is the setting in which Malcolm X has been "rediscovered."

It is perhaps instructive that Malcolmania has come at the same time as Jackson's attempt to embody the Black Leader myth appears to be running out of steam. Suspicion that he and Malcolm contend for the same iconic and affective space is reinforced by popular culture;

Public Enemy's "Bring the Noise," for example, moves between the two in its imagery. A living Leader is handicapped by having at some point to produce real outcomes. Jackson has taken smoke and mirrors about as far as they can go, and he may now be on the verge of exemplifying how gossamer thin is the line between icon and cliché. Malcolm, as I have noted, is exempt from any test of efficacy based on current practice; unlike Jackson, he quite literally can do no wrong. In trying to move into the role previously assigned to King, Jackson seems to have overlooked an essential point: King had to die before attaining the status of iconic Leader. One can in fact only secure it in retrospect, as a posthumous garland. To that extent, Malcolm is much better suited to the position than Jackson. Illustratively, Spike Lee may hold Jackson in high regard, but he ended *Do the Right Thing* with supposedly hortatory quotations from Malcolm and King, whose images recur throughout the film.

I do not mean to be either callous or pointlessly irreverent in stressing the all-too-obvious fact that King and Malcolm are dead. I do so only in service to a less obvious point. The King, Jackson, and Malcolm iconologies that have spread during the Reagan/Bush era— as well as the mythos of the singular Black Leader that connects them—are most meaningfully expressions of the tendency toward evasiveness that has undermined development of critical vision in black politics in the postsegregation era. Yes, the turn to Malcolm in part reflects deepening frustration with material conditions and Jackson's failure, but more importantly, it reproduces the vicarious, or even apolitical, approach to politics that undergirded the earlier romanticizations of King and Jackson.

Three weeks before the 1992 Illinois primaries I attended an all-day public forum on Malcolm X in Chicago. (An earlier one on a similar format had been held in New York.) The organizers had in mind that the gathering and discussions would shed light on serious issues confronting Afro-Americans today. Speakers generally applauded young people for their interest in Malcolm X but also challenged them to dig beneath the X and Afrocentric fashion items to apprehend and emulate Malcolm's "real" essence. Tacitly or explicitly, this challenge presumed that proper orientation toward Malcolm would usefully inform contemporary action. During the entire day, however, there was only one direct reference to current political issues and events, and all the discussions proceeded as if the institutions of public authority were peripheral, if not entirely alien, to Afro-American concern.

Old warhorses often have remained stuck in rituals of opposition that do not take account of important shifts—inspired by consequences of the Voting Rights Act—in the institutional and ideological environment of racial subordination over the 1970s and 1980s. Those old rituals cannot help to make sense of the rise of black governance's complex meanings. For example, even construed as Bantustan administration, black control of public institutions creates black constituencies for those institutions by democratizing access to the spoils and perquisites of government. If only by virtue of increasing the likelihood of their sharing social networks with pertinent functionaries, black government increases black citizens' access to zoning variances, summer jobs in municipal agencies, waivers on code enforcement, breaks in the criminal justice system, special parks and recreation services, and a host of other nonroutine benefits as well as public contracts. But this improved access does not trickle uniformly through the black citizenry, and black control of those agencies whose principal function is management of the dispossessed does not alter their ultimately repressive function. Black control also does not alter the way those agencies socialize their personnel; few speak less sympathetically of black poor people than black service-providers in housing authorities, welfare departments, and school systems. Neither generic Black Power radicalism nor its more elaborate descendants (most prominently now, for example, Afrocentricity) can provide categories that capture these or comparable subtleties associated with the construction of political meaning in the postsegregation era. Nor can they conceptualize productively the subtle ways that social position, point of view, and political interest interact within the Afro-American population.

That the old rituals cannot account for the dynamics that have shaped the environment within which contemporary black politics has developed just makes bad matters worse. They induce blindness to the import of such factors as the intricate logics of reorganization at work in domestic and global political economy since World War II: the consolidation of a domestic political model—joining national and local levels—that cements interest group loyalties and legitimizes state power through participation in a regime of public stimulation of private economic growth; the subsidiary role of defense spending, transportation, and urban redevelopment policy in recomposing regional and metropolitan demographic, economic, and political organization. The result is a radicalism that gives away some of the most important conceptual ground to defenders of the status quo. This is a radicalism that cannot effectively challenge questionable reifications such as the manufacturing sector/service sector job dichotomy, the representation of deindustrialization as if it were natural law, the series of mystifications that run through imagery surrounding the terms "high tech" and skill and their bearing on debates about education, training, unemployment, and income inequality. There is nothing that understanding the "real" Malcolm X—an impossibility in any event—could do to clarify or to help formulate positions regarding any of those phenomena, neither the internal nor the external forces shaping black political life. Invoking his image in these circumstances amounts to wishing away the complexities that face us. So, for instance, when Spike Lee (at the end of his "Epilogue" to *Do the Right Thing*) denounces the regime of racial subordination represented by then–New York Mayor Ed Koch, he poses the trite juxtaposition of Malcolm and King, standing for violence and nonviolence, as the available alternative. But that juxtaposition does not suggest what was substantively wrong with the Koch regime (hardly a difficult task if Lee had but attended to it), hint at how governance of New York City might proceed more equitably, or even imply anything really concrete about mobilization for change. His statement is vague on all the questions central to the sort of call to arms he obviously intends it to be, the questions bearing on the who, what, when, where, and why of political action. Despite its hortatory form, Lee's injunction is pointlessly evocative. The reference to King and Malcolm is just filler, conveying a specious appearance of substance. The reference substitutes for analysis and critique of an obviously objectionable political situation; it is an evasion.

Lee's presentation of the violence/nonviolence dichotomy as a proper frame for organizing political response calls on style and emotional posture to do the work of critical argument, program, and strategy. In doing so, and especially by retailing the hackneyed King/Malcolm trope in the process, he links the defects of the old rituals of opposition to the particular form of political evasion that has developed during the Reagan/Bush era, the discourse of cultural politics. This discourse avoids the problem of black demobilization by redefining the sphere of political action to center on everyday practices of self-presentation and popular cultural expression. Repeating a move of the previous generation, it sidesteps the thorny issues surrounding Afro-Americans' relation to the exercise of public authority in the postsegregation era by dismissing the domain of official politics and governance as inauthentic and therefore not pertinent to radical concern.

As with the different manifestations of the earlier turn to ideology as well, the cultural politics discourse's main analytical weapon is taxonomy; its critical edge consists principally in reclassifying, or recoding, conventional understandings of apparently mundane practices. An important difference, however, is that the objective to which cultural politics' discourse harnesses taxonomic revision is much more celebratory than hortatory. In the other narratives of political evasion, reclassification of conventionally recognized phenomena (for example, the Swahili relabeling in Kawaida nationalism, the domestic colony analogy, attempts to impose a map of reified class categories onto the black population) is directed toward winning adherents to a specific program of action; the thrust of countertaxonomy runs, therefore, to exhorting people to change their perceptions as a step toward redirecting or otherwise altering their behavior. The rhetoric of cultural politics, by contrast, exalts existing practices as intrinsically subversive and emancipatory; it neither calls to action nor proposes sharp changes in quotidian activity. From this standpoint it is the ultimate concession to the fact of political demobilization; it is a construction of radical opposition that naturalizes the demobilized state as outside the scope of intervention and limits itself to celebrating moments of resistance supposedly identifiable within fundamental acquiescence.

Because it rejects distinctions between style and substance, form and content, this new rhetoric of evasiveness gives an intellectual justification for conflating political commitment and consumer market preference. Similarly, in focusing on the expressive dimension of action to the exclusion of the instrumental, it refuses at all to distinguish symbolic and purposive activity. In defining participation in popular culture as political action, this stance merges the avant-garde in fashion and ideological radicalism, thus vesting fad with strategic political significance. It consequently makes a fetish of youth as a social category (another failure to learn from mistakes of the 1960s) and idealizes trends in inner-city fashion as emancipatory expression. These characteristics work to reduce politics to purely affective and symbolic endeavor. And that is a construction of politics in which appeal to icons readily takes the place of careful argument and critical analysis. The youth fetish is especially revealing in this regard.

To represent youth as a status group is to forget the inherently transitory character of that status. Treating youth as authentic bearers of the principle of opposition, moreover, confuses existential rebellion and political rebellion. The former can be pacified through mass marketing; the latter cannot. This romantic view also elides the problem that the coherence of youth as a group in American society derives mainly from its status as a market fraction. Consumption figures so prominently in youth culture because that is the main arena that exists for young people's autonomous action and, relatedly, because the category itself is a creation of the sales effort. Perhaps the most problematic aspect of the youth fetish in cultural politics discourse, though, is the premise that we should look to those who know the least about and have the least experience in the world for our salvation. (This premise even seemed ridiculous to me when I was in a position to benefit from it.)

The climate thus created nurtures the nightmarish absurdity in which rappers project themselves as political sages. Confused and depressingly ignorant performers such as KRS-One, Public Enemy, X-Clan, and Sister Souljah spew garbled compounds of half-truth, distortion, Afrocentric drivel, and crackerbarrel wisdom, as often as not shot through with reactionary prejudices, and claim pontifical authority on the basis of identity with the props of their stage and video performances. Interviews raise the disturbing possibility that many of these "raptivists," the purportedly authentic voices of politically astute youth, in their minds construe the scenes staged in their message videos as identical with actual political experience.

Malcolmania arises in this environment, as the image of Malcolm X, for reasons I and others have described, increasingly takes on a talismanic quality. But not only does the Malcolm iconology support continued evasion of tough political questions; attempts to draw on Malcolm for guidance reproduce his inaccurate, simplistic reading of Afro-American history and reinforce inadequate and wrongheaded tendencies in the present. Few images from the 1960s, for example, have had such broad and lasting resonance as Malcolm's construction of the difference between the "house Negro" and the "field Negro." This construction gave an institutional foundation to the image of the Uncle Tom and has provided a powerful metaphor for characterizing class and ideological cleavage among black Americans. The fact is, though, that this metaphor is historically wrong, obfuscatory, and counterproductive.

Whether or not Malcolm meant the house Negro/field Negro antagonism to be an accurate description of a dominant historical pattern
rather than simply a rhetorical device, the metaphor draws its force
from the implication of sedimented tension and historical continuity.
But the reality of slave acquiescence and resistance was much more
complex and mediated. Nat Turner, Denmark Vesey, and Gabriel
Prosser—leaders of the best-known slave revolts—all were house
slaves. More important, the distinction itself was one imposed from
outside the slave population. When they could, slaves were as likely
as not to try to avoid assignment to work in the house; such work could
be especially demeaning, and it represented a further erosion of the
already exceedingly limited autonomy slaves could fashion for themselves. This is not a merely pedantic point; Malcolm's metaphor also
implies an ontological claim about an original position of organic unity
among Afro-Americans.

The field Negro in Malcolm's rendition stands not only for the
"masses"; he (and the image is male) also represents authentic racial
unity. The house Negro is therefore not simply wrong, or even just
duped, but is also a race traitor. This construction presumes that unity
of purpose is black Americans' "natural" condition and that disunity,
as a result, must spring from treason or some comparably pathogenic
force, such as brainwashing, personal ambition, moral laxity. In addition to its historical falsity (which ironically reflects the prerevisionist
portrayal of black slaves as a brutalized, undifferentiated mass hud-
dled around a campfire) and its implicit intolerance of dissent, there
are two things grievously wrong with this view. First, it reduces political differences to a matter of individual psychology and morality. This
biases political criticism to allegations concerning personal virtue or
mental health and disconnects it from examination of functional relation to structures of power and the autonomous effects of social position. Second, the tacit ontological premise of an originally organic
unity establishes racial authenticity as a primary criterion for political
judgment. The combined effect of these two problems is to sustain an
impoverished form of debate that revolves around assessing whether
individuals or positions are "really" black. This pattern of debate
stands in the way of making sense of the dynamics propelling Afro-
American political life and is, of course, a demagogue's dream.

Malcolm's injunction that black disagreements and problems
should be resolved "in the closet"—that is, quietly among Afro-
Americans themselves—at the same time acknowledges the reality of

difference within the race and seeks to subordinate it to a naive vision of perfect unity. He repeatedly employed family imagery to appeal to a notion of unity that is not purposive but is instead an independent ethical, for the most part racially grounded, imperative. But any unity must exist on some terms, and Malcolm's dicta do not inform the articulation of those terms, especially not under postsegregation-era conditions when no clear objective such as destruction of Jim Crow impels toward consensus. Malcolm never developed a sophisticated or coherent strategy, even for his times; he certainly could not predict the changed conditions that would prevail after his death. Indeed, none of Malcolm's formulations can provide the basis for effective commentary on contemporary Afro-American politics.

Not surprisingly, Malcolm nevertheless is frequently invoked, particularly since the spread of Malcolmania, as a luminous product endorsement for one or another current political program. These are, moreover, often—but not exclusively—programs whose substance is in present circumstances reactionary. Self-reliance or self-help is one such case. In current political debate self-reliance is a code for a Booker T. Washington–style forfeiture of the right to make claims on public authority. In this vein black conservatives such as Clarence Thomas or Tony Brown are at least as likely to annex Malcolm's authority as are nationalists who prefer not to be thought of as conservative.

Malcolm's image is attractive also to those concerned to advance the cause of black men. His appeal to some degree always has had a distinctively male inflection. The alternative that he posed to the Civil Rights movement's passive resistance was bound up with constructions of masculine assertiveness in at least two ways. On the one hand, as I have noted, he appealed to the urban male sensibility that associated failure to fight back with cowardliness. On the other hand, he embodied a sort of Afro-American version of republican manhood; he projected civic virtue, respect for and protection of home and hearth (including women), and the patriarchal vision that defines public life as a masculine realm. He spoke often of manhood rights. It is no accident, therefore, that Ossie Davis's eulogy was steeped in masculine imagery; that imagery had a great deal to do with what Malcolm meant to black men.

Malcolm's image as vicarious redeemer of the suppressed prerogatives of black manhood received a boost from, of all sources, Daniel Moynihan's nefarious report, *The Negro Family: A Case for National*

Action. Nationalists and other petit bourgeois black sexists began incorporating Moynihan's charges concerning the existence of a debilitating black matriarchy that crushed male spirit and arrested masculine development. By 1972 this line underwrote opposition to Shirley Chisholm's entry into presidential primaries, on the ground that she usurped a male prerogative. Worry about the dangers of excessive feminine influence was already an old chestnut. At the turn of the century many scholars fretted that the upper classes would slide into degeneracy because of the "feminization" of their men. The trope is rooted in the gendered dichotomy of nature and culture. Moynihan extended it to blacks (who already had a special place in the nature/culture dichotomy, of course).

The Moynihan line was attractive because it gave a race-conscious foundation to black sexism, though most of its proponents would never acknowledge their ideological debt to him. (For his part Malcolm remained at best an unexamined, paternalistic sexist to his death, and his paternalism bordered on misogyny in its insistence on female subservience.) Beginning in the 1980s we have seen the stirrings of another wave of antifeminist backlash from black men. Under the guise of rhetoric alleging the "crisis of the black male" and proclaiming black men an "endangered species," calls for male assertiveness and discussion of men's special needs have returned. From William Julius Wilson, to Glenn Loury, to entertainers and athletes a popular consensus is forming, across the ideological spectrum, that black men need gender-inflected help.

Role-model rhetoric meshes with this concern and authorizes practices such as sending male buppies into inner-city schools and neighborhoods to propagate "authentic" (and respectable) models of black manhood. Malcolm has been enlisted in these efforts as a version of the ideal black man. His image very well may be etched onto the club used to try to beat black women toward the background so that damaged black manhood may be repaired, or to drive them—by making the presently existing alternatives still more horrible and repressive—into economic dependence on men through marriage.

Because he has no agency at all, Malcolm is now even more a hologram of social forces than he was for my generation. The inchoate, often apparently inconsistent trajectory of his thought makes him an especially plastic symbol in the present context. It is all too tempting to play the what-Malcolm-would-do-if-he-were-alive game, but the temptation should be avoided because the only honest response is that

ave no idea. Part of what was so exciting about Malcolm, in
ct anyway, was that he was moving so quickly, experimenting
eas, trying to get a handle on the history he was living. Recog-
, that he never did does not demean him, but it does underscore
eality that—while we all certainly have our own favorite scenar-
ios—no one can have any hint of where he would have wound up
politically. If he had not been killed when he was, what developed as
Black Power radicalism may have taken a somewhat different form
and so, therefore, would the responses it generated. Yet even imagining that everything would have happened as it did, it is still impossible
to say what course Malcolm would have taken. One irony in the present
appropriation of his image does stand out, however. Despite Malcolm's
own ambivalence about his status as a race spokesman and the legitimacy of black leadership as a category (and notwithstanding his rhetoric about unity), Malcolm made his reputation by attacking entrenched
elites and challenging their attempts to constrain popular action and
the vox populi. Now he is canonized as an icon, an instrument of an
agenda that is just the opposite of popular mobilization.

It seems to me that the best way to think of the best of Malcolm
is that he was just like the rest of us—a regular person saddled with
imperfect knowledge, human frailties, and conflicting imperatives, but
nonetheless trying to make sense of his very specific history, trying
unsuccessfully to transcend it, and struggling to push it in a humane
direction. We can learn most from his failures and limitations because
they speak most clearly both of the character of his time and of the
sorts of perils we must guard against in our own. He was no prince;
there are no princes, only people like ourselves who strive to influence
their own history. To the extent that we believe otherwise, we turn
Malcolm into a postage stamp and reproduce the evasive reflex that
has deformed critical black political action for a generation.

The Autobiography of Deidre Bailey: Thoughts on Malcolm X and Black Youth*

AS TOLD TO MARPESSA DAWN OUTLAW AND MATTHEW COUNTRYMAN

My first introduction to black history was *The Autobiography of Malcolm X*. Probably about 90 percent of young people get their first introduction to black history through the *Autobiography*. For me, it's an amazing book, just truly amazing. I look at Malcolm's life, and I think about the things that I have gone through, and I say if he could do it, then I know I can do it, because I haven't gone through half of the things Malcolm did.

I have had struggles, though. Malcolm's father died; my mother has been hospitalized since I was in the second grade. I'm the youngest of twelve, only six of whom grew up in the same household with me. The others are from my father's first marriage. My father raised us but he was always busy working two jobs, trying to keep a roof over our heads. There were plenty of times we were lucky to have dinner or hot water or lights on in the house.

---

*After reading my story, many of my friends will realize they know little about me. Some of my friends will read this and not be surprised, but they will question why I've allowed my background to be exposed this way. I ask all of you to understand that without talking honestly about what we've seen, our voices—the voices of young people—will seem as meaningless as the voices of those who attempt to speak for us today. That's why I've chosen to speak out.

I was influenced by the drug culture, too. In high school I wanted to have a drug dealer for a boyfriend. I wanted fancy clothes and big earrings and to drive around in a fancy car. At the time I thought it was prestigious, a status symbol. Unfortunately, a lot of our young black men and women—and many of my friends—are thinking this way. I would have to say at least 80 to 85 percent of the people I knew during high school were involved in drugs. A lot of us weren't able to make a conscious decision to say "I'm out of this." When I was in high school, there was a handful of five or six girls I hung out with. Out of those girls, two of us are in college. The rest are mothers now or just hanging out.

It's mostly black men who are drug sellers. There are some instances where you find black women who are selling drugs, but it's black men who are more visible. I can't speak for them, I can only interpret when I say that they're feeling some of the same things that Malcolm was feeling. Malcolm obviously serves as a role model first to black men. Just like what Malcolm went through—drug dealing, pimping, stealing, robbing—that's what so many of our black men are doing now. They look at Malcolm and they can relate to his life. A sense of wanting to get out but also of feeling trapped in a society that has offered no other alternative but to turn to the streets. "How can I get out of this? How can I be successful without doing this?" These are the dilemmas that young black men are faced with today. The main thing is they want to be successful. Unfortunately, the only means that many see is through selling drugs. They say, "Hey, Malcolm sold drugs, I sold drugs. He pimped for a living, I had to pimp for a living. He was in jail. I was in jail."

They use Malcolm as a justification. These are the guys who are not ready to get out of it. They feel like they're living too well at this time. In effect, they are living out the American dream. The money is coming in, the lifestyle is good—fancy cars, nice houses and stuff. You constantly hear guys saying, "The time is just not right, I'm making too much money now." They sell drugs for other reasons, too, not just material wealth. The fact that the money a dealer earns also allows him to support his family makes it very difficult to choose an alternate route when the only other option is to work at McDonald's and not have money to buy the basic necessities of life.

Still, some of the dealers also say, "Okay, this is my situation now, this was Malcolm's situation at one point, too. He was able to get out of it, I have hopes of getting out of it also." For a lot of them, though, the time is probably never going to be right. And they'll just end up either dying young or in prison. I think Malcolm was lucky that he was incarcerated because otherwise he would probably have ended up dead sooner than he was. My high school prom date was shot and killed a couple of years ago, right after my freshman year of college. I was in finals when I was called and told, and I had just spoken to him the night before.

Guys like this can't relate to Jesse Jackson's life. They can't relate to Frederick Douglass's life or Martin Luther King's. These guys don't know what it was like to be in slavery so they can't relate to Nat Turner or Sojourner Truth. And they don't know what it's like to be in college or to be a part of the political process like Jesse or King. But they *can* relate to Malcolm X—someone who was also a drug dealer, also a pimp, also incarcerated. I think when these men bring Malcolm's life forward, what they're trying to say is, "Look, life doesn't always have to be like this. I can make a decision to overcome this. I have to make a conscious decision to change my lifestyle."

There aren't many stories about black women who have made those same transitions and whose lives are highlighted as Malcolm's is— women we perceive as black leaders or onetime leaders—like Assata Shakur, Angela Davis, Maya Angelou. Angelou, especially, went through a lot in her childhood years. I feel like young girls could use Malcolm, though, as an example to challenge their boyfriends, challenge the drug dealers. Once Malcolm became a Muslim, his whole attitude toward women changed and the only thing he had for women was love. He was a strong proponent of respect for black women. These are the things we need to begin articulating to our black men. I know that once I read *The Autobiography of Malcolm X*, I started holding brothers accountable. There's no way that after this man went through all this that brothers and sisters should be talking about "This money is too good." We should be able to make similar changes in our lives, ones that would allow us to move in a positive direction.

There were several factors that inspired me to change my life. One of the first persons to have an impact on my decision to get out was a drug dealer. He was my boyfriend. The day is still clear in my mind when he called me out on the back porch of a friend's house where we were hanging out and told me that he was no good for me, that I was smart enough to make a better life for myself and that I should stay in school. I honestly didn't know what had moved him to say that, but it really brought what he said home. This was a guy whose lifestyle was the streets, and I was a part of his assets, I was a good thing for his image. If he was willing to sacrifice that to see me make it, I could at least go on with my life. I didn't see him again until I was on my way to college, when I thanked him for influencing my life.

I had always had a hope of going to college. Out of the six of us, I'm the first. My older sister, from my father's first marriage, did graduate from college and is a successful speech pathologist. When Malcolm's brother introduced him to Islam, the influence his brother had on him, his words, meant a lot to Malcolm. His brother helped him make his transition. My sister served as motivation for me, by pushing me academically and providing a quiet place for me to study.

She also supported my initial involvement in student activism when I was still in high school and trying to convince my peers to register and vote. At the time, Jesse Jackson was seeking the presidential nomination from Connecticut. I was instrumental in getting over 200 students to register, with the help of the school administration, my youth council advisors and my sister.

I remember later that same summer, a woman named Althea Jackson Tyson, the deputy registrar of voters in New Haven, ran for registrar. I had been reading about her in the paper. She was seeking the community's help, so I went down as a volunteer. Then I got involved with a voter registration drive with some other community leaders. At the time I was also a member of the NAACP Youth Council. After I started working with the campaign, I talked about it to the group and they made a decision to help Mrs. Tyson out also. We were twenty or thirty students.

It was a good experience for all of us, being introduced to the political process at a preliminary stage. We learned a lot about voter registration, campaigning, politics in general. The campaign really taught me the importance of fighting for causes that are right in an unjust situation. In New Haven politics, it has been traditional for the deputy registrar to take over once the registrar has stepped down. But that changed once it was time for Althea Tyson to take over. The decision was made by the Democratic town chairman at the time. He made up excuses like, "Ms. Tyson possesses an attitude problem," and he felt the position should be offered to some other interested people. The way I interpreted that was that Ms. Tyson had made it known that she would promote voter registration and voter education in the African-American community; and the power structure in New

Haven, which was predominantly white male, just didn't want to let that happen. Had she been this submissive, obedient black woman who would listen to everything *they* said she would have been fine, but she wasn't that. The fact was, this woman was entitled to the position, and it was being denied her. It was outright racism, and I felt that to just let something like that happen would be wrong.

I think the key to our involvement in New Haven was the fact that we had this group of people in their late twenties and early thirties who were willing to take an interest in us and show us what the process was all about. With their help, our group stayed together after that for two years, even after Tyson lost. We eventually got involved with John Daniels's race for mayor. I was on his exploratory committee and then we did some voter registration.

Our group served as a youth voice for the Daniels campaign. The youth are what pulled him over the hurdle. If it weren't for us, he wouldn't be in office now. But when it comes down to politics, we usually don't get involved because we don't have too many people taking an interest in us. Politics is something that is considered an adult issue. Only adults can be involved in politics. In politics, young people aren't even considered, so they get discouraged. They don't have any faith in the process or in the leadership, and that's basically the fault of the leadership. Students, even if they want to be involved, kind of just back off because they don't have people motivating them. When they do make independent efforts, they are usually shot down by the older generation.

Instead, the biggest outlet for our voice has been rap. Rap has been sending a message very strongly to the black leadership and leadership in general—if they would only listen—that this is our time and we're not going to accept this exclusion as the norm anymore. But the leadership doesn't take the time to listen, or they've heard some rap that's not positive and want to wipe it all out as a result. Otherwise, they'd understand the hostility and the concerns people today have.

Rap is a key. It has the potential of starting a mass movement. KRS-One and Public Enemy, for instance, are two strong rap artists who have used their music to send out a political message and also to educate young people about black history. I have a saying that once you learn your history, your true African history, your conscience won't allow you to fail. It was rap that brought Malcolm and a bunch of others to young people. I think that is one of the things that rap music tries to do—to put black history out there. To educate young people about black leadership, both past and present, and to show us that we're a positive race: we *do* have a part in the country, and we *do* have people who have made accomplishments, who have helped to build America.

Still, too many of our young people don't get past this stage. They cling to the *symbol* of Malcolm without taking the time to read about him thoroughly. If they read outside of the *Autobiography*, some other literature, they would find that Malcolm's life changed a great deal. He went from hating all white people to realizing that even white people, if their intentions are good, can be your brother or sister also. A lot of young people don't know about that side of Malcolm. They just know violent Malcolm—hating white people and calling white people devils. You have T-shirts where you have Malcolm surrounded by guns. That's the type of negative publicity the media gives you.

The people who feel that they can really relate to Malcolm's rage, who understand how he could be provoked to violence, are poor people. A lot of them invoke that statement of his, "By any means necessary." They aren't middle class people—those folks have somewhat different value systems because they were able to make it in the system. In Atlanta, you have this large college complex surrounded by housing projects. There are tensions. All these black students who are supposedly middle and upper class and all these poor people—they feel that we're coming into their community, trying to take over. "You don't live here or anything. You're just here for four years." There's a lot of hostility, but I don't think that it's something that we can't overcome.

I think we can find common ground. I know I say "By any means necessary" all the time. But I don't use it to imply violence. I use it to imply that something has to be done and it's by any means necessary. The Rodney King verdict, for instance, made a lot of young people stop and think, "Hey, this isn't about you and I beefing"—it's a racial issue. And that encompasses all black people and all minorities. Especially when you have blatant incidents like what happened to Rodney King. It wakes people up to what's really happening in our society. The best thing we can do is to try to work together, to try to come to some type of truce, because we have this big struggle ahead of us. "By any means necessary" means I have to do whatever I can in my power to make sure this happens.

Malcolm has a saying that if the power structure likes you, then there is something wrong. He doesn't expect them to like him. And a lot of young people feel the same way. When I see people with X hats on, I ask them, "What does Malcolm mean to you? Who *is* Malcolm?" Just to start a dialogue with them about the clothing they are wearing. If there's a problem, what can we do about it? Is wearing a hat enough? No. We should be doing this and we should be doing that. The interest is there. I think if we can find some way to begin organizing young people beyond wearing the T-shirts and the hats—even if it's just around Malcolm and his life—that would help us use the energy of all these young people. We could begin to get young people reading. If you wear the T-shirt, you *must* know the man. If we get a campaign around Malcolm, I'm certain something would come out of it. We don't want to have young people using Malcolm's life to justify their lifestyles now, but to move beyond Malcolm the drug dealer, Malcolm the pusher, the guy who was in jail—to the man he was after all that. Just look at what he was able to become. That's what we need to mirror our lives against. If we could be like Malcolm in that respect— educated man, orator, black nationalist, solely interested in the better- ment of himself and his community—there wouldn't be any stopping us.

Notes on Contributors

Hilton Als is a staff writer at *The Village Voice*. His work has also appeared in *The Nation* and *The New Yorker*.

Deidre Bailey is a student and activist at Spelman College in Atlanta. She grew up in New Haven, Connecticut, and first became involved in politics there as a high school junior.

Amiri Baraka (LeRoi Jones) is a poet, dramatist, novelist, essayist, editor and educator. His work includes *Blues People, Dutchman and the Slave*, and *Home: Social Essays*.

Patricia Hill Collins is Associate Professor of African Studies at the University of Cincinnati. She is the author of *Black Feminist Thought: Knowledge, Consciousness, & the Politics of Empowerment*.

Matthew Countryman is a doctoral candidate in History at Duke University.

Angela Davis is a Professor of the History of Consciousness at the University of California–Santa Cruz. She is the author of *Women, Culture, Politics*, and the forthcoming *Ma Rainey, Bessie Smith and Billie Holiday: Black Women's Music and the Shaping of Social Consciousness*.

Robin D. G. Kelley is Professor in the Department of History and CAAS (Center for Afroamerican and African Studies) at the University of Michigan. He is the author of *Hammer and Hoe: Alabama Communists During the Great Depression*.

Marpessa Dawn Outlaw is a writer living in Brooklyn, New York.

Arnold Rampersad is Woodrow Wilson Professor of Literature and Director of the Program in American Studies at Princeton University. He is the author of a two-volume study, *The Life of Langston Hughes*.

Adolph Reed is Professor of Political Science and History at Northwestern University. He is the author of *The Jesse Jackson Phenomenon: The Crisis of Purpose in African American Politics*, and the forthcoming *Fabianism and the Color Line: The Political Thought of W. E. B. Du Bois*.

Marlon Riggs is a filmmaker and writer. His works include *Ethnic Notions* and *Tongues Untied*.

Ron Simmons is a writer and photographer. His essay "Some Thoughts on the Challenges Facing Black Gay Intellectuals" appeared in the anthology *Brother to Brother: New Writings by Black Gay Men*.

Greg Tate is a Staff Writer with *The Village Voice*. He is a co-founder of the Black Rock Coalition, and the author of a collection of essays, *Flyboy in the Buttermilk*.

Cornel West is Professor of Theology and Director of the Afro-American Studies Program at Princeton University. He is the author of *Prophetic Fragments* and *The American Evasion of Philosophy: A Genealogy of Pragmatism*.

John Edgar Wideman writes fiction and nonfiction, and currently teaches at the University of Massachusetts at Amherst. His books include *Damballah, Hiding Place,* and *Brothers and Keepers*.

Patricia J. Williams is Associate Professor of Law and Women's Studies at the University of Wisconsin at Madison. She is the author of *The Alchemy of Race and Rights: Diary of a Law Professor*.

Joe Wood writes a column for *The Village Voice*. His work has also appeared in *Essence* and *The Nation*.

Index

affirmative action, 192, 197
African independence, 73-4
African National Congress (ANC), 37
African women, 37, 40, 46*fn*
afrocentrism, 140, 213, 225
American society, 48, 49, 50, 53, 77, 142, 153, 201; democracy of, 55; legal system, 55, 198, 201; modern politics, 193-194, 196; as white devil, 67, 144

Baldwin, James, 28
Baraka, Amiri, 40, 148
black affirmation, 42, 48, 49, 102, 109
blacks and class, 22, 51, 63, 174, 228, 238; during WWII, 158-159, 160, 178*fn*
"black" as ideology, 1, 20, 229; *see also* "blackness," *and* Black Power ideology
black community, 59, 77, 81-2, 139, 148, 174, 193-4; as value, 11, 16, 52, 56, 72, 136, 141; *see also* black unity
black consciousness, 27, 28, 210
black culture, 1, 2, 24, 36, 54, 186-7; and black rage, 53; co-optation of, 21; hybridization, 54, 162; and masculinity, 137, 139; role in black struggle, 34; and skin color, 69; and women, 38, 42
black discourse, 7, 8, 10, 11, 15
black exploitation films, 32, 210
black gay men, 141, 151
black hair, 161-2; conk, 19, 156, 172-3
black history, 32, 109, 238; as "therapy," 215-6
black homophobia, 57, 137, 139
black intellectuals, 3, 70, 71; as house negroes, 71

black leadership, 145-7, *see also* Jackson, Jesse; destruction of, 145, 146; and Malcolm X, 146, 147
black liberation movement, 18, 20, 21, 26, 28, 34; co-optation by black middle class, 22, 23, 29, 30, 32, 34; and use of guns, 42
black life, 21, 122, 152; caricatures of, 32; as culturally hybrid, 54, 56, 57
black men, 141, 149-51, 234; as warriors, 150-1; *see also* hip-hop culture, hipster culture, *and* black youth
black middle class, 20, 21, 22, 23, 24, 30, 31, 32, 49-50, 51, 63, 68, 212; co-optation of, 68; and Malcolm X, 31, 144, 146, 172; and psychic conversion, 50
Black Muslims, *see* Nation of Islam
black nationalism, 25, 28, 29, 83*fn*, 210, 211, 215; and internationalism, 61-62; as racialized and masculinist, 41, 231
black political elite, 210-12, 216-18, 219, 225, 238, 239; and Nixon, 218; and Reagan, 217-18
Black Power ideology, 209, 210, 211-12, 213, 214, 225, 226-7, 232; and accommodation, 211-12
black poverty, 57, 59, 67, 73
black rage, 56-57; as commodity, 56; co-optation of, 98; *see also* Malcolm X and black rage
black revolution, 26, 29, 31
black self-determination, 11, 23, 24, 25, 26, 27, 29, 30, 32, 33, 34, 35, 51, 70, 77, 79, 112-113